Be Worshipful

WARREN W. WIERSBE

While this book is intended for the reader's personal
enjoyment and profit, it is also designed for group study.
Study questions are located at the end of the text.

Victor®

The Bible Teacher's Teacher

COOK COMMUNICATIONS MINISTRIES
Colorado Springs, Colorado • Paris, Ontario
KINGSWAY COMMUNICATIONS LTD
Eastbourne, England

Victor® is an imprint of
Cook Communications Ministries, Colorado Springs, CO 80918
Cook Communications, Paris, Ontario
Kingsway Communications, Eastbourne, England

BE WORSHIPFUL
© 2004 by WARREN W. WIERSBE

First printing, 2004
Printed in the UNITED STATES OF AMERICA
2 3 4 5 6 Printing/Year 08 07 06 05 04

Editor: Craig Bubeck
Cover photo: © Edmond Van Hoorick/Getty Images

Library of Congress Cataloging-in-Publication Data
Wiersbe, Warren W.
 Be worshipful : Psalms / by Warren W. Wiersbe.--1st ed.
  p. cm.
 ISBN: 0-7814-4100-5(pbk.)
 1. Bible. O.T. Psalms–Commentaries. I. Title
  BS1430.53.W54 2004
  223'.207--dc22
                          2004002872

CONTENTS

PREFACE

The *Be* series had a modest beginning in 1972 when Victor Books published my commentary on 1 John and called it *Be Real*. Nobody remembers who named the book, but for me it was the beginning of three decades of intensive Bible study as I wrote additional commentaries, all of them with *Be* in the title. It took twenty-three books to cover the New Testament, and they were published in two bound volumes in 1989. Then I started the Old Testament *Be* series, and *Be Obedient*, on the life of Abraham, was published in 1991. Over twenty books are now available in the Old Testament series, and the Lord willing, I hope to complete the Old Testament within a year.

I owe a great debt of gratitude to the editorial staff for their encouragement and cooperation these many years, including Mark Sweeney, Jim Adair, Lloyd Cory, Greg Clouse, and Craig Bubeck. These men have been faithful to "shepherd" me through book after book, and I appreciate the friendship and ministry of each more and more. Every author should be as fortunate as I've been to work with such dedicated, skillful people who always take a personal interest in their authors. To the best of my knowledge, during these years we've ministered together, we've never had a cross word or a serious misunderstanding.

I especially want to thank the Lord for His kindness and mercy in allowing me to minister in this way through the printed page. I can think of many of my friends who could have done a far better job than I in this series, but the Lord graciously gave the privilege to me. He also gave me the wisdom and strength to get each book written on time—and sometimes ahead of time—in the midst of a very busy life as a husband and father, a pastor, a radio Bible teacher, a seminary instructor, and a conference speaker.

This leads me to say that I couldn't have done it without the loving care of my wife, Betty. She manages our household affairs so well and takes such good care of me that I've always had the time needed for studying and writing. When I started this series, our four children were all at home. Now they're all married, and my wife and I have eight wonderful grandchildren! Time flies when you're checking proofs!

The numerous readers of the Be series have been a great source of encouragement to me, even when they have written to disagree with me! I have received letters from many parts of the world, written by people in various walks of life, and they have gladdened my heart. Unless a writer hears from his readers, his writing becomes a one-way street, and he never knows if what he wrote did anybody any good. I want to thank the pastors, missionaries, Sunday school teachers, and other students of the Word who have been kind enough to write. We could compile a book of letters telling what God has done in the lives of people who have studied the Be series. To God be the glory!

As I close, there are some other people who ought to be thanked. Dr. Donald Burdick taught me New Testament at Northern Baptist Seminary and showed me how to study the Word of God. Dr. Lloyd Perry and the late Dr. Charles W. Koller both taught me how to "unlock" a Scripture passage and organize an exposition that was understandable and practical. I recommend their books on preaching to any preacher or teacher who wants to organize his or her material better.

For ten happy years, I was privileged to pastor the Calvary Baptist Church in Covington, Kentucky, just across the river from Cincinnati. One of my happy duties was writing Bible study notes for "The Whole Bible Study Course," which was developed by the late Dr. D. B. Eastep, who pastored the church for thirty-five fruitful years. No church I have ever visited or ministered to has a greater love for the Bible or a deeper hunger for spiritual truth than the dear people at Calvary Baptist. The Be series is, in many respects, a by-product of Dr. Eastep's kindness in sharing his ministry with me, and the church's love and encouragement while I was their pastor. I honor his memory and thank God for their continued friendship and prayer support.

To you who study God's Word with me, "I commend you to God, and to the word of his grace, which is able to build you up, and to give you an inheritance among all them which are sanctified" (Acts 20:32).

Warren W. Wiersbe

ONE

INTRODUCTION
TO THE BOOK OF PSALMS

Psalms

The book of Psalms has been and still is the irreplaceable devotional guide, prayer book, and hymnal of the people of God. The Hebrew title is "the book of praises" (*tehillim*). The Greek translation of the Old Testament (the Septuagint) used *psalmos* for *tehillim*; the word means "a song sung to the accompaniment of a stringed instrument." The Vulgate followed the Septuagint and used *psalmorum*, from the Latin *psalterium*, "a stringed instrument." *The King James* adopted the word, and thus we have the book of Psalms.

Writers. The writers of about two-thirds of the psalms are identified in the superscriptions. David leads the way with 73 psalms. He was Israel's "beloved singer of songs" (2 Sam. 23:1 NIV) and the man who organized the temple ministry, including the singers (1 Chron. 15:16; 16:7; 25:1). The sons of Korah, who served as musicians in the temple (1 Chron. 6:31ff; 15:17ff; 2 Chron. 20:19), wrote 11 psalms (42–49, 84, 85, 87), Asaph 12 psalms, King Solomon two (Pss. 72 and 127), Ethan wrote one (Ps. 89), and Moses one (Ps. 90). However, not all scholars give equal value to the titles of the psalms.

Organization. The book of Psalms is divided into five books, perhaps in imitation of the Five Books of Moses (Gen.—Deut.): 1–41, 42–72, 73–89, 90–106, 107–150. Each of the first three books ends with a double "amen," the fourth ends with an "amen" and a "hallelujah," and the last book closes the entire collection with a "hallelujah." The book of Psalms grew over the years as the Holy Spirit directed different writers and editors to compose and compile these songs and poems. David wrote 37 of the 41 psalms in Book I, so this was the beginning of the collection. Books II and III may have been collected by "the men of Hezekiah" (Prov. 25:1), a literary guild in King Hezekiah's day that copied and preserved precious Old Testament manuscripts. Hezekiah himself was a writer of sacred poetry (Isa. 38). Books IV and V were probably collected and added during the time of the scholar Ezra (Ezra 7:1–10). As with our modern hymnals, there are "collections within the collection," such as "The Songs of Degrees" (120–134), the writings of Asaph (Pss. 73–83), the psalms of the sons of Korah (42–49), and the "hallelujah psalms" (113–118, 146–150).

Poetry. Hebrew poetry is based on "thought lines" and not rhymes. If the second line repeats the first line in different words, as in Psalm 24:1–3, you have *synonymous parallelism*. If the second line contrasts with the first, as in Psalms 1:6 and 37:9, it is *antithetic parallelism*. When the second line explains and expands the first, the writer has used *synthetic parallelism* (Ps. 19:7–9), but when the second line completes the first, it is *climactic parallelism* (Ps. 29:1). With *iterative parallelism*, the second line repeats the thought of the first (Ps. 93), and in *alternate parallelism*, the alternate lines carry the same thought, as in Psalm 103:8–13. You don't bring these technical terms into the pulpit, but knowing what they mean can give you great help when you study. To interpret Psalm 103:3 as God's promise to heal every sickness is to ignore the synonymous parallelism of the verse: the forgiveness of sins is like the healing of disease (see Ps. 41:4).

Some of the psalms are laments to the Lord, written by people in dire circumstances. There are messianic psalms that point forward to the Lord Jesus Christ. There are also psalms of praise and thanksgiving, royal psalms, wisdom psalms, psalms of affirmation and trust, penitential psalms, and even imprecatory psalms calling down God's wrath on the enemy. We will consider each of these categories as we meet them in our studies.

Value. There are over four hundred quotations or allusions to the Psalms in the New Testament. Jesus quoted from the book of Psalms (Matt. 5:5/Ps. 37:11; 5:36/Ps. 48:3; 6:26/Ps. 147:9; 7:23/Ps. 6:8; 27:46/Ps. 22:1; John 15:25/Ps. 69:4). The Lord gave guidance from the book of Psalms when the church in Jerusalem chose a new apostle (Acts 1:15ff; Pss. 69:25; 109:8). The early church also used the Psalms to buttress their preaching (Acts 2:31; Ps. 16:10) and to find encouragement in times of persecution (Acts 4:23–31; Ps. 2). Singing selected psalms was a part of their worship (Eph. 5:19; Col. 3:16; 1 Cor. 14:26) and should be a part of the church's worship today. It's helpful and interesting to study Bible history from the viewpoint of the psalmists: creation (8), the flood (29), the patriarchs (47:9, 105:9, 47:4), Joseph (105:17ff), The Exodus (114), the wilderness wanderings (68:7, 106:1ff), the captivity (85, 137).

But primarily, the psalms are about God and His relationship to His creation, the nations of the world, Israel, and His believing people. He is seen as a powerful God as well as a tenderhearted Father, a God who keeps His promises and lovingly cares for His people. The psalms also reveal the hearts of those who follow Him, their faith and doubts, their victories and failures, and their hopes for the glorious future God has promised. In this book, we meet all kinds of people in a variety of circumstances, crying out to God, praising Him, confessing their sins and seeking to worship Him in a deeper way. In the book of Psalms, you meet the God of creation and learn spiritual truths from birds and beasts, mountains and deserts, sunshine and storms, wheat and chaff, trees and flowers. You learn from creatures of all sorts—horses, mules, dogs, snails, locusts, bees, lions, snakes, sheep, and even worms. The psalms teach us to seek God with a whole heart, to tell Him the truth and tell Him everything, and to worship Him because of Who He is, not just because of what He gives. They show us how to accept trials and turn them into triumphs, and when we've failed, they show us how to repent and receive God's gracious forgiveness. The God described in the book of Psalms is both transcendent and immanent, far above us and yet personally with us in our pilgrim journey. He is "God Most High" and "Immanuel—God with us."

Note: In these expositions, references to verses in the psalms will not be marked "Ps." (psalm) or "Pss." (psalms). References to verses in other Bible books will be identified in the usual manner. When referring to the book of Psalms, I will use "The Psalms."

TWO

Book I

Psalm 1

The editor who placed this jewel at the beginning of The Psalms did a wise thing, for it points the way to blessing and warns about divine judgment. These are frequent themes in The Psalms. The images in this psalm would remind the reader of earlier teachings in the Old Testament. In Genesis, you find people walking with God (5:21, 24; 6:9; 17:1), the life-giving river (2:10–14), and trees and fruit (2:8–10). The law of the Lord connects the psalm with Exodus through Deuteronomy. Finding success by meditating on that law and obeying it reminds us of Joshua 1:8. The psalm presents two ways—the way of blessing and the way of judgment—which was the choice Israel had to make (Deut. 30:15, 19). Jesus used a similar image (Matt. 7:13–14). Bible history seems to be built around the concept of "two men": the "first Adam" and the "last Adam" (Rom. 5; 1 Cor. 15:45)—Cain and Abel, Ishmael and Isaac, Esau and Jacob, David and Saul—and Bible history culminates in Christ and Antichrist. Two men, two ways, two destinies.

Psalm 1 is a wisdom psalm and focuses on God's Word, God's blessing on those who obey it and meditate on it, and God's ultimate judgment on those who rebel. Wisdom psalms also wrestle with the problem of evil in the world and why God permits the prosperity of the wicked who reject His law. Other wisdom psalms include 10, 12, 15, 19, 32, 34, 37, 49, 50, 52, 53, 73, 78, 82, 91, 92, 94, 111, 112, 119, 127, 128, 133, and 139. While this psalm depicts two ways, it actually describes three different persons and how they relate to the blessing of the Lord.

The Person Who Receives a Blessing from God (vv. 1–2)

God's covenant with Israel made it clear that He would bless their obedience and judge their disobedience (Lev. 26; Deut. 28). The word "blessed" is *asher*, the name of one of Jacob's sons (Gen. 30:12). It's plural: "O the happinesses! O the blessednesses!" The person described here met the conditions and therefore God blessed him.[1] If we want God's blessing, we, too, must meet the conditions.

We must be directed by the Word (v. 1). Israel was a unique and separate people; they were among the other nations but not to be contaminated by them (Num. 23:9; Ex. 19:5–6; Deut. 32:8–10; 33:28). So it is with God's people today: we are in the world but not of the world (John 17:11–17). We must beware of friendship with the world (James 4:4) that leads to being spotted by the world (James 1:27) and even loving the world (1 John 2:15–17). The result will be conforming to the world (Rom. 12:1–2) and, if we don't repent, being condemned with the world (1 Cor. 11:32). Lot looked toward Sodom, pitched his tent toward Sodom, and soon moved into Sodom (Gen. 13:10–12; 14:12). Though he was a saved man (2 Peter 2:7–8), Lot lost all that he had when the Lord destroyed the cities of the plain (Gen. 18–19; 1 Cor. 3:11–23). We move into sin and disobedience gradually (see Prov. 4:14–15 and 7:6ff). If you follow the wrong counsel, then you will stand with the wrong companions and finally sit with the wrong crowd. When Jesus was arrested, Peter didn't follow Christ's counsel and flee from the garden (Matt. 26:31; John 16:32; 18:8), but followed and entered the high priest's courtyard. There he stood with the enemy (John 18:15–18) and ultimately sat with them

(Luke 22:55). The result was denying Christ three times. The "ungodly" are people who are willfully and persistently evil; "sinners" are those who miss the mark of God's standards but who don't care; the "scornful" make light of God's laws and ridicule that which is sacred (see Prov. 1:22; 3:24; 21:24).[2] When laughing at holy things and disobeying holy laws become entertainment, then people have reached a low level indeed.

We must be delighted with the Word (v. 2). We move from the negative in verse 1 to the positive. Delighting in the Word and meditating on the Word must go together (119:15–16, 23–24, 47–48, 77–78), for whatever we enjoy, we think about and pursue. "Meditate" in the Hebrew means "to mutter, to read in an undertone," for orthodox Jews speak as they read the Scriptures, meditate and pray. God's Word is in their mouth (Josh. 1:8). If we speak to the Lord about the Word, the Word will speak to us about the Lord. This is what is meant by "abiding in the Word" (1 John 2:14, 24). As God's people, we should prefer God's Word to *food* (119:103; Job 23:12; Jer. 15:17; Matt. 4:4; 1 Peter 2:2), *sleep* (119:55, 62, 147–148, 164), *wealth* (119:14, 72, 127, 162), and *friends* (119:23, 51, 95, 119). The way we treat the Bible is the way we treat Jesus Christ, for the Bible is His Word to us. The verbs in verse 1 are in the perfect tense and speak of a settled way of life, while in verse 2, "meditate" is the imperfect tense and speaks of constant practice. "He keeps meditating."[3]

The Person Who Is a Blessing (v. 3) God blesses us that we might be a blessing to others (Gen. 12:2). If the blessing stays with us, then the gifts become more important than the Giver, and this is idolatry. We are to become channels of God's blessing to others. It's a joy to *receive* a blessing but an even greater joy to *be* a blessing. "It is more blessed to give than to receive" (Acts 20:35).

The tree is a familiar image in Scripture, symbolizing both a kingdom (Ezek. 17:24; Dan. 4; Matt. 13:32) and an individual (52:8; 92:12–14; Prov. 11:30; Isa. 44:4 and 58:11; Jer. 17:5–8; Matt. 7:15–23). Balaam saw the people of Israel as a "garden by a river" with trees in abundance (Num. 24:6). Like a tree, the godly person is alive, beautiful, fruitful, useful, and enduring. The most important part of a tree is the hidden root system that draws up water and nourishment, and the most important part of the believer's life is the "spiritual root system" that draws on the hidden resources we have in Christ (Eph. 3:17; Col. 2:7). This is known as "abiding in Christ" (John 15:1–9).

In Scripture, water for drinking is a picture of the Spirit of God (John 7:37–39; 1 Cor. 10:4), while water for washing pictures the Word of God (119:9; John 15:3; Eph. 5:26). Thirst for water is an image of thirst for God (42:1; 63:1; 143:6; Matt. 5:6; Rev. 22:17), and the river is often a picture of God's provision of spiritual blessing and help for His people (36:8; 46:4; 78:16; 105:41; Ex. 17:5–6; Num. 20:9–11; Ezek. 47; and Rev. 22:1–2). We can't nourish and support ourselves; we need to be rooted in Christ and drawing upon His spiritual power. To meditate on the Word (v. 2) is one source of spiritual energy, as are prayer and fellowship with God's people. "Religion lacks depth and volume because it is not fed by hidden springs," wrote Alexander Maclaren.

Trees may wither and die, but the believer who abides in Christ stays fresh, green, and fruitful (see 92:12–14). "Fruit" speaks of many different blessings: winning people to Christ (Rom. 1:13), godly character (Rom. 6:22, Gal. 5:22–23), money given to the Lord's work (Rom. 15:28), service and good works (Col. 1:10), and praise to the Lord (Heb. 13:15). It's a tragedy when a believer ignores the "root system" and begins to wither. We must remember that the tree doesn't eat the fruit; others eat it. We must also remember that fruit isn't the same as "results," because fruit has in it the seed for more fruit. Fruit comes from life, the life of God flowing in and through us.

The godly person described in verses 1–3 is surely a picture of our Lord Jesus Christ, who, according to John 14:6 is the way (v. 1), the truth (v. 2), and the life (v. 3).

The Person Who Needs a Blessing (vv. 4–6)
The first half of the psalm describes the godly person, while the last half focuses on the ungodly, *the people the godly must seek*

to reach with the gospel. How desperately these people need to know God and receive His blessings in Christ! The wicked are pictured in many ways in Scripture, but the image here is *chaff*. In contrast to the righteous, who are like trees, the ungodly are dead, rootless, blown about, and destined for the fire. Chaff is worth nothing. When the grain is winnowed, the wind blows the chaff away, and what chaff remains is thrown into the fire. John the Baptist used these same images of the tree, fruit, and chaff to warn sinners to repent (Matt. 3:7–12). The wicked of this world seem rich and substantial, but from God's point of view, they are cheap, unsubstantial, and destined for judgment. (See Ps. 73.) No wonder Jesus used the garbage dump outside Jerusalem (gehenna) as a picture of hell, because that's where the cheap waste ends up in the fire (Mark 9:43–48). The chaff is so near the grain, but in the end, the two are separated, and the chaff is blown away or burned. But until that happens, we have the opportunity to witness to them and seek to bring them to Christ.

There is a coming day of judgment, and the Lord, the Righteous Judge, will separate the wheat from the tares, the sheep from the goats, and the trees from the chaff, and no unbeliever will be able to stand in the assembly of the righteous. The verb *knows* in verse 6 doesn't mean that God is aware of them intellectually and has the godly in his mind. Rather, it means that God has chosen them and providentially watched over them and brought them finally to His glory. The word *know* is used, as in Amos 3:2, to mean "to choose, to enter into covenant relationship with, to be personally acquainted with."[4] The Jewish Publication Society translation of Acts 3:2 is: "You alone have I singled out of all the families of the earth." That same translation gives verse 6 as "For the Lord cherishes the way of the righteous ... ." At the last judgment, Jesus says to the wicked, "I never knew you; depart from Me, you who practice lawlessness" (Matt. 7:23 NKJV).

This psalm begins with "blessed" and ends with "perish." True believers are blessed in Christ (Eph. 1:3ff). They have received God's blessing, and they ought to be a blessing to others, especially to the chaff that will one day be thrown into the fire. Let's seek to win as many of them as we can.

Psalm 2

Psalm 1 emphasizes God's law while Psalm 2 focuses on prophecy. The people in Psalm 1 delight in the law, but the people in Psalm 2 defy the law. Psalm 1 begins with a beatitude and Psalm 2 ends with a beatitude. Psalm 1 is never quoted in the New Testament, while Psalm 2 is quoted or alluded to at least eighteen times, more than any single psalm. (See Matt. 3:17; 7:23; 17:5; Mark 1:11; 9:7; Luke 3:22; 9:35; John 1:49; Acts 4:25–26; 13:33; Phil. 2:12; Heb. 1:2, 5; 5:5; Rev. 2:26–27; 11:18; 12:5; 19:15). It is a Messianic psalm, along with 8, 16, 22, 23, 40, 41, 45, 68, 69, 102, 110, and 118. The test of a Messianic psalm is that it is quoted in the New Testament as referring to Jesus (Luke 24:27, 44). But this is also a royal psalm, referring to the coronation of a Jewish king and the rebellion of some vassal nations that hoped to gain their freedom. Other royal psalms are 18, 20, 21, 45 (a royal wedding), 72, 89, 101, 110 and 144. According to Acts 4:25, David wrote this psalm, so it may have grown out of the events described in 2 Samuel 5:17–25, 8:1–14, and 10:1–19.

Israel was ruled directly by the Lord through His prophets and judges until the nation asked for a king (1 Sam. 8). The Lord knew this would happen (Gen. 17:6, 16; 35:11; Num. 24:7, 17) and made arrangements for it (Deut. 17:14–12). Saul was not appointed to establish a dynasty, because the king had to come from Judah (Gen. 49:10), and Saul was from Benjamin. David was God's choice to establish the dynasty that would eventually bring the Messiah into the world (2 Sam. 7). However, both Psalm 2 and 2 Samuel 7 go far beyond David and his successors, for both the covenant and the psalm speak about a universal kingdom and a throne established forever. This can be fulfilled only in Jesus Christ, the Son of David (Matt. 1:1).

Some psalms you *see* (114, 130, 133), some psalms you *feel* (22, 129, 137, 142), but this one you *hear*, because it is a record of four voices.

Conspiracy—The Voice of the Nations (vv. 1–3)

David didn't expect a reply when he asked this question, because there really is no reply. It was an expression of astonishment: "When you consider all that the Lord has done for the nations, how can they rebel against Him!" God has provided for their basic needs (Acts 14:15–17), guided them, kept them alive, and sent a Savior to bring forgiveness and eternal life (Acts 17:24–31; see Dan. 4:32). Yet, from the tower of Babel (Gen. 11) to the crucifixion of Christ (Acts 4:21–31) to the battle of Armageddon (Rev. 19:11ff), the Bible records humanity's foolish and futile rebellions against the will of the Creator. The kings and minor rulers form a conspiracy to break the bonds that the Lord has established for their own good. The picture is that of a stubborn and raging animal, trying to break the cords that bind the yoke to its body (Jer. 5:5; 27:2). But the attempt is futile (vain) because *the only true freedom comes from submitting to God and doing His will.* Freedom without authority is anarchy, and anarchy destroys. I once saw a bit of graffiti that said, "All authority destroys creativity." What folly! Authority is what releases and develops creativity, whether it's a musician, an athlete, or a surgeon. Apart from submitting to the authority of truth and law, there can be no true creativity. The British theologian P. T. Forsythe wrote, "The first duty of every soul is to find not its freedom but its Master."

But the nations' rebellion isn't against "God" in some abstract way; they defy the Messiah, Jesus Christ, the Son of God. The one thing the nations can agree on is "We will not have this man to reign over us" (Luke 19:14). The word "Messiah" comes from the Hebrew word meaning "to anoint"; the Greek equivalent is "Christ." In the Old Testament, kings were anointed (1 Sam. 10:1; 2 Kings 11:12), as were prophets (1 Kings 9:16) and priests (Ex. 28:41). Jesus said that the world hated Him and would also hate those who followed Him (John 7:7; 15, 18–19, 24– 25; Matt. 24:9; Luke 21:17). The phrase "set themselves" means "get ready for war." The consequences of this defiance against the Lord and His Christ are described in Romans 1:18ff, and it isn't a pretty picture.

Mockery—The Voice of God the Father (vv. 4–6)

The peaceful scene in heaven is quite a contrast to the noisy scene on earth, for God is neither worried nor afraid as puny man rages against Him. He merely laughs in derision (37:8–13; 59:1–9). After all, to God, the greatest rulers are but grass to be cut down, and the strongest nations are only drops in the bucket (Isa. 40:6–8, 12–17). Today, God is speaking to the nations in His grace and calling them to trust His Son, but the day will come when God will speak to them in His wrath and send terrible judgment to the world (Rev. 6–19). If people will not accept God's judgment of sin at the cross and trust Christ, they will have to accept God's judgment of themselves and their sins.

It was God who gave David his throne on Zion, and it was God who gave David victory after victory as he defeated the enemies of Israel. But this was only a picture of an even greater coronation: God declares that there is but one legitimate King, and that is His Son who is now seated on the throne of glory (Mark 16:19; 1 Cor. 15:25; Eph. 1:19–23). Jesus Christ is both King and Priest after the order of Melchizedek (Heb. 5:5–6; 7:1ff). Today, there is no king in Israel (Hos. 3:4), but there is a King enthroned in the heavenly Zion (Heb. 12:22–24). If we fail to see Jesus Christ in this psalm, we miss its message completely: His death (vv. 1–3, Acts 4:23–28), resurrection (v. 7, Acts 13:33), ascension and enthronement in glory (v. 6), and His return and righteous rule on earth (vv. 8–9, Rev. 2:9, 27; 12:5).

Victory—the Voice of God the Son (vv. 7–9)

The enthroned King now speaks and announces what the Father said to Him. "I will declare the decree" informs the rebels that God rules His creation on the basis of sovereign decrees. He doesn't ask for a consensus or take a vote. God's decrees are just (7:6), and He never makes a mistake. According to Acts 13:33, verse 7 refers to the resurrection of Christ, when He was "begotten" from the tomb and came forth in glory. (See Rom. 1:4 and Heb. 1:5 and 5:5.) In the ancient Near East, kings were considered to be sons of the gods, but Jesus Christ is indeed the Son of

God. (See 89:26–27; 2 Sam. 7:14.) At our Lord's baptism, the Father alluded to verse 7 and announced that Jesus was His beloved Son (Matt. 3:17; Mark 1:11; Luke 3:22).

The Father has promised the Son complete victory over the nations, which means that one day He will reign over all the kingdoms of the world. Satan offered Him this honor in return for His worship, but Jesus refused (Matt. 4:8–11). Christ's rule will be just but firm, and if they oppose Him, He will smash them like so many clay pots. The Hebrew word translated "break" can also mean "shepherd," which explains the *King James Version* translations of Revelation 2:27, 12:5, and 19:15. Before going to battle, ancient eastern kings participated in a ritual of breaking clay jars that symbolized the enemy army, and thus guaranteed the help of the gods to defeat them. Jesus needs no such folly; He smashes His enemies completely (Rev. 19:11ff; Dan. 2:42–44). Jesus is God, Jesus is King, and Jesus is Conqueror.

Opportunity—the Voice of the Holy Spirit (vv. 10–12)

In view of the Father's decree and promised judgment, and the Son's victorious enthronement in heaven, the wise thing for people to do is to surrender to Christ and trust Him. Today, the Spirit of God speaks to mankind and pleads with sinners to repent and turn to the Savior.

Note that in verses 10 and 11, the Spirit speaks first to the kings and leaders, and then in verse 12, He addresses "all" and urges them to trust the Son. The Spirit starts his appeal with the world leaders, because they are accountable to God for the way they govern the world (Rom. 13). The people are enraged against God mainly because their leaders have incited them. They are ignorant because they follow the wisdom of this world and not the wisdom that comes from God (1 Cor. 1:18–31). They are proud of what they think they know, but they really know nothing about eternal truth. How can they learn? "Be instructed" (v. 10) from the Word of God. The word also means "to be warned." How gracious the Lord is to save sinners before His wrath is revealed!

Once the Spirit has instructed the mind, He then appeals to the will and calls the rebels to serve the Lord and stop serving sin (v. 11). True believers know what it means to have both fear and joy in their hearts. Love for the Lord casts out sinful fear (1 John 4:18) but perfects godly fear. We love our Father but still respect His authority. The third appeal is to the heart and calls for submissive love and devotion to the King. In the ancient world, vassal rulers would show their obedience to their king by kissing his hand or cheek. Judas kissed Jesus in the garden, but it meant nothing. This is the kiss of submission and even reconciliation. The Spirit ends with a word of warning and a word of blessing. The warning is that this loving King can also become angry and reveal His holy wrath suddenly and without warning (1 Thess. 5:1–4). The theme of wrath is connected with the Father (v. 5) and the Son (vv. 9, 12).5

Psalm 1 opens with "blessed" and Psalm 2 concludes with promised blessing for all who put their trust in the Son of God. That promise still stands (John 3:16–18; 20:31).

Psalm 3

This is the first time we find the word *psalm* in the book. The Hebrew word is *mizmor* and means "to pluck strings." This is also the first prayer in the Psalms, and the first psalm attributed to David. All the psalms in Book I (Pss. 1–41) are attributed to David except 1, 10, and 33. (Ps. 2 is assigned to him in Acts 4:25.) Psalm 3 is categorized as a "personal lament," and there are many of these in the collection (3–7, 13, 17, 22, 25–28, 35, 38–40, 42–43, 51, 54–57, 59, 61, 63–64, 69–71, 86, 88, 102, 109, 120, 130, 140–143).6 David wrote the psalm after he had fled Jerusalem when his son Absalom took over the throne (2 Sam. 15–18). The king and his attendants had crossed the Jordan River and camped at Mahanaim. This is a morning psalm (v. 5); Psalm 4 was written during the same events and is an evening psalm (4:8). It's possible that Psalm 5 also fits into the same time period, as well as 42, 43, 61, 62, 63, 143. (See 5:3, 8–10.)

Conflict: He Admits His Troubles (vv. 1–2)

The prayer begins very abruptly with "Lord." Like Peter sinking into the sea (Matt. 14:30), David didn't have time to go through a long liturgy, for his own life was at stake and so was the future of the kingdom. David knew that God is a "very present help in trouble" (46:1). Absalom had taken a long time to build up his support for taking over the kingdom and the number increased day by day (2 Sam. 15:12–13; 16:7–8; 17:11; 18:7). Absalom was handsome, smooth-spoken, and a gifted liar who knew how to please the people and steal their hearts (2 Sam. 15:1–6). British statesman James Callaghan said, "A lie can be halfway around the world before the truth has got its boots on." There's something in the heart of mankind that enjoys feeding on lies.

Not only were David's enemies increasing but the news was getting worse. People were saying, "The king is beyond help." (See 31:13; 38:19; 41:4–9; 55:18; 56:2; 69:4 and 71:10–11.) The word "help" in the Hebrew (yeshua) is translated "save" in verse 7 and "salvation" in verse 8 and gives us the names "Jesus" (Matt. 1:21) and "Joshua." It's used 136 times in the Psalms.

Why had God permitted this dangerous and disgraceful uprising? It was part of David's chastening because of his sins of adultery and murder (2 Sam. 12:1–12). God in his grace forgave David when he confessed his sins (2 Sam. 12:13–14; Pss. 32 and 51), but God in his government allowed David to reap the bitter consequences of those sins. He experienced painful family problems (2 Sam. 12–14), including the death of the son Bathsheba bore him, the rape of his daughter Tamar, and the slaying of his sons Amnon, Absalom, and Adonijah.

This is the first use of "Selah" in Scripture (vv. 2, 4, 8); it is used seventy-one times in the Psalms and three times in Habakkuk 3. Hebraists aren't agreed whether it comes from words meaning "to lift up" or "to be silent." If the first, then it might be a signal for louder voices or the lifting and blowing the trumpets, perhaps even the lifting of hands to the Lord. If the second, it could signal a pause, a moment of silence and meditation.

Confidence: He Affirms His Trust in the Lord (vv. 3–4)

But David wasn't a man easily beaten. Without ignoring his problems, he lifted his eyes from the threatening situation around him and looked by faith to the Lord. David knew he was in danger, but God was his shield (see Gen. 15:1). Israel's king was referred to as a "shield" because he protected the nation (84:9; 89:18), but David depended on God as his shield (7:10; 18:2; 47:9; 59:11; 84:11; Deut. 33:29). David was in disgrace because of his own sins and his son's treachery, but God was the source of David's glory. Absalom turned his father's "glory into shame" (4:2), but one day that glory would be restored. The situation was discouraging, but the king knew that God would lift up his head and restore him to his throne (27:6; 2 Sam. 15:30). His faith was in the promises God had made to him in the covenant recorded in 2 Samuel 7, and he knew God would not forsake him.

The temple had not yet been built on the "holy hill of Zion," but the ark was there (see 2 Sam. 15:25) and that was God's throne (80:1 NASB). David may have been forced off his throne, but Jehovah was still on the throne and in control, and Absalom had attacked God's anointed king (2:2). That was a dangerous thing to do. David kept crying out to God in prayer, knowing that God had not forsaken him in the past and would not forsake him now. "This poor man cried out, and the Lord heard him, and saved him out of all his troubles" (Ps. 34:6 NKJV).

Celebration: He Anticipates the Victory (vv. 5–8)

When David awakened the next morning, his first thought was of the Lord and how He had protected him and his attendants during night. This was a sign to him that the Lord was with them and would see them through the crisis. It reminds us of Jesus asleep in the storm (Mark 4:39) and Peter asleep in the prison (Acts 12). If we trust Him and seek to do His will, God works on our behalf even while we're asleep (121:3–4; 127:2). David affirmed that he would not be afraid if tens of thousands of people were set in battle array against him, for God would give him victory (Deut. 32:30).

The morning was the most important time of day for David, as it should be for us today.

It was in the morning that he met with the Lord and worshiped Him. It was his time to pray (5:3), to sing (57:7–8; 59:16) and to be satisfied by God's mercy (90:14). "For His anger is but for a moment, His favor is for life; weeping may endure for a night, but joy comes in the morning" (30:5 NKJV). Abraham arose early in the morning (Gen. 19:27; 21:14; 22:3), and so did Moses (Ex. 24:4; 34:4), Joshua (Josh. 3:1; 6:12; 7:16; 8:10), Samuel (1 Sam. 15:12), Job (Job 1:5), and our Lord (Mark 1:35).

God not only rested David but He also rescued him. David's prayer in verse 7—"Arise, O Lord"—takes us back to the years when Israel was in the wilderness, as David was at that time. When the guiding cloud of glory began to move and the camp set out, Moses would say (or sing): "Rise up. O Lord! Let Your enemies be scattered, and let those who hate You flee before You" (Num. 10:35 NKJV). David had sent the ark back to Jerusalem (2 Sam. 15:24–29), but he knew that the presence of a piece of sacred furniture was no guarantee of the presence of the Lord (see 1 Sam. 4). David had no access to the tabernacle or the ministry of the priests, but he was spiritual enough to know that *the love and obedience of His heart was what God wanted.* He didn't have the ark of God, but he had the God of the ark! He couldn't offer animal sacrifices or incense, but he could lift his hand to worship God (141:2). The glory of God was with him (v. 3) and so was the blessing of God (v. 8). Let the enemy arise! (v. 1). God will also arise and give victory!

Some translations render the verbs in verse 7 as past tense (KJV, AMP, NASB), indicating that David was looking back at the many past victories God had given him. "You saved my life many times in the past, so why would you abandon me now?" The *New International Version* sees this as a prayer for present and future victories. Either way, David had the faith to trust God to go before him and defeat the army of Absalom, and God did. Striking the enemy on the cheek—a "slap in the face"—was an act of humiliation. David saw the rebellious army as a pack of animals that needed their teeth broken (7:2; 10:9; 17:12; 22:12–13, 16, 20–21; 35:17; 57:4; 58:6).

Jonah quoted verse 8 when he was in the great fish (Jonah 2:9) and then experienced that salvation. Though he had used brilliant strategy in opposing Absalom's plans, David refused to take the credit. It was the Lord alone who would receive the glory. David also refused to carry a grudge against his people, but asked the Lord to bless them. This reminds us of our Lord's prayer on the cross (Luke 23:34) and Stephen's prayer as he was being stoned to death (Acts 7:60). God restored David to his throne and enabled him to prepare Solomon to succeed him. David was also able to bring together his wealth so that Solomon would have what he needed to build the temple. (See 1 Chron. 22–29.)

Psalm 4

When you compare the wording in this psalm with Psalm 3, you cannot but draw the conclusion that they deal with the same situation in David's life: foes/distress (v. 1), many/many (vv. 6, 2), glory (vv. 2, 3), call/answer (vv.1, 4), lie down/sleep (vv. 8, 5). Psalm 3 is a morning psalm (v. 5) and Psalm 4 an evening psalm (v. 8). For the historical setting, review the introduction to Psalm 3. This is the first mention of "the chief musician," who is included in the titles of fifty-three psalms. He was the "minister of worship" and custodian of the sacred psalms at the tabernacle and then the temple (1 Chron. 6:31–32; 15:16–22; 25:1, 7). The Hebrew word *neginoth* means "accompanied by stringed instruments" (4, 6, 54, 55, 61, 67, 76) and refers to the harp and lyre (1 Chron. 23:5; 25:1, 3, 6). It's a wonderful thing that David could turn this distressing experience into song, to the glory of God. His example shows us what our responses ought to be in times of crisis.

Look to the Lord (v. 1)

"Hear me" is a passionate and concerned call that means "Answer me!" David had been praying for God's help and was desperate to receive an answer. (See 18:6; 50:15; 55:16; 145:18.)

During his youthful days of exile, he had a priest with him to consult the Urim and Thummim and determine God's will, but not during Absalom's rebellion. "God of my righteousness"7 implies not only that God is righteous and will do what it best ("my righteous God"), but also that David's righteousness came from God, and therefore God should vindicate him ("God of my innocence"). Yes, David was being chastened because of his disobedience, but God had forgiven his sins. God had called David to be king, and God alone could vindicate him.

David reminded the Lord that He had often delivered him in times past, so He was able to deliver him now. "Distress" means "pressed into a corner, in a tight place." But God "enlarged him" or "set him in a broad place," for David grew spiritually in difficult situations (18:19, 36; 25:17; 31:8; 118:5; 119:32). David knew he didn't deserve any help from the Lord, but he prayed on the basis of God's mercy and favor. God in His grace gives us what we don't deserve, and God in His mercy doesn't give us what we do deserve.

Confront the Enemy (vv. 2–3)

David wasn't at the scene of the revolt, but he spoke out to those who had turned against him and made Absalom king. The phrase "sons of men" refers to the leading men of rank who had been seduced by Absalom and with him were leading the people astray. David understood their thinking and how Absalom had deceived them. David had no glory of his own, for all his glory came from the Lord (3:3). The enthusiastic mob was following vanity and would pay dearly for their sins. When you follow vain things and believe falsehood, you can only go astray. The people weren't just deposing a king; they were fighting against the Lord Jehovah who had placed David on the throne. Absalom certainly wasn't a man of God, nor was he God's chosen one to rule over Israel. The rebels were actually following a false god when they listened to Absalom's flattery and lying promises (2 Sam. 15:1–6). David didn't try to compromise with the rebels; he knew what they were, and he rejected them.

Encourage Your Friends (vv. 4–5)

In these verses, David speaks to his own followers, some of whom were so overcome by their emotions that they were about to get out of hand. David gave them six instructions, all of which are useful to us today when we find ourselves getting angry.

Tremble before the Lord (4a). Believers who fear the Lord need not fear anything else. Absalom's followers neither trembled before the Lord nor before their rightful king.

Don't sin (4b). Sinful anger leads to sinful words and deeds, and even to murder (Matt. 5:21–26). Paul quoted this verse in Ephesians 4:26, using the Septuagint (Greek Version of the Old Testament). It reads, "Be angry, and do not sin" (NKJV), which reminds us that not all anger is sinful. There is a holy anger against sin that ought to be in the heart of every believer (Mark 3:5), but we must be careful not to be guilty of unholy anger.

Search your own hearts (4c). It's easy to get angry at the sins of others and ignore our own sins (Matt. 7:1–5). In fact, David himself was guilty of doing this (2 Sam. 12:1–7). Some translate this phrase "Speak to your own heart" (see 10:6, 11, 13). Instead of tossing and turning in bed because of the things others are doing, take inventory and see if there aren't sins in your own heart that need to be confessed.

Be still (4d). The *Amplified Bible* translates this, "Be sorry for the things you say in your heart." Another translation is "say so in your own heart," that is, "Say to your own heart, Sin not." The honest searching of the heart should lead us to confess our sins to the Lord and claim His gracious forgiveness (1 John 1:9).

Offer right sacrifices (5a). They couldn't offer them there in the wilderness, but they could promise the Lord they would do so when they returned to Jerusalem. This is what Jonah did (Jonah 2:9). Absalom was offering insincere and hypocritical sacrifices to impress the people (1 Sam. 15:12), but God didn't accept them. (See 50:14–15.)

Trust the Lord (5b). Absalom was trusting his leadership, his army, his clever strategy, and his popularity with the people, but he wasn't trusting the Lord. His plans were destined to fail.

David was not only a great king and military strategist, but he was also a loving shepherd who cared for his people and wanted them to walk with the Lord. David knew that the spiritual condition of his people was far more important than their military skill, for the Lord gives victory to those who trust and obey (51:16–19).

Praise the Lord (vv. 6–8)

David's leaders reported to him what many of the people were saying, so he knew that there was discouragement in the ranks (see also 3:2). "Who will show us any good?" means "O that we might see some good!" (AMP), or "Can anything good come out of this?" or "Who can get us out of this plight?" The tense of the verb indicates that this discouraging statement was repeated again and again by the complainers, and the more they complained, the more others took up the strain. The Jewish Publication Society version reads, "O for good days!" It's well been said that "the good old days" are a combination of a bad memory and a good imagination. What kind of "good" were the people looking for—material wealth, peace and security at any price, a godly king, a successful new king?

David knew what kind of good he wanted: the light of God's smile upon him and his people. To see the glorious face of God and know that He was well pleased would take care of everything. This statement refers to the priestly blessing in Numbers 6:24–26, and see also 31:16; 44:3; 67:1; 80:3, 7, 19; and 119:135. There was no priest present to bestow this blessing, but David knew that God would answer the prayer of his heart. The king wanted to see the Lord change darkness into light, and that's exactly what He did. But not only did David's darkness become light, but his discouragement was replaced by joy (v. 7). The Israelites experienced great joy at weddings and bountiful harvests (Isa. 9:3; Jer. 48:33); but the joy God gave David exceeded even those times. (See Rom. 15:13 and John 16:24.) Finally, David praised God for the peace the Lord placed in his heart before the battle had been fought and won (v. 8; see 3:5). God had given him rest the night before, and now he would rest again, knowing that God was his shield (3:3). The Hebrew word for "peace" (*shalom*) means much more than the absence of conflict. It carries with it the ideas of adequacy for life, confidence and fullness of life. Perhaps the Lord brought Deuteronomy 33:12 to David's mind—"The beloved of the Lord shall dwell in safety by Him, who shelters him all day long ..." (NKJV). This promise is even more meaningful when you recall that David's name means "beloved."

Psalm 5

Like Psalm 3, this is a morning psalm (v. 3). David may have written it during the crisis caused by Absalom, but we have no indication that he did. However, the description of David's enemies given in verses 4–6 and 9–10 suggests the period prior to David's flight from Jerusalem. The *New International Version* translates verse 10, "Let their intrigues be their downfall," and there was certainly a great deal of deception and intrigue going on at that time.[8] The Hebrew words for "house" and "holy temple" (v. 7) are also used for the tabernacle in Exodus 23:19, Deuteronomy 23:18, Joshua 6:24, 1 Samuel 1:9, 3:3, and 3:15, so we don't have to date the psalm from the time of Solomon. "Nehiloth" in the title is a musical instruction that probably means "for flutes."

Because of the prayer in verse 10, Psalm 6 is classified as one of the "imprecatory psalms" (see 12, 35, 37, 58, 59, 69, 79, 83, 109, 139, and 140). In these psalms, the writers seem to describe a God of wrath who can hardly wait to destroy sinners. The writers also seem to picture themselves as people seeking terrible revenge against these enemies. But several facts must be considered before we write off the psalmists as pagan brutes who cannot forgive, or God as a "dirty bully." To begin with, the enemies described are rebels against the Lord (5:10), and in some instances, against the Lord's anointed king. The Jews were a covenant people whom God promised to protect as long as they obeyed Him (Lev. 26; Deut. 27–29). In His covenant with

PSALMS

Abraham, God promised to bless those who blessed Israel and to curse those who cursed them (Gen. 12:1–3). When the Jews asked God to deal justly with their wicked enemies, they were only asking Him to fulfill His covenant promises. "God is love" (1 John 4:8, 16), but God is also "light" (1 John 1:5), and in His holiness, He must deal with sin. Ever since the fall of man in Genesis 3, there has been a battle going on in the world between truth and lies, justice and injustice, and right and wrong; and we cannot be neutral in this battle. "If the Jews cursed more bitterly than the Pagans," wrote C. S. Lewis in *Reflections on the Psalms*, "this was, I think, at least in part because they took right and wrong more seriously. For if we look at their railings we find they are usually angry not simply because these things have been done to them but because these things are manifestly wrong, are hateful to God as well as to the victim" (p. 30).

Those who have difficulty accepting the "imprecations" in The Psalms must also deal with them in Jeremiah (11:18ff; 15:15; 17:18; 18:19ff; 20:11ff) and in the preaching of John the Baptist (Matt. 3) and Jesus (Matt. 23), as well as in the requests of the martyrs in heaven (Rev. 6:9–11). However, no one will deny that these servants of God were filled with the Spirit and wanted the Lord's will to be accomplished. Perhaps our problem today is what C. S. Lewis pointed out: we don't hate sin enough to get upset at the wickedness and godlessness around us. Bombarded as we are by so much media evil and violence, we've gotten accustomed to the darkness.

If this psalm did grow out of the time in the wilderness when David was fleeing from Absalom, then he teaches us an important lesson: no amount of danger or discomfort should keep us from our time of morning fellowship with the Lord. In this psalm, David gives us three valuable instructions to encourage our daily fellowship with the Lord.

We Prepare to Meet the Lord (vv. 1–3)

If we had an invitation to enjoy a private visit with the President of the United States, or perhaps Queen Elizabeth, we would certainly prepare for it; yet many believers rush into their morning devotional time as if no preparation were necessary. David was open with the Lord and admitted his inward pain ("meditation" can be translated "groaning") and his prayer was a cry for help. David was King of Israel, but he saw the Lord alone as his King (Ex. 15:18). David was a man with a broken heart, but he knew that the Lord understood his sighs and groanings (see Rom. 8:26). We may come to God's gracious throne with "freedom of speech" ("boldly" in Heb. 4:16, and see 10:19, 35) because the Father knows our hearts and our needs and welcomes us. Like our Lord Jesus Christ (Mark 1:35), David kept this appointment "morning by morning" and allowed nothing to interfere. (See 55:18, 59:17; 88:14 and 92:3.)

David was not only *faithful* in his praying each morning but he was also *orderly* and *systematic*. The word translated "direct" in verse 3 was used to describe the placing of the pieces of the animal sacrifices in order on the altar (Lev. 1:8). It also described the arranging of the wood on an altar (Gen. 22:9), the placing of the loaves of bread on the table in the tabernacle (Lev. 24:8), and the setting of a meal before the guests (Ps. 23:5). David wasn't careless in his praying; he had everything arranged in order. The word also has a military connotation: a soldier presenting himself to his commander to receive orders, and an army set in battle array on the field. In past years, many soldiers had presented themselves to David to get their orders, but David first presented himself to the Lord. In order to exercise authority, leaders must be under authority. "I will look up" conveys the idea of waiting expectantly for God to come and bless (see NIV). In our daily morning meetings with the Lord, we should come like priests bringing sacrifices to the altar and soldiers reporting to our Captain for duty.

We Seek to Please the Lord (vv. 4–6)

God has no pleasure in wickedness nor can He be neutral about sin; therefore, rebel sinners couldn't enter into His presence (15:1ff; 24:3–6). God delights in those who fear Him (147:11) and who offer sincere praise to Him (69:31). To please

God, we must have faith (Heb. 11:6) and be identified with His Son in whom He is well pleased (Matt. 3:17). When you read verses 5–6 and 9–10, you meet a crowd of people who deliberately and repeatedly disobey God and think nothing of the consequences. It's the crowd John describes in Revelation 21:8, the people who are going to hell. God loves the world of lost sinners (John 3:16) and sent His only Son "to be the Savior of the world" (1 John 4:14, and see 1 Tim. 2:3–4 and 2 Peter 3:9). Jesus died on the cross for the sins of the world (1 John 2:1–2), and His invitation to salvation is sent to all who will believe and come (Matt. 11:28–30; Rev. 22:17). Such are the vast dimensions of God's grace and love (Eph. 3:18–19).

But the glorious truth of God's love doesn't change the fact that God hates sin and punishes sinners. He has no pleasure in them, and they cannot dwell with Him (v. 4) or stand before Him as they are (v. 5; see 1:5–6). He abhors murderers and liars and destroys them if they don't trust His Son (v. 6). It isn't necessary to dilute the word "hate" in verse 5 because you find it also in 11:5 and 45:7, and see 7:11. In fact, the Lord expects those who love Him to love what He loves and hate what He hates (97:10; 119:113; 139:21; Prov. 6:16–17; Amos 5:15; Rom. 12:9). There is no such thing as "abstract evil" except in dictionaries and philosophy books. Evil is not an abstraction; it's a terrible force in this world, wrecking lives and capturing people for hell. God's hatred of evil isn't emotional; it's judicial, an expression of His holiness. If we want to fellowship with God at His holy altar, then we need to feel that same anguish (anger plus love) as we see the evil in this fallen world.

We Submit to the Lord (vv. 7–12)

When he wrote "But as for me," David contrasted himself with the wicked crowd that rebelled against the King. David had come to pray, and he had three requests.

He prayed for guidance (vv. 7–8). Because he wasn't a member of the tribe of Levi, David couldn't actually enter the tabernacle as could the priests, but he used that phrase to describe his approach to the Lord. David was in the wilderness, but he came to the Lord with the kind of awe that the priests and Levites displayed in the tabernacle. In the worship of our great God, there's no place for cuteness and flippancy. For believers to enter into the presence of God to worship and pray, it cost Jesus His life (Heb. 10:19–20), and to treat this privilege lightly is to cheapen that sacrifice. David knew he needed guidance from God, for he had to put the kingdom back together again. (See James 1:5.)

He prayed for justice (vv. 9–10). David didn't issue orders to his officers to go out and slaughter his enemies; instead, he turned them over to the Lord. During that tragic battle in which Absalom was slain, "the forest devoured more people that day than the sword devoured" (2 Sam. 18:8). David's prayer was answered: "let them fall by their own counsels" (v. 10). But it was not because they rebelled against David; their great sin was that they had rebelled against God. "The Lord loves righteousness and justice" (Ps. 33:5 NIV; and see 36:6; 58:11; 97:2; Isa. 30:18; Luke 18:7–8; Rom. 1:32). Anybody who resents this kind of praying can't honestly pray, "Hallowed be Thy name. Thy kingdom come, Thy will be done in earth, as it is in heaven" (Matt. 6:9–10). In Romans 3:13, Paul quoted "their throat is an open sepulcher" as part of his proof that the whole world is guilty before God (Rom. 3:19)—and that includes all of us! Instead of being upset over God's treatment of David's enemies, we need to examine our own relationship with the Lord!

He prayed for God's blessing (vv. 11–12). David didn't rejoice because some of God's covenant people were evil and were judged by the Lord, but because Israel's God had been glorified and His king vindicated. The future of God's great plan of salvation rested with Israel, and if the Davidic dynasty was destroyed, what about God's gracious Messianic covenant with David (2 Sam. 78)? The outcome of our fellowship with the Lord should be joy in His character, His promises, and His gracious answers to prayer. Even though some of his own people had turned against him, David prayed that God would bless and protect them! This sounds like our Lord on the cross (Luke 23:34) and Stephen when he was stoned to death (Acts 7:60). Note that verse 11 emphasizes faith and love, and verse 12 gives the assurance of future hope. The shield in verse 12 is the large rectangular shield, like a door, and not the smaller round shield of 3:4.

David began his devotions seeking help for himself but ended by seeking blessing for all the people, including his enemies. That's the way our devotional times ought to end.

Psalm 6

The inscription tells us that David wrote this psalm but we aren't sure when he wrote it. It could have been composed during the time of Absalom's rebellion when David was old, sick, and unable to handle all the complex responsibilities of the kingdom. David's gradual failure as a visible leader was one of Absalom's "selling points" as he stole the hearts of the Israelites (2 Sam. 15:1–6). But the psalm might have been written at any time during David's reign when he was ill and being attacked by his enemies. He describes his plight—"foes without, fears within"—and cries out to God for mercy. He was sure he was facing death (v. 5), which indicates that his experience was real and that he wasn't using sickness and war only as metaphors for his personal troubles. Neginoth means "stringed instruments," and Sheminith means "eighth," which may refer to the number of a familiar melody, a lower octave for men's voices or the number of strings of the instrument to be played. You find Sheminith also in the title of Psalm 12, and see 1 Chronicles 15:21. Psalm 6 is the first of seven "penitential psalms" in which the writers are being disciplined by God and experiencing suffering. The other psalms are 32, 38, 51, 102, 130, and 143, and all of these psalms are helpful to us when we need to confess our sins and draw closer to the Lord. In this psalm, David records the stages in his difficult experience of moving by faith from trial to triumph.

The Pain of Discipline (vv. 1–3)

Eight times in the psalm David addresses God as "LORD—JEHOVAH," the covenant name of God, and the address in verse 1 is repeated in 38:1, and see Jeremiah 10:24. When God deals with His children, usually He first rebukes and then chastens, just as parents first warn disobedient children and then discipline them (Heb. 12:5–6; Prov. 3:11–12). According to Hebrews 12:1–13, chastening is not punishment meted out by an irate judge but discipline given by a loving Father to help His children mature (see Rev. 3:19). Sometimes God chastens us in order to deal with our disobedience, but at other times, He chastens us to prepare us for what lies ahead. It's like the training of an athlete for a race. David thought God was angry with him, but that wasn't necessarily true. However, when you consider that he was surrounded by foes (v. 7), evildoers (v. 8), and enemies (10), and that his body was weak and in pain and his soul troubled, you can see why he felt like he had a target on his back.

Three times he used the Hebrew word *bahal*, which means "faint, weak, troubled, terrified." It is translated "vexed" in the *King James Version* (vv. 2, 3, 10), but in the 17th century, the word "vex" was much stronger than it is today. The translators of the Greek Old Testament used *tarasso*, which is the word used in the Greek of John 12:27, "Now is my soul troubled ..." (and see Matt. 26:38 and Mark 14:34). Knowing that he deserved far more than what he was enduring, David begged for mercy (see 103:13–14) and asked God to send help speedily. The painful question "How long?" is asked at least sixteen times in The Psalms (6:3; 13:1–2; 35:17; 62:3; 74:9–10; 79:5; 80:4; 82:2; 89:46; 90:13; 94:3). The answer to the question is, "I will discipline you until you learn the lesson I want you to learn and are equipped for the work I want you to do." According to Hebrews 12, when God disciplines us, we can despise it, resist it, collapse under it and quit, or accept it and submit. What God is seeking is submission.

The Futility of Death (vv. 4–5)
David felt that God had turned His back on him and deserted him, so he asked Him to return; and then he began to reason with Him. Every Jew knew that the Lord was "merciful and gracious"

(Ex. 34:6–7), so David asked God to manifest that mercy to him and spare his life. Furthermore, what would the Lord gain by allowing David to die? (See 30:9–10; 88:10–12). King Hezekiah used a similar approach when he prayed for deliverance from death (Isa. 38:18–19). The word "grave" in verse 5 (KJV) is *sheol*, a word that can mean "the grave" or "the realm of the dead." Here it means the latter. In Old Testament times, people didn't have the clear revelation of the after-life that was brought through Jesus (2 Tim. 1:10), although there were glimpses of what God had in store for His people (16:9–11; 17:15; 49:14–15; 17:24). A body in the grave can't praise or serve God, and David wasn't certain what his spirit could do for the Lord in sheol. Conclusion: it would be wiser for the Lord to deliver him and let him live. David still had work to do.

The Strain of Despair (vv. 5–7)

We have gone from a morning psalm (3:5) to an evening psalm (4:8) and back to a morning psalm (5:3). Now we have another evening psalm (6:6). But whereas in the previous psalms, the Lord gave sleep and peace to David, here we find the king sleepless because of fear and pain. He was worn out from groaning, tossing, and turning, and he spent a good deal of time weeping. "I soak my pillow … I drench my couch" (v. 6, AMP; see 38:9–10). Sleeping had been replaced by suffering. Sleep is important for healing (John 11:11–12), so David's lack of sleep only made the condition worse. David's weakened condition was revealed by the dullness of his eyes (v. 7; see 1 Sam. 14:27, 29). It's remarkable how much physicians can discover about our physical condition by looking into our eyes.

A man I considered to be a godly spiritual leader once said, "I hear Christians say that their pain and sickness brought them closer to God, but in my case, that didn't always happen." That encouraged me! From my own experience and pastoral ministry, I've learned that sickness and pain either make us better or bitter, and the difference is *faith*. If we turn to God, pray, remember His promises, and trust Him, we will find His grace sufficient for our needs (2 Cor. 12:9). The Lord may not do what we ask, when we want it, but He will do what needs to be done and help us glorify His name. The question we should ask isn't "When will I get out of this?" but "What can I get out of this?"

The Joy of Deliverance (vv. 8–10)

At this point, there's a sudden and surprising change from suffering to joy, an experience recorded in other psalms (22:22; 56:10; 69:30). It doesn't matter whether this change occurred later or immediately after David prayed, but he felt healing in his body and peace in his heart and mind. Perhaps word came to him that the enemy had retreated or, better yet, had been defeated, and he knew God had heard his cries. Or maybe his circumstances hadn't changed at all, but David felt God's witness in his heart that all would be well. The Lord had heard his weeping and requests and had accepted his prayer.

He used this experience to glorify the Lord as he witnessed to his enemies. How this message was conveyed to them, we don't know; but David was quick to honor the Lord for what had occurred. Perhaps the words in verses 8–10 are an apostrophe, a speech addressed to persons not present but meaningful to those people hearing or reading it. His enemies said that David was done for, but the failure of their prediction would leave them ashamed and defeated. The phrase "Depart from me" is quoted in Matthew 7:23 and Luke 13:27 and seems quite final.

Psalm 7

Cush the Benjamite was among King Saul's fawning flatterers. He was one of a group of evil men from Saul's tribe who reported what they heard about David during those years when Saul was out to capture and destroy his rival. Saul played on the sympathy of his leaders and bribed them into serving as spies (1 Sam. 22:6ff; 23:21; 24:8ff; 26:18–19). To earn the king's approval and rewards, they even lied about David, and Saul believed them. We don't know what lies Cush told Saul, but David was concerned enough to cry out to God for deliverance and vindication. "Shiggaion" is used only here in the Psalms (but see Hab. 3:1) and could mean "a passionate psalm with strong emotion." Some believe it comes from a word meaning "to wander, to cry aloud." The theme is God's vindication of His servant and judgment on his enemies (vv. 6, 8, 11). The psalm described four different judgments.

Other People Judge us Wrongly (vv. 1–2)

Cush lied about David; therefore, Saul persecuted and pursued David (vv. 1, 5, 13). David fled to the Lord for refuge (see 11:1; 16:1; 31:1; 57:1; 71:1l; 141:8) because the Lord knew that David was innocent of Saul's accusations. David had saved his father's sheep from the attacks of dangerous beasts (1 Sam. 17:34–37), and now he felt like he was the victim. (For animals as symbols of enemies, see 10:9; 17:12; 22:12–13, 16, 20–21; 35:17; 57:4; 58:6; 124:6.) David saw himself as a "dead dog," a "flea," or a hunted bird (1 Sam. 24:14; 26:20). Note that the *King James Version* and the *New American Standard Bible* move from the plural (v. 1) to the singular (v. 2), from Saul's men to Saul himself. Saul's judgment of David was false, and David trusted the Lord to protect and save him. When today, people falsely accuse us and create problems for us, we should follow David's example and find refuge in the Lord. But let's be sure that we are suffering *wrongfully* and not because of our own foolishness or disobedience (Matt. 5:11–12; 1 Peter 3:13–17).

We Judge Ourselves Honestly (vv. 3–5)

David affirmed his integrity before the Lord and asked the Supreme Judge to vindicate him because his hands were clean. David wasn't claiming to be sinless; he was stating that he was blameless in his motives and actions (v. 8; see 18:16–26; Phil. 2:12–15). If indeed David was guilty of sin, he was willing to accept God's discipline; but he knew that his hands were pure. David had two opportunities to kill King Saul and refused to do so (1 Sam. 24, 26). This was proof enough that his heart was not filled with personal malice and a desire for revenge. How important it is that we are open and honest with both our Lord and ourselves. If he was proved guilty, then David was willing for his own honor to be laid in the dust; but David knew that his hands were clean (Isa. 1:15; 59:3; Ezek. 23:37, 45; Acts 20:26).

God Judges Sinners Righteously (vv. 6–13)

David didn't take the situation into his own hands; rather, he turned Saul and his scheming men over to the Lord. Only God's holy anger could truly vindicate David (Rom. 12:17–21). "Arise, O Lord" reminds us of the words of Moses when the camp of Israel began their march with the ark leading the way (Num. 10:35; see also 2 Chron. 6:40–42). David knew that danger was near, and he wanted the Lord to move into action. (See 3:7; 9:19; 10:12; 17:13; 44:26; 68:1.) It's during those times when God seems inactive that we get impatient and want to see things happen immediately. But God is more longsuffering than we are, and we must wait for Him to work in His time. "Let God convene the court! Ascend Your throne on high! Let all the people gather together to witness the trial! Let the Lord try me and prove to all that I am innocent!" David knew that Almighty God could test the minds and the hearts (v. 9; see Rev. 2:23), and he wanted to see the wickedness of his enemies exposed and stopped. David's defense was with the Lord.

How can God both love the world (John 3:16) and hate the wicked? (On God's hatred of evil, see 5:5.) The *King James Version* puts "with the wicked" in italics, which means the phrase was added by the translators, but both the *New International Version* and the *New American Standard Bible* translate the text without it. Their emphasis is that God expresses His anger at sin every day, so He doesn't have to summon a special court to judge sinners. He allows sinners to reap the sad consequences of their sins day by day (v. 16; see Rom. 1:24, 26–27, 32), but sometimes their persistent rebellion causes Him to send special judgment when His longsuffering has run its course (Gen. 6:5ff). God's love is a holy love, and if God loves righteousness, He must also hate wickedness.

Note that God is called "God Most High" (vv. 8, 10, 17), which is *El Elyon* in the Hebrew. This divine name is used twenty-three times in the Psalms and goes back to Genesis 14:18–22. (See also Deut. 32:8; 2 Sam. 22:14, and 23:1.) Jesus was called "Son of the Most High" (Mark 5:7; Luke 1:32, 35; 8:28).

Sin Itself Judges Sinners Ultimately (vv. 14–17)

The image of sin as pregnancy is frequently found in Scripture (Job 15:35; Isa. 33:11; 59:4, 13; James 1:13–15). Sinners "conceive" sin that, like a monstrous child, eventually grows up and destroys them. They dig pits and fall into them themselves (see 9:16; 37:14–15; and 57:6; 1 Sam. 25:39; Prov. 26:27; Ec. 10:8; Ezek. 19:4). The trouble they cause comes back on their own heads (Gal. 6:7). There is a work of divine retribution in this world, and nobody can escape it. "Though the mills of God grind slowly, yet they grind exceeding small" (Friedrich von Logau).

God abandoned King Saul to his own ways (1 Sam. 15), and ultimately both the arrow and the sword caught up with him (vv. 12–13; 1 Sam. 31:3–4). He wanted to kill David, but his own sword killed him. Pharaoh ordered the male Jewish babies to be drowned in the Nile, and his own army was drowned in the Red Sea. Haman built a gallows on which to hang Mordecai, and Haman himself was hanged on it (Est. 7).

The psalm closes with David extolling the Lord, not for the fact that sinners have been judged, but because the righteousness of God has been magnified. The fact that people are ensnared by their own sins and ultimately judged brings no joy to the hearts of believers, but the fact that God is glorified and His righteousness exalted does cause us to praise Him. God judges sin because He is holy, and His decrees are just (v. 6). "Even so, Father, for so it seemed good in Your sight" (Luke 10:21). Finally, keep in mind that God gave His own Son to die for the sins of the world, so that He might uphold His own holy law and at the same time offer His mercy and grace to all who will believe. People may not like the way God runs His universe, but, as Dorothy Sayers expressed it, "for whatever reason God chose to make man as he is—limited and suffering and subject to sorrows and death—He had the honesty and the courage to take His own medicine" (*Christian Letters to a Post-Christian World* [Eerdmans, 1969], p. 14).

Psalm 8

In this beautiful expression of praise to God, David stands amazed that the God of creation, the great and glorious Jehovah, would pay any attention to frail people on earth. David understands that God glorifies Himself in the heavens, but how can He glorify Himself on earth through such weak, sinful people? This is a "nature psalm" (see 19, 29, 65, 104), but it is also a Messianic psalm (Matt. 21:16; Heb. 2:6–8; 1 Cor. 15:27; Eph. 1:22). The answer to the question "What is man?" is ultimately answered by Jesus Christ, the "Last Adam," through whom we regain our lost dominion. "Gittith" means "winepress" and may identify a vintage tune (see 81 and 84). As they worship and serve Him (Matt. 5:13–16), the faithful people of God glorify His name on earth (vv. 1, 9) and help to defeat His enemies (v. 2). That God, in His remarkable condescension, should focus attention on us is proof of our dignity as creatures made in the image of God. The grandeur of men and women is found only there. Apart from knowing God, we have no understanding of who we are or what we are to do in this great universe.

God Created Us (vv. 1–2, 5a)

The phrase "our Lord" is a threefold confession of faith: there is but one God, all people were created by God, and the Jewish people in particular are "his people and the sheep of his pasture" (100:3). They can call Him "our Lord." (See 135:5, 147:5, and Nehemiah 10:30.) However, Jehovah was not a "tribal god" who belonged only to Israel, for He wanted His name (character, reputation) to be known "in all the earth" (66:1; 83:18; Ex. 9:14, 16; Josh. 3:11). Not only has the Lord set His glory "above the heavens" (beyond the earth's atmosphere), but He has also deigned to share His glory with His creatures on earth. The glory of God dwelt with Israel in the tabernacle and temple, and it was especially revealed in the person and work of Jesus Christ (John 1:14). Wicked people crucified "the Lord of glory" (1 Cor. 2:8), but He was raised from the dead and has returned to heaven in honor and great glory (Phil. 2:5–11).

In verse 2, David moved from God's transcendence to His immanence. Jehovah is so great that He can entrust His praise to infants and children and still not be robbed of glory! Jesus quoted this verse after He cleansed the temple (Matt. 21:16). Words are only sounds plus breath, two very weak things. Yet words of praise even from sucklings (not yet weaned) and babes (children able to play in the streets) can defeat God's enemies! The cry of baby Moses ultimately brought Egypt to her knees, and the birth of Samuel was used by God to save Israel and bring David to the throne. Of course, it was the birth of Jesus that brought salvation to this world. Indeed, God has used the weak and helpless to praise Him and help defeat His enemies (1 Cor. 1:27). David himself was but a youth when he silenced Goliath and defeated him (1 Sam. 17:33, 42–43), and he brought great glory to the name of the Lord (17:45–47). God didn't need us, yet He created us and prepared a wonderful world for us. As the Westminster Catechism states it, our purpose is to "glorify God and enjoy Him forever," and if we leave God out of our lives, we miss life's greatest opportunity.

God Cares for Us (vv. 3–4)

The sun rules the day, but its blinding light usually blots out anything else we might see in the heavens, but at night, we are overwhelmed by the display of beauty from the moon, stars, planets, and galaxies. Ralph Waldo Emerson wrote that if the stars came out only once in a century, people would stay up all night gazing at them. What we know today about the size of the universe makes the earth and its inhabitants look even more insignificant than they appeared in David's day. Our knowledge of light years and the reaches of outer space gives us even more reason for appreciating our insignificance in the solar system and God's wonderful concern for us. In His great love, the Lord chose the earth for Himself (Ps. 24:1) and created us in His own image. "Man" in verse 4 is *enosh*, "weak man," and "son of man" is "son of *adamah*—son of the earth, earth-born" (Gen. 2:7). Both titles emphasize the weakness and frailty of humankind.

God spoke the worlds into existence, but David saw creation as coming from God's fingers (v. 3; see Ex. 8:19 and 21:18) and hands (v. 6), the work of a Master Craftsman. It was evil for the Jews to worship the heavenly host (Ex. 20:4–6; Deut. 4:15–19; 17:2–7), but they understood that creation was proof of a caring Creator who prepared the world for the enjoyment and employment of mankind. God is mindful of us ("remembers," see Gen. 8:1; 19:29; 30:22) and cares for us ("visits," see Jer. 29:11; Job 10:12). God completed His creation before He made Adam and Eve and placed them in the garden, so everything was ready for them—their every need.

God Crowns Us (vv. 5–8)

Why does God pay attention to "frail creatures of dust"? Because He has made them in His own image, and they are special! Instead of humans being "a little higher than animals," as science believes, they are actually "a little lower than God." The word *elohim* can mean angelic creatures (see Heb. 2:7), but here it definitely means "God." The Lord crowned Adam and Eve and gave them dominion over the other creatures (Gen. 1:26–27). We are co-regents of creation with the Lord! The angels are servants (Heb. 1:14), but we are kings, and one day, all who have trusted Christ will be like Him (1 John 3:1–3; Rom. 8:29).

People today live more like slaves than rulers, so why aren't we living like kings? Because our first parents sinned and lost their crowns, forfeiting that glorious dominion. According to Romans 5, sin is reigning in our world (v. 21) and death is also reigning (vv. 14 and 17), but Jesus Christ has regained the dominion for us and will one day share it with us when He reigns in His kingdom (Heb. 2:6–8). When Jesus ministered here on earth, He exercised the dominion that Adam lost, for He ruled over the beasts (Mark 1:13; 11:1–7), the fowl (Luke 22:34), and the fish (Luke 5:4–7; Matt.

17:24–27; John 21:1–6). Today He is on the throne in heaven and all things are "under his feet" (1 Cor. 15:27; Eph. 1:22; Heb. 2:8). The phrase means "completely subjected to Him" (47:4; Josh. 10:24; 1 Kings 5:17). Through the exalted Christ, God's grace is reigning today (Rom. 5:21) so that God's children may *"reign in life"* through Jesus Christ (v. 17). He has made us "kings and priests to His God and Father, to Him be glory and dominion forever and ever. Amen" (Rev. 1:6). By faith, "we see Jesus" (Heb. 2:8–9), crowned in heaven, and that assures us that one day we will reign with Him and receive our crowns (Rev. 20:1–6).

To summarize: God the Father created us to be kings, but the disobedience of our first parents robbed us of our crowns. God the Son came to earth and redeemed us to be kings (Rev. 1:5–6), and today the Holy Spirit of God can empower us to "reign in life by one, Jesus Christ" (Rom. 5:17). When you crown Jesus Christ Lord of all, you are a sovereign and not a slave, a victor and not a victim. "O Lord, our Lord, how excellent in your name in all the earth!"

Psalm 9

The emphasis is on joyful praise (vv. 1,2, 11, 14), especially for God's care of Israel and His righteous judgment on the nations that attacked His people. You find the theme of judgment and justice in verses 4, 7–8, 16 and 19–20, and note the mention of the throne of God (vv. 4, 7, 11 NIV). For a parallel passage, see Isaiah 25:1–5. "Muth-labben" means "death of a son," but we don't know how it relates to the psalm. Perhaps it was the name of a familiar melody to which the psalm was to be sung. Ever since the Lord spoke the words recorded in Genesis 3:15 and 12:1–3, there has been a war going on between the forces of Satan and the forces of God, and the focus has been on the nation of Israel. (See Rev. 12.) That battle goes on today.

Personal Praise: God Saves the King (vv. 1–8)

David offers whole-hearted praise to the Lord (Matt. 15:8) for delivering him and his army from the enemy nations that attacked Israel. His aim was to honor the Lord, not to glorify himself. His joy was in the Lord, not just in the great victory that He had been given (Phil. 4:4), and he wanted to tell everybody about God's wonderful works. See verses 14 and 103:1–2; 117:1; 138:1; 1 Peter 2:9; and Ephesians 2:7. "God Most High" is *El Elyon*; see 7:8, 10, 17; 18:13; 21:7. This was the name that Abraham honored after God gave him victory over the kings (Gen. 14).

David describes the victory in verses 3–6, verses that should be read in the past tense: "Because my enemies were turned back ..." Note the repeated "You have" in verses 4–6. God turned the enemy back, and in their retreat, they stumbled and perished before the Lord. Why did the Lord do this? To maintain the right of David to be king of Israel and accomplish God's purposes in this world. God's rebuke is an expression of His anger (2:5; 76:6). To "blot out" a name meant to destroy the person, place, or nation completely (83:4; Ex. 17:14; Deut. 25:19; 1 Sam. 15; and see Deut. 9:14; 25:19; 29:20). In contrast to the wiping out of the nations, the Lord and His great name stand forever. His throne cannot be overthrown. In fact, in the victory God gave David, the king saw a picture of the final judgment and victory when God will judge the world, and Paul referred to verse 8 in his address in Athens (Acts 17:31).

National Praise: God Shelters the People (vv. 9–20)

The focus now centers on the people of the land, whom David calls the oppressed (v. 9), the humble ("afflicted" v. 12), and the needy and the poor (v. 18). These are the faithful worshipers of the Lord who have been persecuted, abused, and exploited by local rulers for being true to the Lord. See 10:17; 25:16; 40:17; 102:1; Zephaniah 2:3; and 3:12–13. David praises the Lord for His faithfulness in caring for His sheep.

The refuge—God will not forsake them (vv. 9–10). The first word means "a high safe place" and the second "a stronghold." During his years of exile, David found the wilderness strongholds to be places of safety, but he knew that the Lord was the safest refuge (46:1). The phrase "times of trouble" means literally "times of extremity" (see 10:1; 27:5; 37:39; 41:1; 73:5; 107:6, 13, 19, 26, 28). To "know God's name" or "love God's name" means to trust Him and be saved (5:11; 69:36; 91:14; 119:132; 1 Sam. 2:12). God forsook His own Son (Matt. 27:46) that He might never forsake His own people.

The avenger—God will not fail them (vv. 11–17). David calls upon the suffering remnant to sing praises to God because He is on their side and fights their battles. He will not fail to hear their cries and execute justice on their behalf. Israel's calling was to bear witness to the nations that Jehovah is the only true and living God (18:49; 44:11; 57:9; 106:27; Isa. 42:6; 49:6). The ark was now in Jerusalem so Jehovah was on His throne in Israel. "Inquisition for blood" refers to the official investigation of murder, to see who was guilty of the crime, symbolized by having blood on the house (Deut. 22:8), the hands (Ezek. 3:17–21; 33:1–9), or the head (Acts 18:6). (See Genesis 9:5 and 10:13.) There was no police force in Israel, but a near kinsman could avenge the murder of a family member. This is why God assigned the six "cities of refuge" to provide havens for people who accidentally killed someone (Num. 35). But when God is the avenger, He has all the evidence He needs to find and punish rebellious sinners. The suffering remnant prays to God in verses 13–17 and asks to be taken from the gates of death (sheol, the world of the dead; see 107:18; Job 17:16; 38:17; Isa. 38:10) and put at the gates of Zion (v. 14). From death to life! They also ask God to catch their enemies in their own traps (vv. 15–16; see 7:14–16) and finally consign them to the grave (sheol). "Higgaion" could mean "meditation," or it may refer to a solemn sound on the accompanying instruments.

The conqueror—God will not forget them (vv. 18–20). "Arise, O Lord" reminds us of the conquering march of Israel (Num. 10:35), when God went before His people to defeat their enemies. "Man" in verse 19 is enosh, "weak frail man," a fact that sinners don't want to admit. (This we will see in Ps. 10.) One day the Lord will put the rebels in their rightful place and they will discover that they are only—dust!

Psalm 10

The problem in Psalm 9 is the enemy invading from without, while the problem in Psalm 10 is the enemy corrupting and destroying from within.[9] There were wicked nations around Israel (9:5), but there were also wicked people within the covenant community (10:4), people who claimed to know God, but whose lives proved they did not know God (Titus 2:16). They know there is a God, but they live as though there is no God or no final judgment. They are "practical atheists" who are their own gods and do whatever they please.

Questioning God (v. 1)

The psalmist wrestles with the age-old problem, "Why doesn't God do something about the prosperity of the wicked (vv. 2, 3, 4, 7, 10, 15) and the misery of the afflicted (vv. 2, 8–10, 12, 14, 17, 18)?" It's also discussed in 13:1–3; 27:9; 30:7; 44:23–24; 73; and 88:13–15, as well as Job 13:24ff and Jeremiah 14. The wicked are marching through the land, but the Lord seems to be distant and unconcerned. During the past century, millions of godly people have lost their homes, jobs, possessions, families, and even their lives because of the ruthless deeds of evil leaders, and where was God? (See 22:1, 11; 35:22; 38:21; 42:9; 43:2; 71:12; 74:1; 88:14.) God has expressed a special concern for widows, orphans, and the helpless (68:5; 82:3; Deut. 10:18; 24:17–21; 26:12–13; 27:19), yet He is not to be found. He "covers His eyes" as though nothing is happening (see Lev. 20:4; 1 Sam. 12:3; Prov. 28:27).

Rejecting God (vv. 2–13)

The psalmist now describes these wicked people, what they do, and why they do it. He gives four statements that express what they believe, because what they believe determines how they behave.

"There is no God" (vv. 2–4, see v. 4 NASB). Believing this lie frees the wicked to do whatever they please, for they become their own god. "You shall be as God" (Gen. 3:5 and 6:5). The wicked cleverly plot against the righteous and hotly pursue them until they get what they want. These evil workers live to please

PSALMS

themselves and fulfill their selfish desires, and then brag about their sins! (Phil. 3:18–21). They revile the Lord (vv. 3, 13 NIV) and "stick their nose up" when anybody challenges them.

"I shall not be moved" (vv. 5–7). This arrogant attitude comes from an ignorance of the laws of God, because unconverted people have no understanding of the Word of God or the ways of God (1 Cor. 2:10–16). Because God is longsuffering, they think they're getting away with their sins (Eccl. 8:11). Peace and prosperity give them a false sense of security that will end very suddenly. (See Luke 12:13–21 and 1 Thessalonians 5:1–3.) Telling lies and swearing oaths they have no plans to keep, they escape the penalties of the law and pursue their devious ways. Like people savoring tasty food, they keep lies under their tongues and enjoy them (Job 20:12–15; Prov. 4:17). Paul quoted verse 7 in Romans 3:14. It is the godly who have God's promise of true security (15:15; 16:8; 21:7; 62:2; 112:6).

"God doesn't see me" (vv. 8–11). Like ferocious lions, wicked people hide and watch for opportunities to pounce on the helpless prey, and like hunters or fishermen, they catch their prey in their nets. They are sure that the law won't catch up with them or the Lord notice what they do. The lion is often used as a picture of ruthless sinners who attack others (17:12; 37:32; 56:6; 59:3; 64:4).

"God will not judge me" (vv. 12–13). At this point, the psalmist cries out to God for help, and he uses three different names for God: Jehovah, the God of the covenant, and El and Elohim, the God of power. The wicked boast that God will not investigate their sins or judge them, but God says, "Be sure your sin will find you out" (Num. 32:23). The Lord will keep His covenant promises to His people, and there will be a day of reckoning when sinners will be judged by a righteous God. "Arise, O God" takes us back to Numbers 10:35 and the triumphant march of Israel.

Read those statements again and see if they don't express the outlook of lost sinners today.

Trusting God (vv. 14–18)

As the psalm draws to a close, the writer expresses his full confidence that God is on His throne and has everything under His control. The Lord may not explain to us why some people seem to get away with their evil deeds, but He does assure us that He will judge sinners and ultimately defend His own. In this paragraph, the Lord answers all four of the statements of the wicked that are quoted in verses 2–13.

God sees what is going on (v. 14). This answers the claim in verses 8–11 that the Lord pays no attention to what the wicked are doing. Even more, God sees the trouble (outward circumstances) and grief (inward feelings) caused by the wicked as they persecute the helpless, and He will take the matter in hand. The poor and needy can safely commit themselves into the hands of the Lord (55:22; 1 Peter 5:7).

God judges sin (v. 15), and this answers the false claim of verses 12–13. The psalmist prays that the Lord will carefully investigate each sinner's life and works, until every evil deed is exposed and judged. But he asks that the sinners be judged in this life and their power removed ("break the arm"). This prayer isn't always answered. (See Rev. 6:9–11.)

God is King (v. 16). The wicked claim that there is no God (vv. 1–4), but the truth is that God is and He rules over all! (See 2:6; 5:2; 24:7–10; 29:10; 1 Sam. 8:6–7.) After their deliverance from Egypt, the Israelites sang praises to their King: "The Lord shall reign forever and ever" (Ex. 15:18).

God defends His own people (vv. 17–18). The wicked boast that they will not be moved (vv. 5–7), but God has other plans for them. He hears the prayers of the persecuted, He sees their plight, He strengthens their hearts for whatever trials He permits (Rom. 8:28), and He eventually judges those who abuse them. People of faith can depend on the God of heaven, but the self-confident and arrogant "people of the earth" have no future with the Lord. Life without the Lord is empty and vain (49:12–20; 62:9). Christians have their citizenship in heaven (Phil. 3:20), and their names are written down in heaven (Luke

10:20). They don't belong to this world, although their ministry is in this world. God's people have been "redeemed from the earth" (Rev. 14:3) and have heaven as their home. The phrase "them that dwell on the earth" is found often in the book of Revelation (3:10; 6:10; 8:13; 11:10; 12:12; 13:8, 12, 14; 14:6; 17:2, 8) and describes not only where these unbelievers live but what they live for—the things of the earth. The "earth dwellers" may seem to have the upper hand today, but wait until the Lord reveals His hand!

Psalm 11

It's difficult to determine the historical background of this psalm. David was often in danger, whether in the court of Saul (1 Sam. 19:1), in the wilderness being chased by Saul, or during the rebellion of Absalom, his son. David did flee from Saul's court and hide in the wilderness for perhaps ten years, and he did abandon Jerusalem to Absalom and take refuge over the Jordan, both of which proved to be wise moves. But during the crisis described in this psalm, David did not flee his post but remained on duty, trusting the Lord to protect him, and He did. Whatever the crisis, the psalm teaches us that we must choose between fear (walking by sight) or trust (walking by faith), listening to human counsel or obeying the wisdom that comes from the Lord (James 1:5).

What David Should Do (v. 1)

When the crisis arose, David's counselors immediately told him to leave Jerusalem and head for the safety of the mountains. They didn't seem to have faith that the Lord could see him through (see 3:2 and 4:6). David used the imagery of the bird in 55:6–7. But David didn't need wings like a dove; he needed wings like an eagle (Isa. 40:31) so he could rise above the storm by faith and defeat his enemies. The verb "flee" is in the plural and refers to David and his court. It's right for us to flee from temptation (2 Tim. 2:22) as Joseph did (Gen. 39:11–13), but it's wrong to flee from the place of duty, as Nehemiah was invited to do (Neh. 6:10–11). The leader who flees needlessly from the crisis is only a hireling and not a faithful shepherd (John 10:12–13). Beware of listening to unwise counsel. Put your faith in the Lord, and He will protect you and direct your paths.

What the Enemy Does (v. 2)

"For, look" (NIV) suggests that these counselors are walking by sight and evaluating the situation from the human perspective. (See 2 Kings 6:8–23.) It's good to know the facts, but it's better to look at those facts in the light of the presence and promises of God. There was a secret plot afoot, not unusual in an eastern palace. The bows and arrows may have been literal, but it's more likely they are metaphors for deceptive and destructive words (57:4; 64:3–4; Prov. 26:18–19; Jer. 9:3, 8; 18:18). Perhaps this psalm was written during the early days of Absalom's campaign (2 Sam. 15:1–6). David was upright before God (v. 2) and righteous (vv. 3, 5), and he knew that the Lord was righteous and would do the right thing (v. 7).

What Can the Righteous Do? (v. 3)

David was God's appointed king, so anything that attacked him personally would shake the very foundations of the nation. God had abandoned Saul as king, and Absalom had never been chosen king, and both men weakened the foundations of divine government. (See 75:3 and 82:5.) Society is built on truth, and when truth is questioned or denied, the foundations shake (Isa. 59:11–15). The question "What can the righteous do?" has also been translated, "What is the Righteous One doing?" God sometimes "shakes things" so that His people will work on building the church and not focus on maintaining the scaffolding (Heb. 12:25–29; Hag. 2:6). But the traditional translation is accurate, and the answer to the question is, "Lay the foundations again!" Each new generation must see to it that the foundations of truth and justice are solid. Samuel laid again the foundations of the covenant (1 Sam. 12), and Ezra laid again the foundations of the temple (Ezra 3). In spite of all his trials, David lived to make preparations for the building of the temple and the organization of the temple worship. During the checkered history of Judah, godly kings cleansed the land of idolatry and brought the people back to the true worship of the Lord. Christ's messages to the churches in Revelation 2–3 make it clear that local churches need constant examination to see if they're faithful to the Lord, and we need to pray for a constant reviving work of the Spirit.

What God Will Do (vv. 4–7)

When you look around, you see the problems, but when you look up to the Lord by faith, you see the answer to the problems. When the outlook is grim, try the uplook! "In the Lord I put my trust," said David, for he knew that God was on the throne in His holy temple in heaven (Hab. 2:20; Isa. 6) and that He saw everything the enemy was doing. The word "try" or "test" in verse 4 carries the idea of "testing metals by fire," as in Jeremiah 11:20 and 17:10. God's eyes penetrate into our hearts and minds (Heb. 4:12; Rev. 2:23). The Lord tests the righteous to bring out the best in them, but Satan tempts them to bring out the worst. When we trust the Lord in the difficulties of life, our trials work for us and not against us (2 Cor. 4:7–18).

David uses three images to describe the judgment that God has prepared for the wicked. First, he saw fire and brimstone descend on them, such as the Lord sent on Sodom and Gomorrah (v. 6a; Gen. 19:24; see also Isa. 30:33; Rev. 9:17). Then he beheld a terrible storm destroying the enemy, a "scorching wind" such as often blew from the desert (v. 6b). David used the image of the storm in his song about his deliverance from his enemies and King Saul (18:4–19). The third image is that of a poisonous potion in a cup (6c KJV and NASB). "Drinking the cup" is often a picture of judgment from the Lord (75:8; Isa. 51:17, 22; Jer. 25:15–17; Ezek. 38:22; Rev. 14:10; 16:19; 18:6). On the Lord's hatred of evil and violent people, see 5:5.

What does God have planned for His own people? "The upright will behold His face" (v. 7 NASB; see 17:15 and 1 John 3:1–3.) To "see the face" means to have access to a person, such as "to see the king's face" (2 Sam. 14:24). For God to turn His face away is to reject us, but for Him to look upon us with delight means He is going to bless us (Num. 6:22–27). When Jesus returns, those who have rejected Him will be cast "away from the presence of the Lord and from the glory of His power" (2 Thess. 1:8–10; Matt. 7:21–23), while His own children will be welcomed into His presence (Matt. 25:34).

Psalm 12

On some university campuses, what once was called "Home Economics" is now "The College of Applied Life Studies." In Tucson, Arizona, potholes are no more, because they're now known as "pavement deficiencies." In politics, new taxes are "revenue enhancements," and in military jargon, "retreat" is "backloading of augmentation personnel." If, while you're backloading, you get shot, the bullet hole is "a ballistically induced aperture in the subcutaneous environment."[10] This kind of artificial evasive language is known as "double-speak" and its popularity in almost every area of human life is evidence that language and communication are in serious trouble. Our ability to speak and write words is a precious gift of God, and this psalm deals with the right and wrong use of that gift. (For "Sheminith," see Ps. 6.)

The Righteous—Despairing Words (v. 1)

In Psalm 11, the foundations of society were shaking (v. 3), but here David cried out for help (salvation, deliverance) because the godly remnant of faithful believers was getting smaller and smaller. This wasn't the complaint of a crotchety old man longing for "the good old days." It was the cry of a truly faithful servant of God who wanted to see his nation Israel fulfill her divine purposes on earth. The faithfulness of Israel involved bringing the Savior into the world and blessing all the nations (Gen. 12:1–3). David wasn't alone in his concern. Elijah thought he was the only faithful prophet left (1 Kings 18:22; 19:10, 18), and the prophets Isaiah (Isa. 57:1) and Micah (Mic. 7:1–7) expressed their concern at the absence of righteous leaders. (See also Psalm 116:1, Ecclesiastes 10:5–7, and Jeremiah 5:1.) When he wrote 1 Timothy, Paul lamented over what "some" were doing in the church (1:3, 6, 19; 4:1; 5:15; 6:10), but in 2 Timothy, that "some" had become "all" (1:15; 4:16). One of the tragedies today is that a new generation of believers doesn't seem to know what it takes to be a godly leader, so they borrow leadership ideas from secular society and all kinds of unequipped and unqualified people to be leaders.

The Wicked—Deceptive Words (vv. 2–4)

One mark of a Spirit-filled believer is the ability to detect lies and liars and avoid them (1 John 2:18–29), and David knew that he was living in a society controlled by deception. It wasn't that only a few people were telling lies; deception was a major characteristic of the whole generation. (See 5:9; 28:3; 34:13; 55:21; 141:3.) What would David say if he were alive today and witnessed the propaganda and promotion that make up what we casually call "the media"? He would probably describe today's "communication" as he did centuries ago: empty and useless words ("vanity"), smooth talk ("flattery"), double-talk from double hearts, and boastful talk or "proud words."

Saul used lies to deceive his leaders about David, and Absalom used flattery to poison the minds of the naïve people of Israel against David. Flattery is not communication, it's manipulation (see Prov. 26:28; 28:23). Even in Christian ministry it's possible to use flattery to influence people and exploit them (1 Thess. 2:1–6; Acts 20:28–31). Flattery plays on the ego and especially influences people who want to appear important (Jude 11). You can flatter yourself (36:2), others (5:9; 12:2), and even God (78:34–37). Of course, what the lips speak comes from the heart (Matt. 12:33–37), and that's why David accuses these liars of duplicity, which is a divided heart (literally "a heart and a heart"). This is the opposite of the "perfect heart," total loyalty to God and His truth (86:11; 1 Chron. 12:33, 38; Rom. 16:17–18).

As for "proud words," this describes boastful speech that impresses people by its oratory and vocabulary. "Great swelling words" is the phrase used in 2 Peter 2:18 and Jude 1:16. Daniel (7:20, 25) and John (Rev. 13:2, 5) both tell us that the Antichrist will speak in this way and rule the world. This kind of speech is motivated by pride and is used by people who think they're in control and will never need to answer to anybody, including the Lord. Their lips are their own, and they can speak just as they please.

The Lord—Delivering Words (vv. 5–8)

But God sees the oppression of the weak (Ex. 3:7) and hears the pain in their cries, and He declares that He will arise and judge the liars and deceivers. "I will arise" takes us back to 3:7, 7:6, 9:19, and 10:12, and see Numbers 10:35 and Isaiah 33:11–12. "Safety" in verse 5 ("protect" NIV) comes from the same Hebrew root as "help" in verse 1 and "deliver" in 6:8, and is the basis for the names "Jesus" and "Joshua" ("Jehovah is salvation"). The last phrase in verse 5 should read as in the *New American Standard Bible*: "the safety for which he longs." When God comes to deliver His people, He will "cut off" those who practice flattery and deception (v. 3), which means separation from the covenant community (Gen. 17:14), like the separation of the goats from the sheep (Matt. 25:31–33).

But can the Lord's promises be trusted? Yes! Unlike the worthless words of the deceivers, the Word of the Lord is like precious silver (19:9–10) that is heated seven times in the crucible before it is poured out into the mold. His Word is flawless and can be trusted; His Word is precious and must be valued (119:14, 72, 127, 162). How paradoxical that society today sees the Scriptures as something relatively worthless and yet pays great sums of money to the people who manufacture deception and flattery. No matter how many lies this generation tells, God's Word is safe, for He said, "I am watching over My word to perform it" (Jer. 1:12 NASB). Furthermore, God is able to protect His godly people from the lies of the enemy. God's people are "the generation of the righteous" (14:5), the generation that seeks God (24:6), the generation of His children (73:15), the generation of the upright

(112:2). If God's people will saturate themselves with God's Word, they won't be seduced by "this lying generation." When the church adopts the techniques and motives of the world system, the church ceases to glorify the Lord.

The final verse issues a call to action, for "the wicked strut about, and evil is praised throughout the land" (NLT). Vileness ("cheapness") is promoted and exalted in the media: immorality, brutality, murder, lies, drunkenness, nudity, the love of money, the abuse of authority. The things that God condemns are now a means of universal entertainment, and the entertainment industry gives awards to the people who produce these things. People boast about things they ought to be ashamed of (Phil. 3:18–19). Is there a way to restrain and overcome this national decay? Yes! God's people are salt and light (Matt. 5:13–16). If there were more light in the land, there would be less darkness, and if we had more salt, there would be less decay. As God's people worship God, pray, and share the Gospel with the lost, more people will trust Christ and increase the salt and light in the land. We must also share the truth of the Word with the next generation (2 Tim. 2:2) and prepare them for the battles and opportunities to come (78:1–8; 102:18). The church is always one generation short of extinction, so we must be faithful to win the lost and teach the believers, or vileness will conquer the land.

Psalm 13

This psalm was probably written during David's difficult years of exile when King Saul was pursuing him. There were times when he confessed, "There is but a step between me and death" (1 Sam. 20:3). By the grace of God, David turned his sufferings into songs and left those songs behind to encourage us in our trials (2 Cor. 1:2–11). In this brief psalm, David deals with his feelings, his foes, and his faith.

The Inward Struggle—His Feelings (vv. 1–2)
God had promised David the throne of Israel, yet that day of coronation seemed further and further away. Saul was doing evil

things, and God wasn't judging him, and yet David was doing good things and felt abandoned by the Lord. David was certainly disturbed by what the enemy was doing, but he was more concerned about what the Lord was *not* doing. "How long?" is a familiar question in Scripture (see 6:3) and is a perfectly good question to ask if your heart is right with God. The saints in heaven even ask it (Rev. 6:10). When we're in trouble and pray for help, but none comes, we tend to feel deserted. David felt that God was ignoring him and that this alienation was final and complete. He also felt that God was hiding His face from him instead of smiling upon him (see 30:7; 44:24; Lam. 5:20). To behold God's face by faith and see His glory was always an encouragement to David (11:7; 17:15; 27:4, 8; 31:16; 34:5; 67:1), but now he felt abandoned.

Feeling like he was left to himself, David tried to devise various ways to overcome the enemy ("wrestle with my thoughts" NIV), but nothing seemed to satisfy him. But faith is living without scheming; it means not leaning on our own experiences and skills and trying to plot our own schedule (Prov. 3:5–6). There were storm clouds in the sky, hiding the sun, but the sun was still shining. It's a dangerous thing to give in to our feelings, because feelings are deceptive and undependable (Jer. 17:9). When Jacob heard the news about Simeon being left hostage in Egypt, he gave up and announced that everything was against him (Gen. 42:36) when actually God was causing everything to work *for* him. We must not deny our feelings and pretend that everything is going well, and there is no sin in asking, "How long?" But at the same time, we must realize how deceptive our feelings are and that God is greater than our hearts (1 John 3:20) and can lift us above the emotional storms of life. David eventually learned to replace the question "How long, O Lord?" with the affirmation, "My times are in your hands" (31:15). This is a lesson that all believers must learn.

The Outward Danger—His Foes (vv. 3–4)

It's good to have peace within you, but you also need protection around you. That's why David prayed to the Lord and made three requests. The first was, "Look on me," a plea for the Lord to fix His eyes on His servant and scrutinize him. David felt that God had hidden His face and he wanted Him to turn His face toward him again. His second request was that the Lord answer Him and send some kind of encouragement. David felt he had been deserted and that his prayers were accomplishing nothing. "Give light to my eyes" was the third prayer. This involved not only spiritual enlightenment (19:8) but also physical and emotional vitality and strength (Ezra 9:8; 1 Sam. 14:24–30). When the mind and body are weary, how easy it is to be discouraged! Perhaps David was even ill and in danger of death (v. 3; see 7:5). If he died, what would happen to the throne of Israel?

As much as David was concerned about his own needs, he was concerned even more with the glory of God (v. 4). After all, God had chosen David and had commanded Samuel to anoint him king, and if David failed, God's name would be ridiculed. "Don't allow the enemy to gloat over me!" was his prayer. The word "moved" in verse 4 means "to waver, to be agitated, to totter and shake" (see 10:6). If David began to waver, the faithful people of the land would think that God was unable to fulfill His own promises. (See 35:19–21; 38:16–17.)

The Upward Look—His Faith (vv. 5–6)

The little word "but" indicates a transition from fear to faith and from questioning to claiming God's promises. In their false confidence, let the enemy rejoice, but David will rejoice in the Lord his God! David's feelings had been on a roller coaster, but God was still on the throne, and His character had not changed. God's mercy (steadfast love) was all that David needed for it would never fail (see 25:6; Isa. 63:9; Lam. 3:22–23). God's people don't live on explanations; they live on promises, and those promises are as unchanging as the character of God. "According to your faith be it unto you" (Matt. 9:29).

Relying on the Lord leads to rejoicing in the Lord and His salvation (yeshua). The word "bountiful" focuses on the goodness of God and His generosity in dealing with His people in grace. (See

103:2; 116:7; 119:17; and 142:7.) The NIV translates it, "The Lord has been good to me." David's circumstances haven't changed, but the Lord has changed him, and that occurred when David stopped looking at his feelings and his foes and by faith started looking to the Lord.

Psalm 14

The psalm deals with the character and conduct of the "practical atheist" and adds to the messages of Psalms 10 and 12. The three psalms present a vivid picture of the ungodly—their proud attitude (10), their deceitful words (12), and now their corrupt deeds (14). All that they are, say, and do comes from their arrogant (and ignorant) belief that "there is no God." Psalm 14 is duplicated in Psalm 53 with two changes: Psalm 53 uses the name "God" (Elohim) instead of "Jehovah" and replaces 14:6 with an addition to verse 5. David contrasted "the workers of iniquity" in Israel with the godly remnant ("the generation of the righteous" vv. 4–5) that sought God and obeyed the terms of His covenant. During the reign of King Saul, the spiritual level of the nation was very low, and many Jews followed the bad example of Israel's first king. But even in the worst of times, God has cared for His faithful remnant and has been their refuge in times of trouble. Note the characteristics of the "practical atheists."

Willful Folly—They Ignore God (vv. 1–3)

Our English word "fool" comes from a Latin word that means "bellows," suggesting that the fool is a person "full of hot air." In the Hebrew language, there are three basic words for "fool": *kesyl,* the dull, stupid fool; *ewiyl,* the unreasonable and perverted fool; and *nabal,* the brutish person who is like a stubborn animal. *Nabal* is the word used in 14:1, and it was the name of a man who was brutish and refused to help David (1 Sam. 25). People who say "There is no God" are not necessarily lacking normal intelligence; in fact, they may have good minds. However, they lack spiritual wisdom and insight. The *nabal* fool has a moral problem in the heart, not a mental problem in the head. The American evangelist Billy

Sunday used to say that sinners can't find God for the same reason criminals can't find policemen—they aren't looking!

Nabal fools are self-righteous and don't need or want God. They want to live their own lives the way they please. Their problem is willful ignorance and not lack of normal intelligence (2 Peter 3:5; Rom. 1:18–28). But this decision causes sad consequences in both their character and their conduct. By leaving God out of their lives, they cause their inner person to become more and more corrupt—the heart (v. 1), the mind (vv. 2, 4), and the will (v. 3). The Hebrew word means "rotten, putrid, decayed." It is used to describe Jeremiah's useless sash (Jer. 13:7). When God looks down to investigate (Gen. 6:5, 11–12; 11:15; 18:21), He sees people who are filthy (v. 3), a word that describes milk that has become rancid. "Gone aside" means they have turned their backs on God (Jer. 2:21) and refuse to fulfill the purpose for which they were created—to glorify God.

This indictment is universal: all people, individually or all together, cannot do anything at all that is good enough to merit heaven—no one, no, not one. Paul quotes from this passage in Romans 3 as part of his proof that the whole world is guilty before God and can be saved only by the grace of God as revealed in Jesus Christ (Rom. 3:9–26). Human depravity doesn't mean that all persons are as wicked as they can be, or that all are equally bad, or that no man or woman can ever do anything good (Luke 11:13). It simply means that all have a fallen nature they cannot change, and that apart from the grace of God, none can be saved from eternal judgment.

Sudden Fear—They Meet God (vv. 4–6)

Someone asked the agnostic British philosopher Bertrand Russell what he would say if, when he died, he suddenly found himself standing before God. Russell replied, "You did not give us sufficient evidence!" If the heavens above us, the earth beneath our feet, the wonders of nature around us, and the life and conscience within us, don't convince us of the existence of a wise and powerful Creator, how much more evidence must the Lord give? An atheistic Russian cosmonaut said he'd looked carefully while in space and didn't see God. Someone commented, "If he'd opened the door of the space capsule, he would have met Him!" The time comes when God and the sinner suddenly meet. See Belshazzar in Daniel 5, the rich farmer in Luke 12:13–21, and the people in Revelation 6:12–17.

Verse 4 gives us two more indictments: these practical atheists take advantage of the weak and the poor, and they will not call upon the Lord. To "eat people like bread" is a biblical metaphor for exploiting the helpless (27:2; 35:25; 53:4; Mic. 3:1–3; Lam. 2:16; and see Isa. 3:12, Jer. 10:25, Amos 2:6–8, and Mic. 2:2 and 7:3). People must never be used as a means to an end or "treated as consumer goods," as Eugene H. Peterson expresses it.[11] Instead of praying to God, the wicked prey on the godly. But then the Lord suddenly appears in judgment, and He identifies Himself with the remnant of faithful believers. We don't know what event David was referring to, but the parallel passage in 53:5 suggests a great military victory that left all the enemy dead, unburied, and therefore humiliated. Some interpret the scene as a metaphor of a court case and connect it with verse 6, "You evildoers frustrate the plans [counsel] of the poor" (NIV). Imagine God suddenly appearing in court and ousting the crooked judge! Whatever the meaning, this much is clear: God is in the generation of the righteous, God is their refuge when the enemy attacks, and God will protect His own people.

Joyless Future—They Have No God (v. 7)

God has promised that the Redeemer will one day come to Zion and deliver His people in mighty power (Isa. 59:16–21; Jer. 31:33–34), and Paul affirmed this at the close of his great discussion of the future redemption of the Jewish nation (Rom. 11:25–32). The word "captivity" in verse 7 doesn't refer to the Babylonian captivity, for Jeremiah made it clear that it would end in seventy years (Jer. 25:8–14). The phrase "bring back the captivity" means "to restore the fortunes, to radically change circumstances from bad to very good." The day will come when

Jesus Christ will return, defeat His enemies, cleanse the nation of Israel, and establish His righteous kingdom on this earth (Zech. 10–14). What a time of rejoicing that will be when the prayer "Thy kingdom come" is fulfilled!

But what about the wicked? They have no future with the Lord because they preferred not to know the Lord or live for Him. They lived according to the desires of their own heart, not to please the Lord and glorify Him. Those who reject Jesus Christ will spend eternity apart from the Lord and will honestly be able to say in hell, "There is no God—here!"

Psalm 15

Psalm 14 informs us that there were two groups in Israel: the "workers of iniquity" and "the generation of the righteous" (vv. 4–5). The former group forsook the law, but the latter group was a believing remnant that kept faith alive in the nation of Israel (Mal. 3:16–18). Today, the church is that "righteous generation," citizens of that heavenly Zion (Heb. 12:19–25), that ought to make a difference in this world (Phil. 2:12–16). Psalms 10 and 12 focus on those who are not acceptable to the Lord while Psalm 15 describes those who are acceptable and are invited to dwell in His tabernacle. David may have written this psalm after his second—and successful—attempt to bring the ark of the covenant to Mt. Zion (2 Sam. 6) where it was housed in a tent.

The rabbis taught that there were 613 commandments for the Jewish people to obey if they wanted to be righteous, but this psalm brings that number down to eleven. Isaiah 33:15–16 gives six requirements, and Micah 6:8 lists three. Habakkuk 2:4 names but one—faith—for faith in Jesus Christ is the only way to have your sins forgiven and be welcomed into the Lord's presence (John 14:6; Rom. 1:7; Gal. 3:11; Heb. 10:38). The psalm says nothing about offering sacrifices, for spiritual Israelites knew that it was their personal faith that brought them salvation (Mark 12:28–34). It's important to note that Psalm 15 is not a *prescription* for being saved but a *description* of how saved people ought to live if they want to please God and fellowship with Him. The list contains both positive and negative qualities, and these qualities must be present in all of life at all times. Believers who would fellowship intimately with God must follow David's example and meet three personal requirements.

Seeking God's Presence (v. 1)

After his men captured Mt. Zion, David made it the site of his residence and of the sanctuary of God, and Jerusalem became "the city of David" (2 Sam. 5:1–16). The tabernacle, the throne, and the "holy hill" belonged together (see 24:3–6; 2:6; 3:4; 43:3). To the believer today, Mt. Zion speaks of the heavenly city where God's people will dwell forever (Heb. 12:19–25). David asked this question because he loved the house of the Lord (26:8; 27:3–5; 65:4) and desired in his heart to know God better and fellowship with Him in a deeper way. The priests could come and go in the house of the Lord, but David, though he was king, had to keep his distance. "Abide" means "to sojourn as a stranger," while "dwell" suggests a permanent residential status, but here the verbs are probably synonymous. Knowing about eastern hospitality, David wanted to enjoy the benefits of being a resident in God's house—enjoying God's fellowship, God's protection, and God's provision. The word "dwell" in the Hebrew is *shakan* and gives us the word *shekineh*, referring to the presence (dwelling) of God's glory in the sanctuary (Ex. 25:8; see also 29:46; 1 Chron. 22:19; Pss. 20:2; 78:69; 150:1). David's great desire was to be with God in heaven and dwell in His house forever (23:6; 61:4), for God is our eternal home (90:1). Believers today can enjoy intimate fellowship with God through Jesus Christ (John 14:19–31; Heb. 10:19–25).

Obeying God's Precepts (vv. 2–5a).

Three basic areas of life are named in verse 2—blameless character, righteous conduct, and truthful conversation—and then these are applied specifically and practically in verses 3–5a. If we are right in these basic virtues, we will "work them out" in every area of life and be obedient to the Lord. Walk, work, and speak are present participles, indicating that the dedicated believer is constantly obeying the Lord and seeking to please Him.

Integrity—blameless character (vv. 2a, 4a, 4b). What we *are* largely determines what we *do* and *say*, so the first emphasis is on godly character. (See Isa. 33:14–16; 58:1–12; Jer. 7:1–7; Ezek. 18:5–9; Hos. 6:6; Mic. 6:6–8; Matt. 5:1–16.) "Blameless" doesn't mean "sinless," for nobody on earth is sinless. Blameless has to do with soundness of character, integrity, complete loyalty to God. Noah was blameless (Gen. 6:9), and the Lord admonished Abraham to be blameless (Gen. 17:1), that is, devoted wholly to the Lord. (See 18:13, 23–25; 101:2, 6; Deut. 18:9–13; Luke 16:13.) People with integrity will honor others who have integrity and who fear the Lord (15:4; 119:63). They will not be deceived by the flatterers (12:2–3) or enticed by the sinful (1:1). When godly people endorse the words and deeds of the ungodly, there is confusion in the church. "Like a muddied fountain and a polluted spring is a righteous man … who compromises his integrity before the wicked" (Prov. 25:26 AMP).

Honesty—righteous conduct (vv. 2b, 5a, 5b). People who "work righteousness" are honest in their own dealings and concerned that justice be done in the land. In the ancient Jewish monarchy, there wasn't much the average citizen could do about crooked judges or extortion (Eccl. 3:16–17; 4:1–3), but in today's democracies, each qualified citizen at least has a vote. Someone defined "politics" as "the conduct of public affairs for private advantage," and too often that is true. In verse 5, David applied the principle of honesty to two areas: asking for exorbitant interest and accepting bribes. Both were "sins in good standing" in the days of the divided kingdom, and the prophets preached against both sins (Isa. 1:23; 5:23; 10:2; Ezek. 22:12; Amos 5:11–12). The Jews were not permitted to charge other Jews interest (Ex. 22:25; 23:7–8; Lev. 25:35–38; Deut. 23:20), and judges were warned not to accept bribes (Ex. 23:8; Deut. 10:17–18; 27:25; 2 Chron. 19:5–7). There can be no justice in a society where money tells the court what is right or wrong.

Sincerity—truthful conversation (vv. 2c, 3–4c). Truth is the cement that holds society together. If people can get away with lies, then every promise, agreement, oath, pledge, and contract is immediately destroyed. The false witness turns a trial into a travesty and causes the innocent to suffer. But we must speak truth in love (Eph. 4:15) and use truth as a tool to build relationships as well as a weapon to fight deception. When truth is in the heart, then the lips will not speak lies, spread gossip (Lev. 19:16), or attack the innocent. People with truthful hearts will keep their vows and promises (Deut. 23:22–24; Eccl. 5:1–5). People of integrity don't have to use oaths to strengthen their words. A simple yes or no carries all the weight that's needed (Matt. 5:33–37). More trouble is caused in families, neighborhoods, offices, and churches by gossip and lies and the people who keep them in circulation than by any other means. The Lord wants truth in our innermost being (51:6), and He wants us to love the truth and protect it.

The Lord is blameless in what He is (1 John 1:6), righteous in what He does (Ezra 9:15), and truthful in what He says (1 Sam. 15:29), and He wants His guests to have the same characteristics.

Trusting God's Promise (v. 5c)

"He who does these things will never be shaken" (NASB). This means that the godly described in this psalm have security and stability in life and don't have to be afraid of earthquakes or eviction notices. "Moved" comes from a Hebrew word that refers to a violent shaking (46:3–4; 82:5; 93:1; 96:10; Isa. 24:18–20). God's promise to the godly is that they are firmly grounded on His covenant promises and need not fear. "He who does the will of God abides forever" (1 John 2:17 NKJV). In these last days, God is shaking things so that the true will remain and the false will be exposed (Heb. 12:18–29). Jesus closed the Sermon on the Mount with a parable about two builders (Matt. 5:24–27) whose structures (lives) were tested by the judgment storm, and only one stood strong. It was the life built by the person who did the will of God. The godly life that our Lord discussed in the Sermon on the Mount parallels the characteristics of the godly person described in Psalm 15,[12] and in both places, the promise is given: "You shall never be moved."

Psalm 16

This is a very personal hymn of joy that focuses on the goodness of the Lord. The personal pronoun "my" is used over a dozen times (my trust, my goodness, my cup, etc.). David's joy (vv. 9, 11) is expressed in words like "delight" (vv. 3, 6), "pleasant" and "pleasure" (vv. 6, 11), and glad (v. 9). David finds his delight only in the Lord and confesses that everything good in his life has come from God. This psalm may have been written shortly after the Lord gave His gracious covenant to David and assured him of an enduring throne (2 Sam. 7). That covenant was eventually fulfilled in the Lord Jesus Christ, the Son of David (Luke 1:32–33). The style of David's response to the covenant (2 Sam. 7:18–29) matches that of Psalm 16, a combination of joy, praise to God, humility, and submission to the divine will. This is the first use of Michtam in The Psalms; it is repeated in the inscriptions to 56–60. Students don't agree on the meaning of the word: engraved in gold, to cover, secret treasure, a poem containing pithy sayings. All six of the Michtam psalms end on a happy and triumphant note. This is also a Messianic psalm, for in his message at Pentecost (Acts 2:25–28), Peter said it referred to Jesus, and so did Paul in his sermon in the synagogue at Antioch of Pisidia (Acts 13:35). As he praised God for His grace and goodness, David presented three descriptions of the Lord, and all three may be applied to Jesus Christ today.

The Lord of Life (vv. 1–8)

"Preserve me" ("Keep me safe" NIV) doesn't suggest that David was in trouble or danger, as in Psalms 9 and 13. It simply means that he needed God's constant care and oversight so that he might honor the Lord and enjoy all the good things that only God could give him. God alone is good (Matt. 19:17), and apart from Him, we have nothing good.

A good relationship (vv. 1–2). The Lord is our highest good and greatest treasure (73:25, 28), the giver of every good and perfect gift (James 1:17). To know Him through Jesus Christ is the highest privilege in life. If we have anything that we think is good, and it doesn't come from God, it isn't good. God meets us with "the blessing of good things" (21:3 NASB), and His goodness follows us until we reach the Father's house (23:6). When Jesus Christ is your Savior (refuge) and Lord, you experience God's goodness even in the midst of trials. Our relationship to ourselves, our circumstances, other people, and the future depends on our relationship to the Lord.

A good companionship (vv. 3–4). We don't live the Christian life alone, because we're part of a great spiritual family and need each other. As in previous psalms, two groups are depicted: the believing remnant ("saints") and the unbelieving worshipers of idols (10:8–10; 11:2–3; 12; 14:5–6). The saints are those who trust God and obey His covenant, those who are set apart for the Lord. They take seriously God's command, "Be holy, for I am holy" (Lev. 19:2; 20:7–8, 26; 21:8). Israel was a kingdom of priests (Ex. 19:6; Deut. 7:6) and a holy nation, just as the church is today (1 Peter 2:9). David called them "the majestic ones" (NASB), a word that carries the meaning of excellence, nobility, and glory. In spite of our faults and failures, believers are God's elite, His nobility on earth. We must all love one another and use our God-given abilities and resources to minister to the family of God (Gal. 6:1–10). Like David, we must not compromise with those who disobey the Lord and worship idols (money, success, fame, etc.) but should seek to lead them to Jesus Christ, the source of all that is good and lasting. Multiplied gods only bring multiplied sorrows. David didn't even want to speak the names of the false gods of those in Israel who forsook the covenant (Ex. 23:13; Josh. 23:7). We are not to be isolationists, for the Lord has left us in this world to be salt and light; but we must be careful not to be defiled by their sins (James 1:27; 4:4; Rom. 12:2). No church is perfect, because no believer is perfect; but let's still give thanks for the people of God and seek to encourage them all we can.

A good stewardship (vv. 5–6). After Israel conquered the Promised Land, each tribe except Levi was assigned a special inheritance (Josh. 13–21). Because they served in the sanctuary and ate of the holy sacrifices, the priests and Levites had the Lord as their special inheritance (Num. 18:20–32; Deut. 10:8–9; 14:27–29; Josh. 13:14, 23), and David saw himself in that privileged position. "The Lord is the portion of my inheritance and my cup" (v. 5 NASB). To possess great wealth but not have the Lord is poverty indeed (Luke 12:13–21), and to enjoy the gifts but ignore the Giver is wickedness indeed. If Jesus is the Lord of our lives, then the possessions we have and the circumstances we are in represent the inheritance He gives us. The measuring lines marked off the inheritance of the tribes, clans and families in Israel, and then each individual lot was marked with a "landmark" that was not to be moved (Deut. 19:14; 27:17; Prov. 15:25; 22:28; 23:10–11). David rejoiced that God had caused the lines of his inheritance to fall in pleasant places, and that he had a "delightful inheritance" (NIV). He wanted to be a good steward of all that the Lord had given him.

A good fellowship (vv. 7–8). David's personal fellowship with the Lord was his greatest joy. This was when God instructed and counseled David and told him what to do and how to do it. David even went to "night school" to learn the will of God. (See 17:3; 42:8; 63:6; 77:2, 6.) "Night" is plural, suggesting "dark nights" or "night after night" learning from God. The word "instruct" carries with it the idea of discipline and chastening, for David learned many lessons when God's loving hand chastened him (Heb. 12:1–12). The Lord at his right hand suggests God as his advocate and defender. (See 73:23; 109:31; 110:5; 121:5; 1 John 2:2; Acts 2:33; 5:31.) With the Lord as his guide and guard, he had nothing to fear; he would not be moved (10:6; 15:5). The future is your friend when Jesus is your Lord.

The Conqueror of Death (vv. 9–10)

To delight in the Lord and His goodness and then lose all these blessings at death would be a great tragedy. "If in this life only we have hope in Christ, we are of all men the most pitiable" (1 Cor. 15:19 NKJV). But in His death and resurrection, Jesus has conquered death, and through faith in Him we have a "living hope"

(1 Peter 1:3ff). When David wrote "My body will rest secure" (v. 9 NASB), he was referring to Messiah and not to himself. Using these verses, Peter proved that Jesus had been raised from the dead, for it's obvious that David was dead and his body had decayed in his tomb (Acts 2:22–31). But Jesus did not see corruption! When He arose from the dead on the third day, He had a real and substantial body, but it was a glorified body that could ingest food (Luke 24:36–42) and was also able to appear and disappear (Luke 24:28–31) and pass through locked doors (John 20:19–29). David could face death with a glad heart and soul, and could rest in the grave in hope, knowing that one day, he, too, would have a new glorified body. Paul used this same text to prove the resurrection of Jesus Christ from the dead (Acts 13:26–39). The full light of revelation about death and resurrection had not yet been revealed in Old Testament times, although there are hints in verses like 17:15 and 73:24–26, but through Jesus Christ, God had brought "life and immortality to light through the gospel" (2 Tim. 1:10).

The Joy of Eternity (v. 11)

The noted philosopher and Harvard University professor Alfred North Whitehead once asked a friend, "As for Christian theology, can you imagine anything more appallingly idiotic than the Christian idea of heaven?"[13] But the focal point of heaven is not gates of pearl, streets of gold, or even angels and glorified saints. The central glory and joy of heaven is Jesus Christ (Rev. 4–5). The path of life that He shows us on earth today will end in even greater life when we enter heaven. Then we shall be in His presence and experience fullness of joy and pleasures forevermore. A foolish caricature of heaven shows white-robed saints with halos and harps, resting on little white clouds; but the Bible gives no such description. In our glorified bodies, we shall be like Jesus Christ (Phil. 3:20–21; 1 John 3:1–3), and we shall worship and serve Him forever. The pleasures of heaven will be far beyond any pleasures we have known here on earth, and as we enjoy the Lord and serve Him, we will not be restricted or encumbered by time, physical weakness, or the consequences of sin. So magnificent are the glories of heaven that the apostle John had to ransack human language to find words to describe it (Rev. 21–22).

Is Jesus Christ the Lord of your life? Have you accepted your inheritance and are you making the most of it for His glory? Do you anticipate being with Christ in glory? Is He the joy of your life today; for if He isn't, when will you be prepared to enjoy Him for all eternity?

Psalm 17

This is one of five psalms identified as "prayers" (17, 86, 90, 102, 142). The title is also used in Habakkuk 3:1 and Psalm 72:20. Since most of the psalms contain prayers to the Lord, we wonder why these five were singled out for this special title. Except for 90, written by Moses, they describe the writer in dangerous situations and crying out to God for deliverance. Only 17, 86, and 142 are attributed to David, and they were probably written during the years when Saul pursued him. There are at least a dozen words for prayer in the Hebrew language, and this one (*tepilla*) can also mean "to intervene." Perhaps the title also told the temple musicians what melody to use when using these psalms in public worship. Psalm 17 has definite connections with Psalm 16—"keep me" (16:1/17:8); the night (16:7/17:3); the use of El as the name for God (16:1/17:6); the hand (16:8/17:7, 14); God's presence (16:11/17:15); maintain or hold up (16:5/17:5). While there are suggestions of danger in Psalm 16 (vv. 1, 8, 10), the atmosphere is much more calm than what we find in 17. In this prayer, David deals with three pressing concerns and makes three major requests to the Lord. Each section opens with David addressing the Lord.

Vindication—"Examine Me" (vv. 1–5)

The psalm begins and ends with "righteousness" (vv. 1 and 15), because David wants God to examine him and vindicate him before his enemies. He saw God as a righteous judge who would give him a fair trial. King Saul and his leaders believed and circulated all kinds of lies about David, but the Lord and David knew the truth. David asked God to hear his plea, examine his life, and declare his integrity by giving him victory over the forces of Saul. Then everybody would know that God was with David, the man He has chosen to be Israel's king. God knew that David's prayer was sincere and that his life, though not sinless, was blameless. He was a man of integrity whose cause was a righteous one. During those years of exile, God had proved David's heart, visited and examined him, and tested him the way gold and silver are tested and refined in the crucible ("tested by fire"). (See 26:2; 66:10; 81:7; 95:9; 139:23–24; also Job 23:10; Rev. 3:18.) No matter what Saul and his men had said about him, David was able to affirm to the Lord that he had not spoken evil of the king. In fact, on at least two occasions, David could have slain Saul, but he refused to lay hands on God's chosen and anointed leader (1 Sam. 24, 26). Saul would have killed David (v. 9, "deadly enemies"), but David obeyed the Word of the Lord and kept himself from violence. Though he was a fugitive in the wilderness, David walked on the paths of the Lord and obeyed God's law.

David's declaration of righteousness was not evidence of pride or hypocrisy but of faithfulness to the Lord in difficult situations. You find similar language in 18:19–28, and see John 18:22–23 and Acts 23:1 and 24:16. David had a good conscience toward God.

Protection—"Keep Me" (vv. 6–12)

The enemy had surrounded him (vv. 9, 11; and see 1 Sam. 23:19–29), and though David was a masterful military tactician, he knew that without the Lord's help, he could not escape. God was not only the righteous judge, but He was also the powerful defender who could shelter David and his men from the enemy. He used the Hebrew name *El* as he addressed the Lord, a name that emphasizes God's great power, for He is "the Mighty God." His request in verse 7 reminds us of the "Song of Moses" in

Exodus 15:1–19. Jehovah is a God of marvels and wonders (Ex. 15:11) and great unfailing love (15:13), and His right hand works for His people (15:12). If God could deliver His people from Egypt, He could deliver David from the hand of Saul. (In Ps. 18, David will celebrate that victory.) David asked for "a marvelous demonstration of God's love" in the defeat of his enemies.

In verse 8, David used two images—the eye and the wings—to remind God that he was precious to Him. The "apple" of the eye is the pupil, the most delicate part of the eye. The Hebrew says "the little man of the eye," for when you look into someone's eyes, you can see yourself. Just as we protect the eye from injury, so David wanted the Lord to protect him. David may have borrowed this image from Deuteronomy 32:10. The phrase "under the shadow of thy wings" sometimes pictures the mother hen protecting her young (Matt. 23:37), but often it refers to the wings of the cherubim in the Holy of Holies of the tabernacle (Ex. 25:18–20). David asked the Lord to make his hiding place into a Holy of Holies, the place of God's throne and God's glory, protected by the angels of God (see 36:7–8; 57:1; 61:4; 63:7; Ruth 2:12). Because of the heavenly intercession of Jesus Christ, God's people today can enter into the Holy of Holies and fellowship with God (Heb. 10:1–25).

The enemy had arrogant mouths and hearts that were "enclosed in fat" (v. 10), that is, they had hearts that were callous from repeated disobedience to the Lord. In Scripture, "fatness" is sometimes associated with a selfish and worldly lifestyle (73:1–9; 119:70; Isa. 6:10). These people were morally and spiritually insensitive to what was right and weren't upset when they did something wrong. Paul called this "a seared conscience" (1 Tim. 4:2), for a heart covered with fat would not be sensitive to the needs of others (1 John 3:17). David's heart was sensitive to God's will; he knew that God wanted him to have "a broken and a contrite heart" (51:17). David was a compassionate shepherd, but Saul was a ravenous beast (v. 12; see 57:3 and 2 Sam. 1:23). Twice Saul threw his spear at David (1 Sam. 18:11; 19:10), on four occasions he sent soldiers to capture him, and

Saul went personally to lay hold of him (1 Sam. 19:11–23). Now, like a lion, Saul tracked his prey and waited for the right time to pounce; but the Lord protected David.

Salvation—"Rescue Me" (vv. 13–15)

David now sees the Lord as his gracious Redeemer, rescuing him and his men from the wicked hands of Saul. These verses contrast the "people of this world" to the "people of God" who live for that which is eternal. "Arise, O Jehovah" reminds us of 3:7, 7:6, 9:19 and 10:12, all of which go back to Numbers 10:35. He asks the Lord to confront Saul and his army, cast them down, and use His sword to defeat them. "Cast down" (v. 13) can be translated "make him crouch down like a lion that has been subdued." (See v. 12.) Except for his son Jonathan, Saul and his leaders were not spiritually minded but thought only of the things of this fleeting world (39:5; 49:1; 89:47). As "men of the world," they lived for time, not for eternity, and for their own pleasures, and not for the glory of God. (See Luke 16:8, 25 and James 5:5.)

Verse 14 is difficult to translate, but the sense seems clear: God was storing up judgment for David's enemies (Matt. 23:32; 1 Thess. 2:16), and their only reward would be in this life, not in the afterlife. They were full, they had many children who lacked nothing, and they would leave their wealth to their descendents. But the consequences of their sins would also be inherited by their descendents (Ex. 34:7; Num. 14:18). "May they have their punishment in full. May their children inherit more of the same, and may the judgment continue to their children's children" (v. 14 NLT). But verse 15 describes David's glorious future: seeing God's face and sharing God's likeness. This is one of the few texts in The Psalms that touches on the future life (see 16:11 and 73:23–26). "Awake" is a metaphor for the resurrection of the human body (2 Kings 4:31; Job 14:12, 14 and 26:19; Dan. 12:2; John 11:11; 1 Thess. 4:13–18). David seems to be saying, "Even when I die, the Lord won't desert me; for I shall be awakened and given a glorified body. I shall see His face, and I shall be satisfied!"

Psalm 18

This psalm of praise and victory was written and sung after the Lord made David king of all Israel and gave him victory over the nations that opposed his rule (2 Sam. 5, 8, 10). Another version of the psalm is found in 2 Samuel 22, and quotations and allusions are found in Psalm 116. No matter how much Saul persecuted David, David did not consider Saul his enemy. "Deliver" is one of the key words in the psalm; it is found in the title as well as in verses 2, 17, 19, 43, and 48 (KJV). It's possible that the new king used this song at a national day of prayer and praise to give thanks to the Lord for His manifold mercies to Israel. The psalm opens (vv. 1–3) and closes (vv. 46–50) with a doxology. David the servant of God (78:70; 89:3, 20, 39; 132:10; 144:10) addressed the Lord in verses 1, 25–29, 35–36, 39–40, 43, and 48, and in the rest of the psalm, he told the people what God had done for him, so the song blends worship and witness. The focus of the psalm is on the Lord and what He graciously did for His servant, but it also tells us what He can do for us today if we will trust and obey.

God Delivers When We Call on Him (vv. 1–18)

When David expressed his love for the Lord, he used a special word that means "to love deeply, to have compassion." It's related to the Hebrew word for "womb" (see Jer. 21:7) and describes the kind of love a mother has for her baby (Isa. 49:15), a father has for his children (103:13), and the Lord has for His chosen people Israel (102:13; Hos. 1:7; Deut. 13:17). It's a deep and fervent love, the kind of love all of us should have for the Lord (31:23). David expressed his love (v. 1), his faith (v. 2), and his hope (v. 3). The seven metaphors he used certainly reflect the life of an outdoorsman and a soldier. "Rock" (vv. 2, 31, 46) is a familiar metaphor for the Lord, speaking of strength and stability, a place of refuge (19:14; 28:1; 31:2–3; 42:9; 62:2, 6–7; 71:3; 78:20; 89:26; 92:15; 94:22; 95:1; 144:1; 1 Sam. 23:25). It goes back to Genesis 49:24 and Deuteronomy 32:4, 15, 18, and 30–31. "Fortress" pictures God as a stronghold, like the city of Jerusalem on Mount Zion (1 Sam. 22:4; 24:22; 2 Sam. 5:17; 23:14). "Shield" speaks of God's protection (3:3; 7:10; 28:7; 33:20; Gen. 15:1; Deut. 33:29), but it also is a symbol of the king (84:9; 89:18). David was Israel's shield, but the Lord was David's shield. "Horn" refers to strength (Deut. 33:17; 1 Sam. 2:1, 10; 1 Kings 22:11) and has Messianic connotations (Luke 1:69). This kind of God is worthy of our prayers and praise! (See 48:1; 96:4; 145:3.)

After expressing his devotion, David described his distress (vv. 4–6) and pictured himself as a man who had been hemmed in on every side, caught in a trap, bound with cords, and thrown into the water to drown. (See 88:16–178; 69:2, 15; 124:4; Job 22:11.) But, when he called, God began to act on his behalf. The great deliverance (vv. 7–19) is depicted as a storm. The Lord had been longsuffering with King Saul, but now His anger arose and began to shake things, like an earthquake and an erupting volcano (vv. 7–8; Ex. 15:8; Deut. 32:22). God came down in a storm, like a warrior in a chariot, carried along swiftly by a cherub. (See Gen. 3:24; Ex. 25:18; 2 Kings 19:15; Ezek. 1, 10). He was accompanied by darkness, rain, wind, hail (a rare thing in the Holy Land), thunder, and lightning (His arrows, v. 14; see 77:17, 144:6). All because David called on the Lord! (v. 6). At just the right time, God reached down and delivered David (vv. 16–19). Like Moses, he was drawn out of the water (Ex. 2:10). The enemy fell in defeat, but David stood firm, supported by the Lord (23:4). He was now king of Israel. Ten years of exile were ended, his life had been spared, and his ministry lay before him.

God Rewards When We Obey (vv. 19–27)

The word "distress" in verse 6 means "to be in a tight place, in a corner, hemmed in," but when the storm was over, David found himself in "a large place" where he could take "large steps" of faith in serving the Lord (v. 36). God enlarged David's trials (25:17) and used them to enlarge David! (4:1). David wasn't perfect, nor are we, but he was "a man after God's own heart" (1 Sam. 13:14, and see 15:28) and a man with a shepherd's heart (78:70–72; 2 Sam. 24:17). God delighted in David the way parents delight in the maturing of their children in character, obedience, and service. David was faithful to the Lord (vv. 20–24; 17:3–5), so the Lord faithfully cared for David (vv. 25–29). David knew God's law (v. 22) and obeyed it, in spite of the difficult circumstances of his exile. In the spirit of Samuel (1 Sam. 12:3) and Hezekiah (2 Kings 20:3), his affirmation of righteousness was an evidence of humility and honesty, not pride and deception. Note the use of the words righteousness and cleanness (vv. 20, 24), upright (blameless, vv. 23, 25), and pure (v. 26).

David had clean hands (vv. 20, 24) as well as skillful hands (v. 34; 78:72).

The way we relate to the Lord determines how the Lord relates to us (vv. 25–27). David was merciful to Saul, and God was merciful to David (Matt. 5:9). David was loyal ("blameless"), and God was faithful to him and kept His promises to bless him. David wasn't sinless, but he was blameless in his motives. The "pure in heart" (Matt. 5:8) are those whose hearts are wholly dedicated to God. Saul had been devious in his dealings with God, David, and the people, but David was honest and straightforward. It's true that early in his exile, he lied to Ahimelech the priest and to Achish, king of Gath (1 Sam. 21), but he soon learned that faith is living without scheming. Read verse 26 in the *New American Standard Bible* or the *New International Version* to see that God meets our "perverseness and crookedness" with His own shrewdness. The word translated "astute" or "shrewd" means "to wrestle," which reminds us of the way God dealt with Jacob (Gen. 32). God's character and covenants never change, but His dealings with us are determined by the condition of our hearts.

God Equips When We Submit to Him (vv. 28–45)

What was God accomplishing during those difficult years of Saul's reign? For one thing, He was disciplining His people for running ahead of Him and making Saul king (Hos. 13:10–11). In His longsuffering, He was also giving Saul opportunities to repent. At the same time, He was equipping David for his years of service. God takes time to prepare His servants: thirteen years for Joseph, forty years for Moses, and forty years for Joshua. The lessons David learned about himself and God during those years of exile helped to make him the man that he was. The images in these verses reveal God developing a great warrior, a compassionate leader, and a godly man.

The image of the lamp (v. 28) speaks of God's grace in keeping David alive during those dangerous years (Job 18:5–6; Prov. 13:9). It also speaks of the perpetuity of his family and dynasty (132:17; 2 Sam. 21:17; 1 Kings 11:36, 15:4; 2 Kings 8:19; 2 Chron. 21:7), culminating in the coming of Jesus Christ to earth (Luke 1:26–33). Because David trusted God (v. 30), God enabled him to run, leap, fight, and defeat the enemy (vv. 29, 32–34, 37–45). He could run through a troop, scale a wall, or leap like a deer up the mountains (see Hab. 3:19). This is not a glorification of war, for God trained him to fight His battles (v. 34) and protect Israel so they could accomplish His purposes on earth. David did not invade other countries just to add territory to his kingdom. Whatever land he gained was the result of his defeating armies that first attacked Israel.

Though David was a man of war, he recognized that it was God's gentleness that made him what he was. The word means "condescension." God condescended to look down and call David (1 Sam. 16), bend down and mold David (v. 35), and reach down and save David (v. 16); and then He lifted him up to the throne (vv. 39–45). This reminds us of what Jesus, the Son of David, did when He "stepped down" to come to earth as a servant and die for our sins (Phil. 2:1–11; see also John 8:1–11 and 13:1–11). Because David was submitted to the Lord, God could trust Him with the authority and glory of the throne. Only those who are under authority should exercise authority.

God is Glorified When We Worship Him (vv. 46–50)
After looking back at God's gracious ministry to him, what else could David do but praise Him? "He must increase, but I

must decrease" (John 3:30). David didn't take things into his own hands but allowed the Lord to vindicate him when the time was right (1 Sam. 24:1–7; 26:1–12; Rom. 12:17–21).

Paul quoted verse 49 in Romans 15:9 and applied it to the Jews praising God among the Gentiles. In Romans 15:10–11, the Jews and Gentiles rejoice together—the result of Paul's ministry to the Gentiles—and then Romans 15:12 announces Jesus Christ reigning over both Jews and Gentiles (see Isa. 11:10).

The psalm climaxes with David exalting the Lord for His covenant to him and to his descendants (v. 50; 2 Sam. 7). Little children often use their own names when they ask for something ("Please give Tommy a cookie"), and David used his own name here, just like a little child. (See also 2 Sam. 7:20). David used the word "forever," so he must have realized that it would be through the promised Messiah that the kingdom promises would be fulfilled. "And he shall reign forever and ever" (Rev. 11:15).

Psalm 19

Two quotations help to introduce this psalm. The first is from the German philosopher Immanuel Kant: "Two things fill the mind with ever new and increasing wonder and awe, the more often and the more seriously reflection concentrates upon them: the starry heaven above me and the moral law within me."[14] The second is from the well-known Christian writer C. S. Lewis: "I take this [Ps. 19] to be the greatest poem in The Psalms and one of the greatest lyrics in the world."[15] The church lectionary assigns this psalm to be read on Christmas Day, when the "Sun of Righteousness" came into the world (Mal. 4:2) and the "Living Word" was laid in the manger (John 1:14). The emphasis in the psalm is on God's revelations of Himself in creation, Scripture, and the human heart.

The Worlds Around Us—God the Creator (vv. 1–6)

David focused on the heavens above him, especially the circuit of the sun; but there are many worlds in God's creation. They include the earth beneath our feet, the plant and animal worlds on earth, in the skies and in the waters, the human world, the world of rocks and crystals, worlds visible to the human eye, and worlds so small we need special equipment to see them. World famous biologist Edward O. Wilson claims there may be as many as 1.6 million species of fungi in the world today, 10,000 species of ants, 300,000 species of flowering plants, between 4,000 and 5,000 species of mammals, and approximately 10,000 species of birds.[16] But these large numbers pale into insignificance when you start examining the heavens, as David did, and begin to calculate distances in light years. David knew none of this modern scientific data, and yet when he pondered the heavens, he was overwhelmed by the glory of the Lord.

The Jewish people were forbidden to worship the objects in the heavens (Ex. 20:4–5; Deut. 4:14–19; 5:8–9), nor were they allowed to practice astrology (Isa. 47:13–14; Jer. 10:1–5). They worshiped the Creator, not the creation (Rom. 1:25). The existence of creation implied the existence of a Creator, and the nature of the creation implied that He was wise enough to plan it and powerful enough to execute His plan and maintain what He had made. So complex a universe demands a Creator who can do anything, who knows everything, and who is present everywhere. But even more, *David knew that God was speaking to the inhabitants of the earth by means of His creation.* Creation is a "wordless book" that everybody can read because it needs no translation. God speaks through creation day after day and night after night; His speech "pours out" silently, abundantly, universally.

In Romans 10:18, Paul quoted verse 4 as part of his explanation of why Israel rejected the Gospel and what this rejection did to the nation. The Jewish people could never say that they had not heard God's message, because Psalm 19:4 says that the whole world has heard. Therefore, both Gentiles and Jews stand guilty before God and need to be saved through faith in Jesus Christ, and we must take the salvation message to them (Rom. 10:1–15). Paul quoted from the Septuagint version of the Old Testament, which uses "sound" (voice) instead of "line," but the sense is the same. Some translators use "influence" instead of "line." God's voice of power in creation prepares the way for His voice of grace in the Gospel. When Paul preached to Gentiles, he started with creation and then moved into the Gospel message (Acts 14:14–18; 17:22–31). Phillips Brooks gave the first instructions about God to Helen Keller, who was blind and deaf, and she replied that she had always known there was a God but didn't know what His name was. Our task is to tell the world that His name is Jesus (Acts 4:12).

David was an outdoorsman and often watched the sunrise and sunset, and what he saw day after day reminded him of a bridegroom leaving the marriage pavilion to claim his bride,[17] and a vigorous athlete running a race. The first image speaks of glory (the groom was richly attired), love and anticipation, while the second speaks of power and determination.

But in spite of this universal message that pours out day and night to the entire world, most people ignore it and reject God because they want to live as they please (Rom. 1:18–223). The repeated question, "Are people lost who have never heard about Jesus?" has two answers: (1) Yes, they are lost, because God speaks to them all day long, and they refuse to listen; (2) *What are you doing about getting the message to these people?*

The Word Before Us—God the Instructor (vv. 7–11)

The revelation of God in creation is truly wonderful, but it is limited when it comes to manifesting the attributes of God and His purposes for creation. Following the fall of man, creation has been subjected to futility and bondage (Gen. 3:17–19; Rom. 8:20–22), so we need something that reveals more clearly the character of God. That "something" is the inspired Word of God. When he wrote about creation, David used *Elohim* (v. 1), the name that speaks of God's great power; but when he wrote about God's Word, seven times he used the "covenant" name *Jehovah*, for the God of creation is also the God of personal revelation to His people. Israel was a very special nation, chosen by God to receive His law, covenants, and promises (Rom. 9:4). "He declares His words to Jacob, His statutes and his ordinances to

Israel. He has not dealt thus with any nation" (147:19–20 NASB). The heavens declare God's glory, but the Scriptures tell us what God did so that we may share in that glory. There is no conflict between what God does in His universe and what He says in His Word. It was by His Word that He created the worlds (33:9), and it is by His Word that He controls the worlds (33:11; 148:8). David recorded six different names for God's Word, six attributes of the Word, and six ministries of the Word in the lives of those who receive it and obey it.

Law of the Lord (v. 7a). This is the Hebrew word *torah*, which means "instruction, direction, teaching." Jewish people call the scrolls of the Law "The Torah," but the word refers to all of God's revelation. It comes from a word that means "to shoot an arrow," for a teacher aims to hit the target and achieve specific goals in the lives of the students. Unlike the textbooks that we write, God's Word is perfect, flawless, and complete. Because human language changes, we require new translations of God's Word; but the Word of God never needs revision or improvement. "Restore" is the same word used in Psalm 23:3 and means "to revive, to give new life." The Word of the Lord not only *has* life (Acts 7:3; Heb. 4:12), but it *imparts* spiritual life to all who receive it (1 Peter 1:23), and it *sustains* life as well (119:25, 37, 40, 88, 107, 149, 156, 159).

Testimony of the Lord (v. 7). The Ten Commandments were known by this name (Ex. 25:21), and they are the basis for God's law. But all of the Scriptures are God's witness to us of who He is, what He has said and done, and what He wants us to be and to do. The witness God bears of Himself in the written Word is sure and reliable. Through the Word, we become wise concerning salvation (2 Tim. 3:15) and the principles of successful living (Prov. 2; 8:33; 10:8). The "simple" are not mentally deficient people or the naïve people who believe everything, but the childlike people who humbly receive God's truth (Matt. 11:25; Luke 10:21–24).

Statutes of the Lord (v. 8). These are God's detailed instructions concerning the practical matters of everyday life. For the Old

Testament Jew, the statutes related to what they ate, how they dressed, how they kept clean, and so forth. God laid down certain basic laws and commandments, and the statutes applied them to specific situations. The New Testament epistles repeat nine of the Ten Commandments for believers today, omitting the Fourth Commandment, and then give applications of these principles. (See Eph. 4:20–32.) Some of the statutes that legislators have passed are not right and have brought grief, but the statutes of the Lord bring joy.

Commandment of the Lord (v. 8). The word means "that which is appointed." Because the Lord loves us, He commands us what to do and warns us what not to do, and how we respond is a matter of life or death (Deut. 30:15–20). God's commands are pure and lead to a pure life, if we obey from the heart. The Bible is the *Holy* Scriptures (Rom. 1:2; 7:12; 2 Tim. 3:15), and therefore His Word is "very pure" (119:140; Prov. 30:5). We are enlightened and learn God's truth when we obey what He says (John 7:17) and not just when we read it or study it (James 1:22–25). We are strangers on this earth, and the Word of God is the road map to guide us (119:19). Like a traveler on the highway, if we deliberately make a wrong turn, we go on a detour and fail to reach our destination.

Fear of the Lord (v. 9). This is an unusual name for the Scriptures, but it reminds us that we cannot learn the Word of God unless we show reverence and respect for the God of the Word. To teach the Bible is to teach the fear of the Lord (34:11; Deut. 4:9–10), and the mark of a true Bible student is a burning heart, not a big head (Luke 24:32; 1 Cor. 8:1). While some of the fears people have might be distressing and even defiling, the fear of God is clean and maturing. We do not decay or deteriorate as we walk in the fear of the Lord (2 Cor. 4:16–18).

Judgments of the Lord (v. 9). This can be translated "ordinances" or even "verdicts." It refers to the decisions of a judge. Throughout the Bible we see the Lord passing judgment on what people and nations do, and His rewards, rebukes, and punishments help us understand what pleases Him. In the nation of

Israel, the ordinances instructed the officers and judges in set-tling problems between individuals and in meting out punishments to guilty offenders. Believers today are not under the Old Testament law, but how those laws were applied helps us understand the righteousness of God and our need for His grace.

The way we treat the Bible is the way we treat the Lord, so it isn't difficult to determine if we are rightly related to God. Do we *desire His Word* because it's precious to us (12), even more than wealth (v. 10; 119:14, 72, 127, 162) or tasty food (119:103; 1 Peter 2:2)? Do we find satisfaction in "feeding on" God's Word? (See Matt. 4:4; Job 23:12; Jer. 15:16.) Would we skip a meal to spend time meditating on the Scriptures? Do we attend church dinners but not church Bible studies? Furthermore, do we *accept the warnings of the Word and act upon them?* To know the warning and not heed it is sin (James 4:17). Do we *enjoy the blessing of the Lord* because we've obeyed His will? To have an appetite for God's Word is a mark of a healthy Christian whose priorities are straight. The Lord has sent the Holy Spirit to teach us His Word, and if we walk in the Spirit, we will learn and live the truth (John 14:26; 16:12–15; 1 Cor. 2:9–10; 1 John 2:20–29).

The Witness Within Us—God the Redeemer (vv. 12–14)

Unless we have a personal relationship with the Lord so that God is our Father and Jesus is our Redeemer, what we see in cre-ation and what we read in the Bible will not do us much good. The Magi in Matthew 2:1–12 started on their journey by follow-ing God's star, a special messenger in the sky to direct them. Then they consulted God's Word and found that the King was to be born in Bethlehem; so they went to Bethlehem and there found and worshiped the Savior.[18] When you study God's cre-ation with a Bible in your hand, you can't help but see Jesus! He is seen in the vine (John 15), the sun (John 8:12; Mal. 4:2), the stars (Num. 24:17), the lambs (John 1:29), the apple trees and lilies (Song 2:3, 16; 6:3), the seed planted in the ground (John 12:23–24), and the bread on the table (John 6:35). The Word in the hand is fine; the Word in the head is better; but the Word in the heart is what transforms us and matures us in Christ (119:11; Col. 3:16–17).

The Word is a light (119:105) and a mirror (James 1:22–25) to help us see ourselves, search our hearts (Heb. 4:12), and recognize and acknowledge our sins. "By the law is the knowledge of sin" (Rom. 3:20; 7:7–14). "Secret sins" are those we don't even see ourselves, "sins of ignorance" we don't realize we've committed. The Old Testament law made provision for their forgiveness (Lev. 4; Num. 15:22–29) because the sinners were guilty even though they were ignorant of what they had done (Lev. 5:17). However, the law provided no atonement for presumptuous sins (Num. 15:30–36; Deut. 17:12–13). When David committed adultery and arranged to have Uriah murdered (2 Sam. 11–12), he sinned insolently with his eyes wide open and therefore could bring no sacrifice (Ps. 51:16–17). When he confessed his sins, God in His grace forgave him (2 Sam. 12:13), but David paid dearly for his transgressions. Unconfessed sins, even if committed ignorantly, can grow within the heart and begin to rule over us, and this can lead to our committing willful disobedience ("great transgression"—there is no article in the Hebrew text).

Creation is God's "wordless book," and the Scriptures are God's holy Word to us, but God wants to hear our words as "sacrifices" that please Him (141:1–2; Hos. 14:2; Heb. 13:15). The word translated "acceptable" refers to the priest's examination of the sacrifices to make sure they were without blemish. If the sacrifice wasn't acceptable to the Lord, the worshiper was not accepted by the Lord (Lev. 1:1–9; 22:17–25; Mal. 1:6–8). The words we speak begin with the thoughts in our heart (Matt. 12:33–37), so it's important that we meditate on God's Word and God's works, the first two themes of Psalm 19. If we delight in God's Word, we will naturally meditate on it and give expression of His truth with our lips, and this will help to keep us from sin (119:9–16, 23–24, 47–48, 77–78, 97–99). The usage here refers to the "kinsman redeemer" (*goel* = "one who has the right to redeem") who could rescue a relative from difficult situations (Lev. 25:25–28; Num. 35:11–34; the book of Ruth; Isa. 43:14).

Jesus is our Redeemer (Gal. 3:13; 4:5; Titus 2:14; Heb. 9:12; 1 Peter 1:18), and He became our "kinsman" when He came in sinless human flesh to die for us on the cross. He is both Rock and Redeemer, for He not only paid the price to set us free, but He also keeps us safe.

Psalm 20

This is a prayer before the battle, and Psalm 21 is the praise after the victory. In verses 1–5, the people pray for their king (we/you); David the king encourages the people in verses 6–8 (I/we/they); and both the king and the people speak in verse 9, where "the king" is Jehovah God, *The King*. The psalm begins and ends with a plea for God to hear them as they pray and to give victory to the army of Israel (vv. 1, 9). The anointed king was the very life and breath of the nation (Lam. 4:20) and the lamp of Israel (2 Sam. 21:17), and the enemy soldiers would make him their special target (1 Kings 22:31). Those who have problems with the military aspects of some of David's psalms should remember that David went to war only when the enemy attacked Israel. He did not invade other nations just to gain territory, and he was fighting the Lord's battles (1 Sam. 17:47; 25:28; 2 Chron. 20:15). The covenant God made with David (2 Sam. 7:11) assured him of victory over his enemies. In this regard, David is a picture of our Lord Jesus Christ, the Commander of the Lord's armies (Josh. 5:14–15), who one day will ride in victory against the armies of this world (Ps. 45:3–7; Rev. 3:14; 17:14; 19:11–21). Just as physicians fight a battle against disease and death, so our Lord wages a war against sin and evil. "Lord Sabaoth His name / From age to age the same / And He must win the battle" (Martin Luther). This psalm describes three essentials for victory as God's people fight against the forces of evil.

A Praying People (vv. 1–5)
Before the army went out to battle, the Jewish law of warfare required the officers and soldiers first to dedicate themselves to

the Lord (Deut. 20:1–4), and this psalm speaks of such a dedication service. "Battles are won the day before," said Marshall Foch, commander of the Allied forces in World War I. The word "may" is used six times in verses 1–5 as the people prayed for their king (see NASB, NIV). Not only were the lives of the king and his army involved, but so also was the glory of the Lord (vv. 5, 7). It was a "day of trouble" (see 50:15; 59:16; 77:2; 86:7; 102:2), but Jehovah is a "very present help in trouble" (Ps. 46:1). In verse 1, the people prayed that God would answer the king's prayers and lift him up above the enemy ("defend"). "The God of Jacob" is a familiar title for the Lord (24:6; 46:7, 11; 75:9; 76:6; 81:1, 4; 84:8; 94:7; 114:7; 132:2, 5; 146:5; and see Isa. 49:26 and 60:16). It suggests that God works on behalf of those who are weak and in special need (see Gen. 35:1–3).

David had brought the ark of the covenant to Mt. Zion (2 Sam. 6), which meant that God was enthroned among His people and would help them (Pss. 80:1 and 99:1 NIV). His holy name was upon the sanctuary (Deut. 14:23; 16:2, 11), and therefore His glory was at stake. Many times David had brought sacrifices to the altar and dedicated himself to the Lord (burnt offerings) and given thanks to Him, and he would have offered sacrifices before coming to lead the army. (See 1 Sam. 7:9ff and 13:9ff.) The Lord did not forget these offerings that were given as memorials to His great name (Lev. 2:1–2, 9, 16; 5:12; and see Acts 10:4). But David had done more than worship God; he had also sought the Lord's will concerning strategy for the battle (see 1 Sam. 23). The people prayed that God would bless those plans, for petitions and plans must go together. The central verse in the psalm is verse 5, a confident affirmation of victory before the battle even started. Raising the banners and waving them was a sign of victory, and "Jehovah our banner" was one of God's special names (see Ex. 17:15–16). The theme of salvation (victory) is repeated in verses 6 and 9.

A Confident Leader (vv. 6–8)

"Everything rises and falls with leadership," Dr. Lee Roberson often says, and he is right. Now the king speaks and assures his people that he is confident of success because the Lord has chosen him ("anointed") and heard his prayers. The people had prayed "May the Lord hear" (v. 1) and David's reply was, "He will hear" (v. 6). The Lord would not only send help from Zion (v. 2) but also from the very throne of heaven! (v. 6). Just as God's hand had reached down and saved David in the past (18:9–18), so His hand would deliver him from the enemy. In the covenant God made with David, He had promised him success in battle (2 Sam. 7:11), and David claimed this promise by faith.

Was the enemy coming with horses and chariots? There was no need to fear, for Israel's faith was in the Lord. Israel's kings were commanded not to acquire great numbers of horses and chariots (Deut. 17:16), a law that Solomon disobeyed (1 Kings 10:26–27). Note that the law of warfare even mentions horses and chariots (Deut. 20:1–4, and see 32:20 and 2 Sam. 10:18). God had defeated Egypt's best troops (Ex. 14:6ff; 15:4), and He could defeat the enemy attacking David (Ps. 33:16–17; Prov. 21:31; 2 Kings 19:20–23). "If God be for us, who can be against us?" (Rom. 8:31). God's people don't boast in their human resources but in the God who alone can save them in every situation. Only this kind of faith will honor the strong name of the Lord. The enemy will go down in defeat, but Israel will stand upright as victors.

A Sovereign Lord (v. 9)

Translators don't agree as to whether "king" in this verse refers to David or to the Lord, the King of Israel (5:2; 10:16; 48:1–2; 84:3; 95:3; 145:1). The *Prayer Book Version* of the Psalms reads, "Save, Lord, and hear us, O King of heaven, when we call upon thee"; and the *English Revised Version* reads, "Save Lord: Let the King answer us when we call." The *American Standard Version* also reads "King," and so does the *New American Standard Bible*. But whether "king" refers to David or to the Lord, verse 9 affirms that the Lord is sovereign because He hears prayer and is able to answer. I prefer "King," and I can see David, the people, and the troops acknowledging the sovereignty of the great king of Israel. Unless the Lord is King, there can be no victory. "For the Lord is the great God, the great King above all gods" (95:3 NIV). "The Lord Almighty—he is the King of Glory" (24:10 NIV). David plans his strategy (v. 4), but the Lord alone can determine the outcome.

Psalm 21

This is probably the praise hymn David and his people sang after the victories prayed for in Psalm 20 as they celebrated a day of national thanksgiving. They had prayed for specific blessings and God had granted them. The hymn opens and closes with praise for God's strength granted to His king and the army (vv. 1, 13). Answered prayer ought to be acknowledged by fervent praise. Since only Messiah could win the victories prophesied in verses 8–12, the Jewish Targum states that this psalm is about "King Messiah." Of course, David is a type of Jesus Christ.

Looking Back: Celebration for Past Victories (vv. 1–7)

The people and their king address the Lord and thank Him for what He did for them in answer to their prayers. Compare 21:1 with 21:5, 21:2 with 20:4, and 21:5 with 20:1. The word "salvation" in verses 1 and 5 (KJV) means "deliverance, victory." David had prayed that his life be spared (v. 4), and the Lord answered him (v. 2; 20:1, 6). This blessing was part of God's covenant with David (2 Sam. 7:16). The word "prevent" in verse 3 (KJV) means "to see to it beforehand" (69:10; 79:8). The Lord met Joshua before the battle of Jericho (Josh. 5:13–15), and Melchizedek (a type of Jesus Christ) met Abraham after the battle with the kings (Gen. 14); and God went before David and "welcomed" him (NIV) to the battlefield and the victory. That God goes before His obedient people is a great encouragement (48:14; 77:20; John 10:4; Deut. 8:2).

Some students connect the gold crown of verse 3 with Israel's victory over the Ammonites at Rabbah (2 Sam. 12:26–31), but this victory actually belonged to Joab. David didn't join the siege until the very end. The crown is probably symbolic of God's special "blessings of goodness" upon David (v. 5 and see 8:5). To David, the victory God gave was like a second coronation, assuring him that he was indeed God's anointed. Length of days forever (v. 4) and blessings forever (v. 6) remind us of God's covenant with David that was ultimately fulfilled in Christ (2 Sam. 7:6, 13, 16, 29; Luke 1:30–33; and see Pss. 10:16; 45:17; 48:14; and 133:3). It was customary to attribute endless life to kings (Neh. 2:3; Dan. 2:4). While he reigned, David would not be "shaken" by his enemies, because his faith was in the Lord (v. 7; 10:6; 16:8; 55:22; 121:3). This declaration of faith is the central verse of the psalm.

Looking Ahead: Anticipation of Future Victories (vv. 8–12)

The king trusted in the Lord and so did the people, and they affirmed their faith as they addressed these words to the king. The emphasis is now on the future victories God will give David and Israel because they have faith in the living God. (See 20:7.) God's right hand is more than a symbol of power; it actively works for His people and brings defeat to their enemies (89:13; 118:15–16; Deut. 5:15). "Find out" (KJV) means "dispose of." Just as fire devours what it touches, so the Lord will devour David's enemies as a cook burns fuel under the oven (79:5; 89:46; 97:6; Mal. 4:1). The nation of Israel and David's posterity would be preserved (18:50; 2 Sam. 7:16; Gen. 12:1–3), but there would be no future for the enemy. "Fruit" refers to posterity. (See 127:3, 132:11; Deut. 28:4; Hos. 9:16.) God did give David many victories and he greatly extended Israel's borders and brought peace to the kingdom. The nations might get together and plot against him, but David would still win the battle.

Looking Up: Exaltation of the Lord of the Victories (v. 13)

As in 20:9, the psalm concludes with a statement addressed to the Lord and expressing praise for His greatness. David fought battles and won victories, not to exalt himself, but to magnify the Lord, and his people knew this. David showed this same spirit as a youth when he killed the giant Goliath (1 Sam. 17:36, 45–47).

Psalm 20 closes with the people and the king asking God to hear their prayers, and Psalm 21 closes with the prayer that God would be "lifted up on high" and exalted. "[T]hose who honor Me, I will honor" (1 Sam. 2:30 NKJV).

Psalm 22

Psalms 22, 23, and 24 form a trilogy on Christ the Shepherd. In 22, the Good Shepherd dies for the sheep (John 10:1–18); in 23, the Great Shepherd lives for the sheep and cares for them (Heb. 13:20–21); and in 24, the Chief Shepherd returns in glory to reward His sheep for their service (1 Peter 5:4). *Aijeleth Shahar* (or *Hash-shahar*) is interpreted to mean "the doe (or hind) of the morning" or "help at daybreak." It may have been the name of the tune to which this psalm was sung.

David is the author, but we have a difficult time finding an occasion in his life that would call forth this kind of psalm. According to the record, the Lord never deserted him in his hour of need but always provided friends to help him and deliverance from his enemies. The intense suffering described here isn't that of a sick man in bed or a soldier in battle. *It's the description of a criminal being executed!* Numerous quotations from the psalm in the four Gospels, as well as Hebrews 2:10–12, indicate that this is a Messianic psalm. We may not know how this psalm related to the author's personal experience, but we do know that David was a prophet (Acts 2:30), and in this psalm he wrote about the death and resurrection of Jesus Christ. The first part (vv. 1–21) focuses on prayer and suffering and takes us to the cross, while the second part (vv. 22–31) announces the resurrection and expresses praise to the glory of God. An understanding of Messiah's suffering and glory is basic to grasping the message of the Bible (Luke 24:25–27; 1 Peter 1:11). We will try to see both David and the Son of David as we study the psalm.

Prayer in a Time of Suffering (vv. 1–21)

There were three burdens that moved David to pray for God's help, and they apply to Jesus as well.

He was abandoned by the Lord (vv. 1–5). The opening words of the psalm immediately transport us to Calvary, for Jesus quoted them at the close of a three-hour period of darkness (vv. 1–2; Matt. 27:45–46; Mark 15:34). "I am not alone," Jesus had told His disciples, "because the Father is with me" (John 16:32), and yet He cried out that the Lord had forsaken Him. When He spoke these words, He had been engaged in a mysterious transaction with the Father, dying for the sins of the world (1 John 2:2; 4:14). On the cross, Jesus was "made sin" (2 Cor. 5:21) and made "a curse" (Gal. 3:13) for us. In some inexplicable way He experienced what condemned lost sinners experience "away from the presence of the Lord" (2 Thess. 1:9 NASB; see Matt. 25:41). However, note that both David and Jesus called Him "*my* God," making it clear that they still knew and trusted the Father.

This was not the cry of a complaining servant but the sob of a broken–hearted child asking, "Where is my father when I need him?" As David prayed for help, he wondered why God didn't answer him. After all, He was a God of compassion who was concerned about His people, and He was a holy God who practiced justice. Even more, Israel was God's special covenant nation, and He was "enthroned upon the praises of Israel" (v. 3 NASB; see 80:1; 99:1; Isa. 66:1–2). Only Israel had God's divine law and could worship Him in a way acceptable to Him (John 4:21–24). Many times in the past, the Lord had kept His covenant promises to Israel and fought battles, so why was He distant now? Compassion, justice, and the sacred covenant were strong arguments for God's intervention—but He was silent.

He was despised by the people (vv. 6–11). These words especially apply to our Savior. "I am a worm and not a man" (NASB) is a forgotten "I am" statement that speaks of how little value the leaders of Israel and the Roman officials placed on Jesus of Nazareth. A worm is a creature of the ground, helpless, frail, and unwanted. Isaiah 52:14 predicted that Messiah would be terribly disfigured by His enemies and not even look human. (See also Isa. 49:7, 50:6 and 53:3, and for "reproach," see 69:9 and Rom. 15:3. For the fulfillment of vv. 7–8, see Matt. 27:39 and 43, Mark

15:29, and Luke 23:35–36.) David reminded the Lord that from birth He had cared for him, so why abandon him now? (See 139:13–16.) David had learned to trust in the Lord ("hope" KJV) from infancy, and was not going to relent now. "Trust" is used three times in verses 4–5 and also in verse 8.

He was condemned by the law (vv. 12–21). David looked around and saw his enemies, and so brutal were they that he compared them to animals: bulls (vv. 12, 21), lions (vv. 13, 21; and see 7:2; 10:9; 17:12; 35:17; 57:4; 58:6), and dogs (vv. 16, 20). Bashan was a very fertile area east of the Sea of Galilee and north from the Yarmuk River to Mt. Hermon, now known as the Golan Heights (Jer. 50:19; Deut. 32:14; Ezek. 39:18; Amos 4:1). The wild bulls encircled their prey and then moved in for the kill. The dogs were ravaging savage wild dogs that lived in the garbage dumps and traveled in packs looking for victims. The people involved in arresting and condemning Jesus were only beasts attacking their Creator (2:1–3; Acts 4:23–28). Then David looked within and saw himself (vv. 14–18), and the description is surely that of a man being crucified. He is stripped of his clothing, placed on a cross, and nails are driven through his hands and feet. As he hangs between heaven and earth, his body is dehydrated, intense thirst takes over, and the end of it all is "the dust of death" (v. 15; see Gen. 3:19; Job 7:21; 10:9; 17:16; Eccl. 3:20). Like ebbing water and melting wax, his strength fades away, and he becomes like a brittle piece of broken pottery. (For the application to Jesus, see Matt. 27:35, Mark 14:24, Luke 23:34, and John 19:23–24, 28.) It is remarkable David should describe crucifixion because it was not a Jewish means of capital punishment, and it's unlikely that he ever saw it occur. David the prophetic psalmist (Acts 2:30) saw what would happen to Messiah centuries later.

Finally, David looked up to the Lord and prayed one more time for the strength he needed (vv. 19–21). In verse 1, he mentioned that God was far from helping him, and he repeated this in verse 11, but he asks a third time for the Lord to come near and intervene. "The sword" in verse 20 may refer to the authority of the Roman government (Rom. 13:4), for it was Pilate who authorized Christ's death. "Darling" in verse 20 (KJV) means "my only one," as an only child (Gen. 22:2), and refers to the one and only life that David possessed (see 35:17). Once lost, it could not be regained. We may translate verse 21, "Save me from the lion's mouth, and from the horns of the wild oxen you have delivered me" or "you have heard me." In verse 2, he wrote that God had not answered, but now he almost shouts, "You have answered me!" (See also v. 24.) This is the turning point of the psalm.

Praise in the Time of Victory (vv. 22–31)

We move now from suffering to glory, from prayer to praise (vv. 22, 23, 25, 26). In verses 1–21, Jesus "endured the cross," but now He enters into "the joy that was set before him" (Heb. 12:2, and see Jude 24). He had prayed to be delivered out of death (Heb. 5:7), and that prayer was answered. Jesus sang a Passover hymn before He went to the cross (Matt. 26:30; Mark 14:26), and according to Hebrews 2:12, the risen Christ praised God in the midst of His people after His resurrection (see Matt. 18:20). Note that in His song, our Lord deals with the expanding outreach of the atoning work He finished on the cross.

The great assembly (vv. 22–25). There is no biblical evidence that Jesus appeared to any unbelievers in the days immediately after His resurrection (1 Cor. 15:1–7). "The great congregation" (assembly) included those who believed in Jesus who became a part of His church when the Spirit came at Pentecost. But the church is made up of believing Jews and Gentiles who form one body in Christ (Eph. 2:11ff), so the song included the seed of Jacob (Israel). The first Christians were Jewish believers, and all Gentiles in the church are, by faith, the children of Abraham (Gal. 3:26–29). God did not despise His Son in whom He is well pleased (v. 24), but accepted His work on the cross and proved it by raising Him from the dead (Rom. 4:24–25).

The glorious kingdom (vv. 26–29). The image here is that of a feast and was a familiar picture to the Jews of the anticipated Messianic kingdom (Isa. 25:6–9; Matt. 8:10–12; Luke 13:29;

14:15). When a Jewish worshiper brought a peace offering to the Lord, he retained part of it to use for a feast for himself, his family, and any friends he wanted to invite (Lev. 3; 7:15ff); and this tradition became a picture of the future glorious kingdom. But believing Gentiles will be also included in this feast (v. 27), and Messiah will reign over all the earth. God promised Abraham that his descendants would bring blessing to the whole world (Gen. 12:1–3). This has been fulfilled in the coming of Christ to die for the world, but when He comes again, it will have a glorious fulfillment in the establishing of His glorious kingdom. Both the prosperous and the poor will submit to Him (v. 29) and find their satisfaction in His grace alone. Orthodox Jews close their religious services by quoting Zechariah 14:9—"And the Lord shall be king over all the earth; in that day there shall be one Lord with one name" (Jewish Publication Society translation).

The generations to come (vv. 30–31). The blessings of the atonement and the kingdom will not be temporary but perpetual, from one generation to another. Three generations are listed here: a seed (see Isa. 53:10), a second generation, and a people that shall be born. This reminds us of 2 Timothy 2:2. But the emphasis isn't on what God's children have done but on the fact that the Lord did it all: "He has done it" (v. 31 NIV). "It is finished" is what Jesus cried from the cross (John 19:30).

Psalm 23

This is the psalm of the Great Shepherd who cares for His sheep and equips them for ministry (Heb. 13:20–21), the "great High Priest" (Heb. 4:14) who "ever lives to make intercession for us" (Heb. 7:25). Certainly this psalm has a message for the sorrowing, but it's unfortunate that it's used primarily at funerals, because Psalm 23 focuses on what Jesus does for us "all the days of [our] life" and not just at death (v. 6). It's also unfortunate that people tend to spiritualize the psalm and fail to see it in its true setting. They see David, a "young shepherd boy," lying on his back in the pasture and pondering the things of God, when he probably wrote this psalm late in his life, possibly during the rebellion of Absalom (2 Sam. 13–19). In it, David deals with some of the difficult things he experienced during his long walk with the Lord. While people of all ages love and quote this psalm, its message is for mature Christians who have fought battles and carried burdens.

Abel, the first martyr, was a shepherd (Gen. 4:2) and so were the patriarchs of Israel. Moses spent forty years caring for his father-in-law's sheep, and David, Israel's greatest king, served his father as a shepherd. The image of God as Israel's shepherd begins in Genesis 48:15 (NIV) and 49:24 and continues throughout Scripture (28:9; 80:1; 95:7; 100:3; Isa. 40:11; 49:10; Jer. 31:10; Ezek. 34:11–15; Matt. 10:6; 15:24; Mark 6:34). The promised Messiah was seen as a shepherd (Ezek. 34:16, 23; Mic. 5:4; Zech. 13:7; Matt. 2:6; 26:3; Mark 14:27; John 10). In Psalm 22, David compared the enemy to animals that are clever and strong (22:12–16, 21), but in this psalm, he pictured God's people as lowly sheep. Why? So we would learn about the Shepherd and see how tenderly He cares for us. Sheep are defenseless animals that are prone to get lost, and they need almost constant care. You can't drive sheep, as you do cattle; they must be led. The eastern shepherds know their sheep by name and can call them and they will come (John 10:1–5). The sheep were kept, not for food but for wool, milk, and reproduction. In this psalm, David explains that if we follow the Lord and trust Him, He will meet our every need, no matter what the circumstances may be.

In the Pasture—Adequacy (vv. 1–3)
"The Lord" is Jehovah God, the covenant making God of Israel. The compound names of Jehovah in the Old Testament reflect the contents of this psalm.

> "I shall not want"—Jehovah-Jireh, the Lord will provide" (Gen. 22:14)
> "still waters"—Jehovah-Shalom, "the Lord our peace" (Judg. 6:24)

"restores my soul"—Jehovah-Rophe, "the Lord who
heals" (Ex. 15:26)

"paths of righteousness"—Jehovah-Tsidkenu, "the Lord
our righteousness" (Jer. 33:16)

"you are with me"—Jehovah-Shammah, "the Lord is
there" (Ezek. 48:35)

"presence of my enemies"—"Jehovah-Nissi, "the Lord
our banner" (Ex. 17:15)

"anoint my head"—Jehovah-M'Kaddesh, "the Lord who
sanctifies" (Lev. 20:8)

The verb is a participle and means "is shepherding me."
Eastern shepherds guarded their sheep, led them, provided food
and water for them, took care of them when they were weary,
bruised, cut or sick, rescued them when they strayed, knew their
names, assisted in delivering the lambs, and in every way simply
loved them. What does this say to pastors today? In the Holy
Land, pastures were lush and green following the rainy season but
this didn't last all year. There were no fences, the land was rough
and dangerous, abounding with wild animals and snakes, and the
helpless flock needed constant oversight. Even if he didn't own
the sheep, the shepherd treated them as if they were his and had
to give an accounting for any that were missing. Our Lord called
believers "my sheep" because He died for them (1 Peter 1:18–19)
and because the Father gave them to Him (John 17:12). The
emphasis in verses 1–3 is that Jesus is adequate for every need the
sheep may have as they are in the pasture. Primarily, they need
food (grass), water, rest, and a shepherd who knows where to lead
them. When God's people follow their Shepherd, they have all
that they need and will not lack the necessities of life (37:25;
Matt. 6:33; Phil. 4:19). Sheep will not lie down when they are
hungry, nor will they drink from fast-flowing streams. Sometimes
the shepherd will temporarily dam up a stream so the sheep can
quench their thirst. You can read verse 2 "beside the *stilled* water."
In heaven, our Shepherd will lead us to fountains of living water
(Rev. 7:17).

The word translated "lead" in verse 2 means "to lead gently." You cannot drive sheep. The sheep hear the shepherd's voice and follow him, just as we listen to Christ in His Word and obey Him (John 10:3–5, 16, 27). If a sheep goes astray, the shepherd leaves the flock in charge of his helpers and goes to find the lost animal. (See Matt. 9:36; 18:12–14; and Luke 15:3–7.) The word "paths" in verse 3 means "well-worn paths, ruts." When sheep start to explore an exciting new path, it will lead them into trouble. "Do not be carried about by varied and strange teachings" (Heb. 13:9 NASB). God cares for us because He loves us and wants us to glorify Him ("for his name's sake"). The shepherd cares for the sheep because he loves them and wants to maintain his own good reputation as a faithful shepherd.

In the Valley—Serenity (v. 4)

This is the central verse of the psalm, and the personal pronoun changes from *he* to *you*. David is not speaking *about* the shepherd but speaking *to* the shepherd. In the dark valley, He is not before us but beside us, leading the way and calming our fears. The "vale of deep darkness" represents any difficult experience of life that makes us afraid, and that includes death. Sheep lack good vision and are easily frightened in new circumstances, especially where it's dark; and the presence of the shepherd calms them. The rod was a heavy cudgel with which the shepherd could stun or kill an attacking beast, and the staff was the shepherd's crook, which he used to assist the individual sheep. At evening, he would have the sheep pass under the crook one by one so he could count them and examine them (Lev. 27:32). It gave the flock peace knowing that the shepherd was there and was equipped for any emergency. He is "Immanuel … God with us" (Matt. 1:23). Jesus is not a hireling who runs away at the sight of danger; he is a true Shepherd who lay down his life for his sheep (John 10:11–15). God's sheep have "peace with God" (Rom. 5:1) and may enjoy "the peace of God" (Phil. 4:4–7) as they trust Him. Through life, as we follow the Shepherd, we will have many and varied experiences, some of which will be very trying, but none of them can take the Lord by surprise. We may trust Him and have peace. The closer we are to our Shepherd, the safer we are and the more His peace will fill our hearts. (See Isa. 40:9–11; 43:1–3; Rev. 1:17–18.)

In the Fold—Certainty (v. 5)

Some students believe there is a change of metaphor here, from the shepherd and his sheep to the host and his guest, but this is not necessarily the case. "Table" doesn't necessarily refer to a piece of furniture used by humans, for the word simply means "something spread out." Flat places in the hilly country were called "tables" and sometimes the shepherd stopped the flock at these "tables" and allowed them to eat and rest as they headed for the fold (see 78:19). After each difficult day's work, the aim of the shepherd was to bring the flock safely back to the fold where the weary sheep could safely rest for the night. Sometimes at the fold, the shepherd would spread out food in a trough, because sheep lie down and rest after they have eaten. As they slept, they would be protected by a stone wall that surrounded them, and the shepherd himself would sleep across the opening and be the door (John 10:7–9). During the night, thieves and dangerous animals might approach the fold, but there was no way they could reach the sheep. The Lord doesn't always remove the dangers from our lives, but He does help us to overcome them and not be paralyzed by fear. This is what it means to be "more than conquerors" and have peace in the midst of danger (Rom. 8:31–39).

The shepherd would examine the sheep as they entered the fold to be sure none of them was bruised, injured, or sick from eating a poisonous plant. To the hurts, he applied the soothing oil, and for the thirsty, he had his large two-handled cup filled with water. He would also apply the oil to the heads and horns of the sheep to help keep the flies and other insects away. The sheep knew they were safe and they could sleep without fear.

In the Father's House—Eternity (v. 6)

As the shepherd lay each night at the door of the sheepfold, he looked back over the day and gave thanks that the Lord had blessed them with goodness and mercy. As an old man, David looked back over his long life and came to the same conclusion. In spite of his sins and failures, he had been followed by goodness and mercy, which is the Old Testament equivalent of Romans 8:28. "Surely" means "only." As David looked ahead, he knew he would be in heaven—the Father's house—forever. This isn't a reference to the temple, because the king didn't live in the temple. Furthermore, nobody could live there or anywhere else forever. Jesus used this vocabulary to speak about heaven (John 14:1–6). The things that perplex and disturb us today will all be clear when we get to heaven. We will look back and see "only goodness and mercy." Under the old covenant, the sheep died for the shepherd, but under the new covenant, the Shepherd died for the sheep—*and we shall meet our Shepherd in heaven!* "For the Lamb who is in the midst of the throne will shepherd them and lead them to living fountains of waters. And God will wipe away every tear from their eyes" (Rev. 7:17).

Psalm 24

Most commentators connect this psalm with David's bringing the ark of the covenant into Jerusalem (2 Sam. 6; 1 Chron. 15:1–16:3), and it may well be that David wrote it for that occasion. It appears to be an antiphonal psalm. The people (or a Levitical chorus) opened with verses 1–2, a leader asked the questions in verses 3, 8a, and 10a, and the chorus or the people answered with verses 4–7, 8b and 10b. It was sung in Herod's temple each Sunday, and some connect the psalm with our Lord's entrance into Jerusalem on what we call Palm Sunday. For years, the church has assigned this psalm to be read on Ascension Day, the fortieth day after Easter. Christians see Jesus Christ as "the Lord of Glory," first of all returning to heaven after His passion (Eph. 4:8; Col. 2:15), and then returning in glory to establish His kingdom (Matt. 25:31). This explains the repetition of "Lift up your heads" in verses 7 and 9. The psalm presents a threefold privilege God has given His people.

98

We Are Stewards Who Enjoy His Goodness in Creation (vv. 1–2)

Of all the heavenly bodies created by the Lord, the earth is the one He has chosen to be His own special sphere of activity. Clarence Benson called the earth "the theater of the universe," for on it the Lord demonstrated His love in what Dorothy Sayers called "the greatest drama ever staged." He chose a planet, a people and a land, and there He sent His Son to live, to minister, to die, and to be raised from the dead, that lost sinners might be saved. The earth is God's, everything on it and in it is God's, and all the people on the earth are God's, made in His image and accountable to Him. The divine name "LORD" is used six times in this psalm. "All the earth is mine" (Ex. 19:5), says the Creator, but in His goodness He has shared it with us. He is "possessor of heaven and earth" (Gen. 14:19, 22), and we are guests on His planet, stewards of all that He gives us to enjoy (1 Tim. 6:17) and to employ. This stewardship is the basis for the way we treat planet earth and protect the treasures God has shared with us. Anything we give to Him, He has first given to us (50:10–12; 1 Chron. 29:14). Paul quoted 24:1 in 1 Corinthians 10:25–26 to remind believers that all food was permitted to them (see also Mark 7:14–23; 1 Tim. 4:3–5). The place of "water" in the creation is seen in 104:5–9; 136:6; Genesis 1:1, 6–7, 9; 49:25; Exodus 20:4; Deuteronomy 33:13.

We Are Worshipers Who Experience His Grace in Redemption (vv. 3–6)

Psalm 15 is a parallel text, and both psalms emphasize the fact that to worship God means going up higher. God's Son sits on the throne in the heavenly Zion (2:6), and the mercy seat on the ark was God's throne in the earthly Zion. The Levites carrying the ark had to be ceremonially clean, and God's people must be clean if they wish to worship the King and please Him. "Clean hands" speak of righteous conduct (Isa. 1:15–16, 18) and a "pure heart" of godly character and motives (Matt. 5:8). "Vanity" refers to the worship of idols ("worthless things") and "swearing deceitfully" to all kinds of deception, especially false witness in court.

The reward is the gift of salvation, the righteousness of God (Gen. 15:6). However, nobody on God's earth is able to meet these standards. "All have sinned and come short of the glory of God" (Rom. 3:23). Good works or religious character cannot save us. The only way we can enter into God's presence is through the merits of Jesus Christ, which means we must repent of our sins and put our faith in Him. Only Jesus Christ qualifies to enter the Father's presence, and He has gone to heaven to represent His people and intercede for them before the Father's throne. To "seek God's face" means to have an audience with the King (Gen. 44:23; Ex. 10:28; 2 Sam. 14:24, 28, 32), and this is now possible through the work of Christ on the cross (Heb. 10:1–25). God's righteousness is a gift, not a reward for good works (Rom. 3:21–4:9; 5:17; 10:1–10). David compared the generation of God–seeking people to their ancestor Jacob, who saw the face of God and held on by faith until he received a blessing (Gen. 32:24–32). Jacob certainly wasn't a perfect man, but the Lord saved him and even is called "the God of Jacob" (Ps. 46:7, 11).

We Are Victors Who Celebrate His Glory in Conquest (vv. 7–10)

Five times in this text God is called "the King of Glory." Jesus is the Chief Shepherd who will one day return in glory and give each faithful servant a crown of glory (1 Peter 5:1–4; and see 1:7, 4:11–14 and 5:10; 1 Cor. 2:8). The gates of Jerusalem opened outward, so what is meant by "be lifted up"? Certainly there would be plenty of headroom for the Levites to carry in the ark, and it wouldn't be required to raise the lintels of the gates. Martin Luther translated it, "Open wide the portals," that is, "Give a hearty welcome to the Lord!" Bringing in the ark may have reminded David of what Moses and the leaders of Israel sang when the ark was carried in the wilderness (Num. 10:33–35; Ps. 68:1–3; 132:8). The administration of an ancient city was transacted at the city gates, so the gates were to those people what the city hall is to citizens in the western world today. David was commanding the whole city to welcome the Lord and give honor to Him. The King of Glory is also "the LORD of Hosts," a title used nearly three hundred times in the Old Testament. "Hosts" means "armies," and this can mean the stars (Isa. 40:26), the angels (Ps. 103:20–21), the nation of Israel (Ex. 12:41), or all believers who belong to the army of Christ (2 Tim. 2:3–4; 2 Cor. 10:3–6; Eph. 6:10ff).

But why were the gates of Jerusalem addressed twice (vv. 7 and 9)? The King of Glory is Jesus Christ. When He entered Jerusalem on Palm Sunday, the whole city didn't receive Him and praise Him. This psalm had been sung that morning at the temple, but it wasn't applied to Jesus of Nazareth. Instead of accepting Him and honoring Him, the leaders rejected Him and sent Him to Golgotha to be crucified. However, in His death and resurrection, Jesus won the battle against Satan and sin, and when He ascended back to heaven and entered the heavenly Zion (Heb. 12:18ff), He was received as the victorious Lord of Hosts and the King of Glory. However, Jesus will return to the earth and fight a battle against the armies of the world and be victorious (Rev. 19:11ff; Isa. 63:1–3). He will deliver Jerusalem from her enemies (Zech. 12–14) and establish His kingdom on earth. Then His people will receive Him in Jerusalem, the Lord of Hosts, the King of Glory; and "the LORD shall be king over all the earth" (Zech. 14:9). Meanwhile, we can triumph in life through Jesus Christ (2 Cor. 2:14) and be "more than con-querors" through faith in Jesus Christ (Rom. 8:31–39).

As children of God, we belong to three worlds: the world of creation around us, the world of the new creation within us (2 Cor. 5:17), and "the world to come" of the wonderful final cre-ation that will be our home for eternity (Rev. 21–22).

Psalm 25

This psalm pictures life as a difficult journey that we can't suc-cessfully make by ourselves. The word "way" is used four times (vv. 4, 8, 9, 12) and "paths" once (v. 10), and we find the psalmist crying out to God for wisdom as he makes decisions (vv. 4–5). He is surrounded by enemies (v. 2) who hate him (v. 19), lay traps for him (v. 15), and want him to fail and be ashamed (vv. 2, 3, 20). The psalmist knows he is a sinner who doesn't deserve God's help (vv. 7, 11, 18), but he relies on the goodness and mercy of the Lord. Psychologist M. Scott Peck writes, "Once we truly know that life is difficult—once we truly understand and accept it—then life is no longer difficult."[19] David knew that the path of life wasn't easy, but he succeeded in the journey because he held to three unwavering assurances.

The Help We Need Comes from God (vv. 1–7)

Other people may lift up their hearts to idols (24:4), which are only manufactured substitutes for God, but David lifted his heart up to the Lord, for He is the only true source of encouragement. In one of the darkest hours of his life, when David had lost everything, he "encouraged himself in the Lord his God" (1 Sam. 30:6). It has well been said, "When the outlook is bleak, try the uplook." He affirmed his faith in the Lord and his desire to glorify His name. He didn't want to fail and bring disgrace to the name of the Lord. So, he waited on the Lord, worshiped, and confidently asked for His help. He desperately needed wisdom to make the right decisions, avoid the traps, and reach the goal.

David not only prayed for God's guidance, he asked for insight to understand the Word; for only there could he learn God's ways and understand his own path. "Lead me in your truth" reminds us that the Word and prayer always go together (1 Sam. 12:23; John 15:7). David is referring to God's covenants with His people, the precepts and promises He gave them to keep them in His will so they could enjoy His blessing (v. 10; Deut. 27–30). David knew the history of Israel, that God had graciously helped them when they cried out to Him, and so he prayed with assurance and faith. But he also prayed with contrition, confessing his sins to the Lord (vv. 7, 11). He had regrets about some of his youthful omissions of obedience or commissions of sin, and he wanted forgiveness. He prayed "for your goodness' sake" (v. 7) and "for your name's sake" (v. 11; see 23:3; 31:3; 79:9; 106:8; 109:21; 143:110). "My help comes from the Lord who made heaven and earth" (121:2 NASB).

Our God Can Be Trusted (vv. 8–14)

At this point, David paused to meditate on the character of the Lord his God. After all, why pray to the Lord if He can't be trusted? But He *can* be trusted! To begin with, He is "good and upright" and what He says and does is always right. If we submit ourselves to Him in meekness, He will teach us His ways, but if we are arrogant, He will be silent. In the New Testament, the word "meek" describes a horse that has been broken, a soothing wind on a hot day, and a healing medicine. Meekness is not weakness; it is power under control. God can be trusted to guide those who obey His Word (v. 10), for a willingness to obey is the first step toward spiritual understanding (John 7:17).

God can be trusted to be merciful and gracious to those who repent (v. 11), but we must walk in the fear of the Lord (v. 12). "He [God] will instruct him in the way chosen for him" (v. 12 NIV). Knowing that the Lord has a plan for our lives, and that this plan is the very best for us, should give us great joy and confidence as we seek His will (16:11; 139:13–16; Eph. 2:10). According to God's covenant arrangement, those who obey will receive His provision and protection, and there will be blessing also for the next generations in the family (Deut. 4:1–14). The word "children" is used nearly forty times in Deuteronomy, reminding us that our descendants can receive blessing from our obedience or sorrow because of our sins. If we love Him, fear Him, and obey His Word, He will draw near to us and share His plans with us. "Secret" in verse 14 means "intimate conversation, plans and purposes," what Jesus spoke about in John 15:15 and what Abraham experienced in Genesis 18:16ff. (See also Jer. 23:18 and 22, Prov. 3:32 and Amos 3:7.) As we "walk with the Lord in the light of His Word," we develop a close fellowship with Him and better understand His ways. Yes, the Lord can be trusted to help us; and when He helps, He does it in mercy and truth ("love and faithfulness" NIV).

Trusting God Brings Us Victory (vv. 15–22)

David once again turns to prayer and mentions to the Lord the special burdens that beset him, the dangerous enemies without, and the distressing emotions within. *But he wouldn't mention them to the Lord if he didn't believe the Lord could help him!* What were the enemies that God helped him to conquer?

Danger (v. 15). The enemy had put snares in the path, but David trusted the Lord to protect him. Satan is a destroyer and a murderer and would trap us all if he could, but if we are in God's will, he can't harm us.

Loneliness (v. 16). Those who have never had to exercise authority and make difficult decisions involving other people sometimes overlook the loneliness of leadership. As we obey the Lord, we sometimes see friends and even family members turn against us, and this is painful. Three of David's sons—Absalom, Amnon, and Adonijah—turned against him, and so did his close friend and counselor Ahithophel.

A broken heart (v. 17). If we sit alone and feel sorry for ourselves, we will never grow in the Lord and accomplish greater things for Him. Enlarged trouble will either make us or break us, turn us into giants or crush us into pygmies. Review 4:1 and 18:19 and 36 to see how God helped David to grow. God can heal a broken heart if we give Him all the pieces and let Him have His way.

Regrets (v. 18). As we have seen from verse 7, David may have had deep regrets because of things he had done in the past, and these regrets were robbing him of peace and joy. Satan is the accuser (Rev. 12:10) and wants to remind us of our sins, even though the Lord has forgiven them and holds them against us no more (Heb. 10:11–18).

Fear (vv. 19–20). We don't know what the situation was, but whatever it was, David feared for his life. Even more, he feared that he would fail and bring disgrace to the name of the God he loved. His enemies were increasing and so was his fear, but he trusted the Lord to take care of both.

Despair (vv. 21–22). "I wait on you" also means "I have hope in you." To lose hope is to surrender the future to the enemy, and that only destroys the meaning of the present. David was a man of integrity (7:8; 26:1, 11; 41:12; 78:72); he was wholehearted in his obedience to the Lord. Whatever lies the enemy was spreading about him, David knew that the Lord saw his heart and approved of his character. The prayer in verse 22 may have been added so the psalm could be used in public worship, but it expresses a basic truth: we are never alone in our trials, for as members of God's believing community, we have encouragement from one another. Our brothers and sisters around the world are also suffering trials (1 Peter 5:9), so we are not alone.

David survived his trials and was able to write Psalm 26:12— "My feet stand on level ground; in the great assembly I will praise the Lord" (NIV). May we follow his example!

Psalm 26

Psalms 26, 27, and 28 reveal David's love for God's sanctuary (26:6–8, 27:4–7, 28:2), which in David's day was the tabernacle on Mt. Zion. God didn't permit David to build the temple (2 Sam. 7), but He did give him the plans for the temple and helped him accumulate from the spoils of battle great wealth to provide material for constructing the temple (1 Chron. 22, 28–29). But not all who gathered to worship at the sanctuary were sincere in their walk or their worship, and some of them were openly disobedient and spread lies about the king. It was this situation that led to the writing of this psalm. In it, David makes three requests of the Lord.

Vindicate Me (v. 1)

The enemies who were slandering David are described in verses 4–5 and 9–10. They were deceitful, hypocritical, and wicked evildoers, sinners who schemed to rob others and even accepted bribes (Ex. 25:8; Amos 5:12), murdering those who stood in their way. David the king was a godly man, but not every judge and official in the government was walking with the Lord. Perhaps all of this occurred at the time when Absalom was trying to seize the throne by spreading lies about his father (see 2 Sam. 14–15). David would see these deceitful men at the tabernacle altar, bringing their offerings, and it deeply grieved him. (See 119:28, 115, 136, 150, 158.) Throughout the history of both Israel and the church, there was a "congregation of evildoers" (v. 5; 50:16–21) along with the congregation of true worshipers (v. 12), the tares among the wheat (Matt. 13:24–30, 36–41), and wolves in sheep's clothing (Matt. 7:15, Acts 20:26–31).

"Vindicate" means "give me justice, defend my reputation" (see 7:8; 35:24; 43:1). David was a man of integrity (7:8; 25:21; 41:12; 78:72), a fact that was affirmed by the Lord Himself (1 Kings 9:4–5). The people attacking him were "dissemblers" (v. 4 KJV) or "hypocrites," play-actors who wore masks to cover up their evil character. Integrity means wholeness of character, an undivided mind and heart, completely devoted to the Lord. Without wavering, David stood for what was right, but double-minded people are unstable in all their ways (James 1:8). His life revealed a balance of faith ("I have trusted") and works ("I have walked"), as commanded in James 2:14–26. When your character and conduct are attacked, it isn't wrong to vindicate yourself, as Paul did (2 Cor. 10–12), or to ask the Lord to vindicate you. We aren't just defending ourselves; we're defending the name of the Lord whom we serve. Our vindication is "for his name's sake" (23:3; 25:11).

Examine Me (vv. 2–8)

As with David's words in 18:20–24, this is not an expression of self-righteousness (see Luke 18:9–14), but rather the honest testimony of a real man of God. The words translated "examine" and "try" refer to the testing of metals to determine their true value and also to remove the dross (12:6; 17:3). "Heart and mind" is "kidneys and heart" in the original, the kidneys being the seat of the emotions and the heart the place of moral decision. (See 139:23, Phil. 4:7 and Rev. 2:23.) David's life was motivated and controlled by God's love and truth (faithfulness; see 6:4; 25:5–7, 10; 40:10; 57:3; Ex. 34:6). The Lord was faithful to His covenant and David was faithful to the Lord. Though David occasionally fell, as we all do, the habitual bent of his life was toward the Lord and His Word. He refused to have fellowship with the hypocrites in the congregation, the "men of vanity, nothingness" who pretended to worship the Lord and keep His covenant. This doesn't imply that he was isolated from the real world (1 Cor. 5:10), but rather that he didn't allow it to defile him (1:1–2; 2 Cor. 6:14–7:1). While the assembly of the wicked needs our witness, it's with the congregation of the righteous that we share our worship (35:18; 40:9–10; 89:5; 107:32; 149:1). David was balanced: he hated sin but he loved the things of God (vv. 5, 8). In walking (vv. 1, 3, 11), standing (v. 12), and sitting (v. 4), he kept himself from evil (see 1:1).

The wicked came to the sanctuary to hide their sins; they made it a "den of thieves," the place where criminals run and hide (Matt. 21:13; Jer. 7:1). But David went to the sanctuary to worship God and bear witness to His grace and mercy. His hands were clean (24:4), his sacrifice was acceptable (see Isa. 1:10–17), and his voice was clear as he praised the Lord. Cleansing comes from the blood of Christ (1 John 1:7, 9) and the water of the Word (Eph. 5:26–27; John 15:3). In order to serve God acceptably, the priests were required to wash their hands and feet at the laver (Ex. 30:17–21). Nowhere in the law of Moses do we find instructions about processions and praise around the altar, but neither were they forbidden. David was an enthusiastic worshiper of the Lord (see 43:4; 2 Sam. 6:12–23) and enjoyed his times of worship. (On washing hands to prove innocence, see Deut. 21:1–9.) The king brought sacrifices of thanksgiving (Lev. 3:1–17; 7:11–38) because he loved the Lord and the Lord's house (27:4–6; 42:4; 122:1–4, 9; 1 Chron. 29:3). He glorified God at the place where God's glory dwelt (Ex. 40:35). David is a good example for us to follow in our own worship.

Redeem Me (vv. 9–12)

David couldn't stop the hypocrites from joining the worshiping congregation, but he could help from becoming like them; so he asked the Lord to deliver him from that sin. "Don't sweep me away with the wicked!" The sheep and goats and the wheat and tare may be mixed today, but there is coming a day when God will separate them; on that day, the wicked will perish (1:4–6; Matt. 7:21–23; 25:31–46). The godly must constantly beware of the evil influences of the world and especially of those who profess to love God but are using "religion" as a cover up for their sins. To remain faithful, we must also ask God to be merciful to us and help us to maintain our integrity. Once we begin to waver (v. 1 NASB), it becomes easier to stumble and fall. "Therefore let him who thinks he stands take heed lest he fall" (1 Cor. 10:12 NKJV). David was standing on level ground (see 27:11; 143:10; Isa. 40:4). He would not waver.

Psalm 27

According to the title of this psalm as recorded in the Septuagint, David wrote it "before he was anointed." This means it was probably written when he was exiled from home and being hunted by King Saul and his men. The psalm does reveal that David was in great danger from violent evildoers (v. 2) who were lying about him (v. 12) and wanting to kill him (vv. 2 and 12), and Saul and his men qualified. But in spite of this difficult and dangerous situation, David was confident (v. 3), courageous (v. 14), and unafraid (v. 1). In this psalm, David teaches us that when we know the Lord and trust Him, He helps us overcome the fears that can paralyze our lives.

Fear of Circumstances (vv. 1–6)

David didn't close his eyes to the circumstances around him; rather, he looked by faith to the Lord and examined his circumstances from heaven's point of view (Heb. 12:1–3). The Lord was everything he needed just as He is everything we need today. He is our light, so we need not fear because of darkness; He is our strength (or stronghold; see 18:2; 31:3–2), so we need not fear because of our weakness; and He is our salvation, so the victory is sure. This is the first time in Scripture that light is used as a metaphor for God (see John 1:4, 9; 8:12; 1 John 1:3; Rev. 21:23), although in many texts He is associated with the light (4:6; 18:28; 43:3; 84:11; Isa. 10:17; 60:1, 20; Mic. 7:8). David didn't know if the enemy would make a sudden attack, like a beast devouring its prey (v. 2; see 1 Sam. 17:43–47), or settle down for a long siege (v. 3a), or at a propitious time declare war and attack (v. 3b). No matter what the tactics might be, the enemy didn't frighten David. "If God be for us, who can be against us?" (Rom. 8:31).

The secret of David's public confidence was his private obedience: he took time to fellowship with the Lord and get directions from Him. David knew that the most important part of his life was the part that only God could see, and this was one priority he would not negotiate.[20] David was living in the wilderness of Judea, away from the sanctuary of the Lord, but he was still able to enter into fellowship with his God. God's house was but a tent (vv. 5–6), for the temple had not yet been built, but it was still referred to as "God's temple" (see 1 Sam. 1:9; 33). The imagery in verses 4–6 is the Old Testament equivalent of "abiding in Christ" (John 15:1–8). In the ancient Near East, when a visitor entered his host's tent, the host was personally responsible for his protection and provision, and the flimsy tent became a fortress. The word "beauty" in verse 4 means not only the glory of God's character but also the richness of His goodness and favor to His people (16:11; 90:17; 135:3). David took time to meditate and to contemplate the wonders of God's grace. He came away from his times of worship feeling the rock under his feet and seeing above and beyond the enemy to the victory God had prepared. No wonder he vowed to God that, when he returned to Jerusalem, he would bring thank offerings to Him and joyfully worship Him.

Fear of Failure (vv. 7–10)

David's confidence in the Lord didn't prevent him from being concerned about himself, for he knew he was a sinner and a man of clay. It's one thing to behold the Lord in the sanctuary and quite something else to see the enemy approaching on the battlefield. What if there was something wrong in David's life and the Lord abandoned him in the midst of the battle? When David cried out, God answered him in his heart and said, "Seek my face." (See 24:6; 105:4; Deut. 4:29; 1 Chron. 16:11; 2 Chron. 7:14; Hos. 5:15.) When the Lord's face "shines upon us" (Num. 6:22–27), it means He is pleased with us and will help us; when His face is turned from us, He is displeased (69:16–18; 143:7), and we must search our hearts and confess our sins. David's parents never abandoned him (see 1 Sam. 21:3–4). His statement was a familiar proverb. God cares for us as a father and mother care for their children (Isa. 49:15; 63:16); and though it's unlikely that parents would abandon their children, it's certain that God never forsakes His own (Heb. 13: 5–6).

Fear of the Future (vv. 11–14)

Did David write these words after he had won the battle? As a wise soldier, he realized that one victory did not guarantee that the enemy would stop attacking. Perhaps the enemy had retreated and David was now concerned about their return. "Let us be as watchful after the victory as before the battle," said the godly Scottish preacher Andrew Bonar, and wise counsel it is. He asked the Lord for guidance (see 25:4–5), for a level path without traps in it, and for victory over the liars who were slandering his good name. His statement in verse 13 is incomplete: "If I had not believed in the goodness of the Lord in the land of the living"—then what? Where would I be? David believed that God's goodness followed him (23:6) and also anticipated him (21:3), that God stored up goodness to use when it was needed (31:19). God's goodness never ran out (52:1), for David could go into God's house (presence) and receive all he needed (65:4). The key was *faith in God*.

Instead of rushing ahead, David calmly waited on the Lord, for faith and patience always go together (Isa. 28:16; Heb. 6:12; 10:36). Perhaps in verse 14 he was addressing his soldiers, for the men would need courage and strength for the next battle and for the journey that lay before them. This admonition reminds us of the words of Moses to Joshua (Deut. 31:7, 23), God's words to Joshua (Josh. 1:6–7, 9), and the Jewish leaders' encouragement of Joshua (Josh. 1:18). Stuart Hamblin wrote in one of his familiar songs, "I know not what the future holds / but I know who holds the future." If Jesus is your Savior and Lord, then the future is your friend, and you have nothing to fear.

Psalm 28

Once again, David found himself in difficulty and cried out to the Lord for help. We don't know what caused the problem, but it involved wicked people and workers of iniquity, and deceptive people who pretended to be David's friends but were working for his ruin. The period leading up to Absalom's rebellion would fit this description, but would David pray for his own son's destruction when he asked to have Absalom spared (vv. 4–5; 2 Sam. 18:5)? Regardless of the background, this psalm teaches us some important lessons about prayer and patience.

The Problem of Unanswered Prayer (vv. 1–5)

David had prayed fervently about his dangerous situation, but the Lord hadn't answered him. (See 13:1; 35:22; 39:12; 40:17; 69:3; 83:1; 109:1; 119:82.) It has often been said that "God's delays are not God's denials," and David was learning that important lesson. In verse 1, he "called" on the Lord, and in verse 2, he "cried out" to Him in desperation, but the Lord didn't answer. The unchanging Rock had changed! (19:14; 31:2–3; 62:2). Was the Lord silent because He could no longer hear and speak? David lifted his hands in worship as he prayed toward the sanctuary of God (63:4; 141:2; Ex. 17:19; 1 Kings 8:44ff; Lam. 2:19; 3:41; 1 Tim. 2:8), but the Lord apparently didn't see him. But Jehovah is the "living God" who sees His people, hears their cries, and speaks His Word to them! (115:1–8). David felt like a dead man whose body was in the tomb and whose soul was in sheol, the realm of the departed

(22:20; 30:9; 88:4; 143:7). He also felt like a criminal who was being dragged away with the wicked to be executed (vv. 3–5). They were hypocrites, but he was speaking the truth. They had no regard for the words and works of the Lord, but David was a servant of God who worshiped Him faithfully. According to God's covenant with Israel, David's idolatrous enemies should have been judged and condemned, but the Lord was doing nothing. How could God treat His anointed king like a criminal? But we should remind ourselves that the Father allowed His own Son to be unjustly treated like a common criminal (Isa. 53:7–8, 12; Luke 22:37). David's prayer was not an expression of personal revenge but a call for God to fulfill His covenant and bring righteousness and peace into the land. "Let them reap what they have sown," was his request.

The Joy of Unbounded Praise (vv. 6–7)

Suddenly, the scene changes and David is singing instead of sobbing! The reason is given in verse 7, "My heart trusts in Him, and I am helped" (NASB). Faith in Jehovah made all the difference. The hands of the enemy were busy doing evil (v. 4), but when David believed God and lifted up his hands in prayer (v. 2), then God's hands went to work and met the need (v. 5). Faith moves the hands of God, and God's hands control the universe.

David blessed the Lord for his deliverance and wasn't ashamed to confess it. His testimony was clear: "God heard me and God helped me! I trusted Him and now I praise Him!" David now had the strength to obey God's will, no matter what the enemy might do. He also had the Lord as his shield (3:3; 7:10; 18:2, 30; 33:20; 84:11; Gen.15:1; Deut. 33:29). David had God's power and God's protection. How wonderful that David turned a painful experience into a song of praise to the Lord and that he left behind a witness that has encouraged other believers for centuries.

The Promise of Undeserved Blessing (vv. 8–9)

David closed his song by encouraging his people with what he had learned from the Lord. Not only had God saved His anointed king, but He would also save His people Israel. "God save the king" included "God save the people," so they must trust Him. David saw the nation as God's inheritance (33:12; 78:62, 71; 79:1; 94:14; Deut. 4:20; 9:26, 29; 32:11; Mic. 7:14, 18), God's flock, and God's family. The word "feed" in verse 9 (KJV) means "to shepherd." (see Ps. 23), and "lift up" means "to carry like a child." Of course, the faithful shepherd sometimes has to carry the lambs, so the two images merge (Isa. 40:11). Though he was Israel's king, David always saw himself as a shepherd (2 Sam. 24:17). Indeed, the nation of Israel is God's inheritance, for He has invested in them the spiritual treasures that the bankrupt world needs (Rom. 9:1–5). "Salvation is of the Jews" (John 4:22). God has not forsaken His people.

Psalm 29

David was an outdoorsman who appreciated nature and celebrated the power of Jehovah the Creator. Jewish worshipers today use this psalm in the synagogue as a part of their celebration of Pentecost. When you read Acts 2 and discover the sound of wind, tongues of fire, and the "thunder" of God's voice through His Word, you can see that God's church today can also use Psalm 29 to celebrate Pentecost. Israel's neighbors believed that Baal, the storm god, controlled rain and fertility, but this psalm says otherwise. It magnifies the sovereignty of God and the power of God in His creation, both of which bring glory to God. The word "glory" is used four times in the psalm (1–3, 9), for David saw in the storm God's glory revealed in three different places.

God's Glory in the Heavenly Temple (vv. 1–2)

Heaven is a place of worship (see Rev. 4–5), and here the command is given for the angels ("mighty ones, sons of the Mighty") to ascribe (attribute; 96:7–9) to God glory and strength, because these divine attributes magnify His name. The psalm begins and ends mentioning God's "strength" (v. 11), and verses 4–9 demonstrate that strength in the description of the storm. Angels are called "sons of God" in Job 1:6, 2:1 and 38:7; and see Psalm 89:6.

The Jewish priests and Levites had to dress properly as they served at the sanctuary (Ex. 28:1ff), and even God's angels must come before Him in proper "attire," what is called "holy array" (NASB) and "the splendor of his holiness" (NIV). (See 27:4 and 96:9.) True holiness is a beautiful thing to behold, and certainly the greatest demonstration was in the life of Jesus Christ when He ministered on earth. Sin is ugly, no matter what we may call it, but true holiness is beautiful and brings glory to God.

God's Glory in the Earthly Tempest (vv. 3–9)

This is an inspired and dramatic description of a thunderstorm that started somewhere over the Mediterranean Sea (v. 3) and moved eastward to the Lebanon mountain range in the northern part of the land of Israel (v. 5). The storm continued moving eastward overland to Mount Hermon (v. 6; Sirion, Deut. 3:8–9), where it turned south and traveled about two hundred miles down to Kadesh in the wilderness (v. 8), and there it dispersed. It was accompanied by loud thunder ("the voice of the Lord"— see 18:13–14 and Job 37:1–5; 40:9) and also by lightning (v. 7). Seven times you find the phrase "the voice of the Lord" (see Rev. 10:3–4), and it was "the God of glory" who was thundering and revealing His majesty. He is also "the King of Glory" (24:7).

The Lebanon range was about ten thousand feet above sea level, and the Canaanites believed it was the home of their gods. It was famous for its cedar forests (72:16; 1 Kings 4:33), but the thunder of God broke even those stalwart trees (v. 5). In fact, the thunder made the trees and the mountains skip like calves! (v. 6; see 114:1ff). In Scripture, the cedar tree is sometimes a symbol of a nation or a kingdom, including David's dynasty (Ezek. 17:1–3), Assyria (Ezek. 31:3), and even Israel (Num. 24:6). The prophet Isaiah saw the fall of the proud cedars as a picture of the defeat of the nations in the day of the Lord (Isa. 2:10–17). Note that it was the thunder—the voice of God—that broke the trees, and not the wind or the lightning. The voice of God is powerful and can shake the wilderness like an earthquake (v. 8). So frightened were the animals that the hinds went into premature labor and delivered their calves. Imagine being born in a thunderstorm! During this demonstration of God's great power, the angels were watching with amazement and shouting, "Glory!" The angels learned about God's grace, wisdom, and power by watching the Son of God when He served on earth (1 Tim. 3:16). They also learned during the week of creation (Job 38:7), and they are learning today as they behold the church on earth (Eph. 3:10; 1 Peter 1:12). According to verse 9, after the angels watched the storm described in this psalm, they cried, "Glory!"

God's Glory on the Heavenly Throne (vv. 10–11)

Seeing the rain and the mounting streams of water, hearing the thunder and watching the lightning, David began to meditate on the flood that occurred in the days of Noah (Gen. 6–9). "The Lord sat as King at the flood" (v. 10 NASB); He was in charge, not Baal. He sent the rain, He opened the fountains of the deep, He stopped the rain, He waited for the water to drain off and the land to dry, and then He brought Noah and his family out of the ark. As he watched the storm move down to Kadesh, David rejoiced that the God who created the universe was also in control of the forces of nature, and there was nothing to fear. Eighteen times in these eleven verses, He is called "Lord," and that means He is Lord of heaven and earth, Lord of all.

The Lord is King today and will sit as King forever! He can give strength to His people and see them through the storms of life. After the thunder, lightning, wind, and rain comes the calm after the storm when "the Lord blesses His people with peace" (v. 11 NIV; and see 107:29 and 148:8.) Noah saw the rainbow of the covenant after the storm (Gen. 9:8–17), the apostle John saw it before the storm (Rev. 4:3), and Ezekiel saw the rainbow in the midst of the storm (Ezek. 1:26–28). We always have God's promise to encourage us.

Psalm 30

The psalm opens and closes on a note of thanksgiving (vv. 1, 12; and see 4 and 11).

The emphasis is on praise to the Lord for rescuing David from a dangerous and difficult situation that included sickness (v. 2), being near death (vv. 3, 9), God's anger (v. 5), weeping (vv. 5, 11), and emotional turmoil (v. 7). But the trial also involved the nation, for David addressed them in verses 4–5. Apparently this was a national crisis that David had helped to precipitate because he disobeyed the will of God. It came at a time when he was enjoying ease and security and was proud of himself and his kingdom (vv. 6–7). According to the superscription, David wrote this psalm for "the dedication of the house." The word "house" can be translated "palace," referring to David's house, or "temple," referring to the Lord's house. If it's the first, then perhaps 2 Samuel 5 describes the historical setting, when David captured Mt. Zion and made Jerusalem his capital city. (Note "my mountain" in 30:7.) All Israel had crowned David king, he had won great victories over the Philistines, and he had built himself a palace. He knew that his kingdom was established and exalted by the Lord (5:12). This context has all the ingredients necessary to make David proud and thus invite the chastening of the Lord.

However, if "house" refers to the temple of the Lord, then we must look to 1 Chronicles 21:1–22:1 and 2 Samuel 24 for the context. This is the record of the national plague David caused when he arrogantly numbered the people and 70,000 people died. This caused David great distress (2 Sam. 24:10, 14), and he put on sackcloth and begged God for mercy for the people (1 Chron. 21:16; see Ps. 30:11). David purchased a plot of ground from Ornan and dedicated it to be the site for the temple (1 Chron. 22:1), and he began to use the plot as his own personal place of worship. This second explanation seems to cover the facts better. In either case, the message of the psalm is clear: the Lord forgave David and gave him the blessing of a new beginning. "The victorious Christian life," wrote the noted Scottish preacher George Morrison, "is a series of new beginnings." That definition beautifully fits this psalm.

A New Victory—From Death to Life (vv. 1–3)

David experienced three problems: the sinking mire beneath him that would take him down to the pit, the enemies around him who wanted him to die, and the distress within him that was like a painful sickness—and the Lord delivered him from all three! Because of his disobedience, David was in the depths, and the Lord had to lift him up. (See 18:4–6; 69:1–2, 14–15; 71:20; 88:6; 130:1–3; Lam. 3:55; and Jonah 2:2.) The "grave" or the "pit" refers to sheol, the realm of the departed spirits. (The Greek equivalent is hades.) But instead of allowing David to go down, God lifted him out and brought him up. God had done this for David before (18:16).

David's foes would have been glad to see him die (13:4; 25:2; 41:11), but the Lord saved David's life and silenced their taunts. The "healing" mentioned in verse 2 may not have involved actual physical sickness, because the word is also used to describe not only forgiveness and spiritual restoration (41:4; Isa. 6:10; 53:5; Hos. 6:1 and 7:1) but also deliverance from mental and emotional distress (Jer. 8:21–22; 14:19; Lam. 2:13). It was David's pride that had brought the plague to the land, and he felt the pain of this deeply, so much so that he thought his convicted conscience and broken heart would kill him. But God heard his pleas and brought him from death to life.

A New Day—From Night to Morning (vv. 4–5)

The psalm is not only David's personal expression of praise and thanksgiving, but it was also used by the congregation in worship; and here David addressed them. "Oh, magnify the Lord with me, and let us exalt his name together" (34:3). Personal worship that doesn't enrich our corporate worship may become selfish and lead to more pride! The contrasts in verse 5 are the motivation for David's praise: from God's anger to God's favor; from chastening for only a moment to a lifetime of His grace (Isa. 54:7–8); from a night of weeping to a morning of joy. For David, this was the dawning of a new day after a painful time of suffering in darkness. Each morning, God's mercies are new (Lam.

3:22–23), and God's special help often arrives in the morning. "God will help her when morning dawns" (46:5; NASB; and see 59:16; 143:8). The resurrection of Jesus Christ brought the dawning of a new day for all who trust in Him (Matt. 28:1). Weeping comes as a guest, but God's gracious favor is with us for a lifetime. (See 2 Cor. 4.) As Jesus explained to His disciples, God doesn't *replace* sorrow with joy; He *transforms* sorrow into joy (John 16:20–22). The same baby that causes the mother pain also brings the mother joy.

A New Heart—From Pride to Humility (vv. 6–10)

This is where the story really began, for it was David's pride that made it necessary for the Lord to chasten him. "Prosperity" means "careless ease, a carefree self-assurance because things are going so well." This is frequently the attitude of the unconverted (10:6; 73:12; Luke 12:16–21), but it is a constant temptation to believers also (read Deut. 8). One reason the Lord permits trials is that we might not get comfortable in our faith and stop growing. "I was at ease," said Job, "but He shattered me, and He has grasped me by the neck and shaken me to pieces: He has also set me up as His target" (Job 16:12 NASB). Prosperity without humility can lead to adversity. David's mountain (kingdom, as in Jer. 51:25) seemed strong, but the Lord showed David how weak he was.

When God's face is shining upon us (Num. 6:23–27), then we enjoy His rich blessings; but when we rebel, He may hide His face, and this causes trouble (see 10:11; 13:1; 27:9; 88:14; Deut. 31:17–18; 32:20). The Hebrew word translated "troubled" describes "intense agony, terror, anguish." It's used in 1 Samuel 28:21 to describe King Saul's feelings in the house of the witch. Knowing he had sinned, David kept crying out to the Lord for mercy and even debated with Him. "Am I more useful to you in the grave than I am alive on earth? Can the dead praise you and serve you?" (See 88:7–12; 115:17; Isa. 38:18–19.) David was a great king with a strong kingdom, but he was only dust, one short breath away from the grave. He humbled himself and confessed his sin, and the Lord mercifully forgave him and restored him.

A New Song—From Mourning to Rejoicing (vv. 11–12)

Seven times in the psalm David wrote "You have" (vv. 1–3, 7, 11), bearing witness to the strong and gracious hand of the Lord working on his behalf. Even God's chastening of David was an expression of His love (Heb. 12:1–11). Once David knew he was forgiven and accepted, he moved from the funeral to the feast. He took off the sackcloth of sadness and put on the garments of gladness. In Scripture, a dramatic alteration of one's life was often marked by a change of clothing (Gen. 35:2; 41:14; 45:22; Ex.19:10, 14; 2 Sam. 12:20; Luke 15:22). "My glory" means "my heart, my soul." David was singing to the Lord from the depths of his being. He realized that he would be singing praises to God forever (v. 12), so he wanted to start getting ready now! Every difficult experience of life—and David had many of them—is an opportunity to have a "pity party" or attend a rehearsal for singing in the choirs of heaven! We have a lifetime of grace (v. 5) to prepare us for an eternity of glory.

Psalm 31

The emphasis is on trusting ("taking refuge") in the Lord, no matter how difficult the circumstances might be (vv. 1, 6, 14, 19). David was surrounded by subversive whispering campaigns and wicked conspiracies (vv. 8, 13, 15, 18, 20), and everything seemed against him. Even his best friends and neighbors didn't want to be seen with him (vv. 11–13), and there was "fear on every side" (v. 13). The reference to "a besieged city" in verse 21 (NIV, NASB) has led some students to connect this volatile situation with David's experience at Keilah (1 Sam. 23:1–15) or perhaps at Ziklag (1 Sam. 30). However, it appears that what is described in the psalm best fits what happened during the rebellion led by Absalom (2 Sam. 15–18). Over many months, Absalom led a subversive campaign against his father, and even Ahithophel, David's wisest counselor, deserted the king and followed Absalom. "They took counsel together against me" (v. 13) reminds us of the conference recorded in 2 Samuel 17. If we take the phrase "besieged city" literally, it could refer to Jerusalem.

After fleeing Jerusalem, David had made Mahanaim his head-quarters (2 Sam. 17:24, 27), but it was never under siege. Perhaps the phrase should be taken metaphorically: "God showed me marvelous kindness as if I were in a besieged city." If so, then it would parallel verse 20 which pictures God hiding His faithful ones in the Holy of Holies, which certainly isn't to be taken literally. Out of this harrowing experience, David learned some valuable lessons and recorded them in this psalm. They can be summarized in three statements.

When Others Do Evil, Trust God for His Strength (vv. 1–8)

The first three verses are quoted in 71:1–3, an untitled psalm probably written by David. He affirms his trust in the Lord and asks Him to deliver him and defend him on the basis of divine righteousness. "Shall not the Judge of all the earth do right?" (Gen. 18:25). How can the righteous Lord permit wicked people to prosper and overthrow His anointed king? Such a thing would make David ashamed, a statement he repeats in verse 17. As he often did, he begged God to act speedily (69:17; 70:1, 5; 71:12; 141:1; 143:7) and be to him a rock and a fortress (see 18:1–3). Along with God's protection, David needed God's direction so he would avoid the traps the enemy had set for him. "You are my strength" was his affirmation of faith (v. 4), for his own strength had failed (v. 10).

His prayer of commitment in verse 5 was quoted by our Lord from the cross (Luke 23:46, and see Acts 7:59). Peter also borrowed the idea (1 Peter 4:19) and used the word "commit," which means "to deposit in trust, as money in a bank." The hand of the enemy was against David (vv. 8, 15), but he knew he was safe in God's hand (see John 10:27–30). The God of truth would keep His promises. His enemies were idolaters; they weren't trusting in the living God but in "lying vanities, worthless idols." Note the repeated "but I trust" (vv. 6, 14). The word means to depend on, to lean on. Jonah quoted verse 6 in his prayer from the great fish (Jonah 2:8). In His mercy, God had delivered David from many dangerous places, and David knew he could depend on Him again, and this brought him joy. As in the past, God would deliver him from a "tight place" and enable him to stand in a "spacious place" (v. 8; see 18:19, 36, and 4:1). He would grow because of his trials and his faith in the Lord.

When Others Cause Pain, Ask God for His Mercy (vv. 9–18)

David had prayed, "You are my strength" (v. 4), but now he said, "You are my God" (v. 14) and asked Him for the mercy he desperately needed (v. 16). When you consider the vocabulary he used to describe his plight, you can well understand his need for mercy. He was filled with grief; he was sighing; his physical strength was failing; and his very bones were weakening. His soul and inner being were pained because of the troubles others were causing. He must have examined his heart and discovered sin there, so he confessed it to the Lord. Along with his physical and emotional anguish was the way people were treating him (vv. 11–13). His enemies were spreading malicious lies about him and people believed them. Of course, these lies spread rapidly, and David's close friends and neighbors heard and believed them. Even casual acquaintances avoided him when they saw him coming, for who wants to be seen speaking to an evil man? He became like a dead man who had been forgotten and like a useless piece of pottery that had been thrown away. It didn't take long for "the strife of tongues" (v. 20) to poison the nation and prepare the way for Absalom to take over.

The phrase "fear [terror] on every side" (v. 13) is used six times by the prophet Jeremiah (6:25; 20:3, 10; 46:5; 49:29; Lam. 2:22). In David's day, the disruption of the government and the exile of the king brought great fear to the people, and all sorts of rumors spread throughout the land. David's answer to this confusion? "My times are in your hands" (v. 15 NIV). He had committed himself into God's hands (v. 5), and now he committed his circumstances into God's hands. "My times" refers, not to some special schedule, but to all the events and circumstances that surrounded David (see 1 Chron. 29:30). We would say, "All the affairs and details of my life are in the Lord's hands." This is the

Old Testament version of Romans 8:28. David trusted God to bring light into the darkness and truth into the sea of lies that was overwhelming the people. Instead of the king being ashamed, his enemies would be ashamed when the Lord exposed their wickedness and defeated them.

When Others See the Victory, Give God the Glory (vv. 19–24)

The face of the Lord did smile upon David (Num. 6:22–27), and though he was severely chastened by the Lord, he was not abandoned. David knew that the Lord had laid up a supply of goodness and kindness for him (see 21:3), and that His mercies would never fail. Throughout the tragedy of the insurrection, God had protected David from danger, and he was as safe as if he had hidden in the Holy of Holies. As for the plots of the enemy and the lies they spread about the king, the Lord also took care of them and revealed the truth to the people. God's great goodness and marvelous lovingkindness were all that David needed to weather the storm and survive to lead his people.

However, at one point, David may have been ready to give up: "In my alarm I said, 'I am cut off from your sight!'" (v. 22, and see 30:6). It wasn't the enemy that frightened him but the thought of being abandoned by the God he trusted and served. He did what all of us must do when we sense that God is no longer near: he cried out to the Lord for His mercy, and the Lord answered. When the terrible experience of the rebellion was over, David spoke to the people (vv. 23–24) and gave God the glory for delivering him. David had written about his faith in the Lord (vv. 1, 6, 14, 19), but now he encourages his people to love the Lord and put their hope in Him. Faith, hope, and love always go together (1 Cor. 13:13). The courage and strength we need in the trials of life are available from the Lord if we will put our faith in Him. Let's be sure that we give Him the glory.

Psalm 32

This is the second of the seven penitential psalms (see Ps. 6). David wrote it after confessing to God his sins of adultery, murder, and deception (see 51; 2 Sam. 11–12). In 51:13, he vowed to share what he had learned from this costly experience, and this psalm is a part of the fulfillment of that promise. This is the first "Maschil" psalm (see 42, 44, 45, 52–55, 74, 78, 88, 89, 142). The word had been interpreted many ways: "a skillful song, a song of instruction, a contemplative poem." The word means "instruction" and is translated that way in verse 8. However, Maschil may be a musical direction, the meaning of which is still unknown. This psalm is used by our Jewish friends at the close of the annual Day of Atonement; on the church calendar, it's assigned to be read on Ash Wednesday. Paul quoted verses 1–2 in Romans 4:7–8 as part of his argument for salvation by grace alone, apart from the works of the law. In this psalm, David shared four basic facts about sin and forgiveness that need to be understood by every believer.

The Blessing of Acceptance (vv. 1–2)

Instead of starting with a catalog of his sins, David launched into the psalm with a song of praise for everybody in the assembly to hear. The first beatitude in the Psalms pronounces blessing on the obedient (1:1), but this second beatitude pronounces blessing on the disobedient who have been forgiven. (For other beatitudes, see 34:8; 40:4; 65:4; 84:5, 12; 94:12; 112:1.) Chronologically, his experience of forgiveness came long after he had committed his sins and covered them up for almost a year (vv. 3–5). But having now entered into the freedom of forgiveness, David couldn't wait to shout about it. If we have acceptance with God, it matters not what else may happen to us.

Transgression is "crossing over the line" and rebelling against God. David knew the Ten Commandments and that adultery, murder, and deceit were forbidden. *Sin* means "to miss the mark" and not live up to the standards God has set. *Iniquity* means "twisted" and describes what happens to the inner character of the sinner. *Guile* means "deception." David tried to cover his sins and pretend nothing had happened, but the Lord chastened him until he confessed he had sinned. This vocabulary will reappear in verse 5. *Forgive* means to remove a burden; it's pictured by the "scapegoat" in the Day of Atonement service, for symbolically the goat "carried" the sins of the people into the wilderness (Lev. 16:20–22; Ps. 103:12; John 1:29). Like Adam and Eve (Gen. 3:8), David tried to "cover" his sins, but his schemes didn't work. They never do (Prov. 28:13), but when God covers the sins we confess to Him, they are hidden from sight and never seen again. (See Isa. 38:17, 43:25, 44:22; Jer. 31:34; Mic. 2:18–19; 1 John 1:7–9.) On the Day of Atonement, the blood of the sacrifice was sprinkled on the mercy seat by the high priest, and that covered the sins the people had committed. *Impute* is a bookkeeping term that means "to put on the account, to add to the record." When we confess our sins, God cancels the debt and it's no longer on the books. As the children say, "It doesn't count any more." Why? Because Jesus paid the debt on the cross, and His blood cleanses the record and the heart of the offender. The forgiveness of the Lord is certainly something to sing about! It's unfortunate that too many of God's children take it for granted.

The Folly of Impenitence (vv. 3–4)

Now David tells his own story and honestly admits what a fool he had been to hide his sins for almost a year. Charles Spurgeon said, "God does not permit His children to sin successfully." John Donne wrote, "Sin is a serpent, and he that covers sin does but keep it warm, that it may sting the more fiercely, and disperse the venom and malignity thereof the more effectually." The Lord chastened David for almost a year and made him miserable until he stopped lying, humbled himself before God, and confessed his sins. Chastening isn't a judge punishing a criminal; it's a loving Father dealing with His disobedient children to bring them willingly to the place of surrender. According to Hebrews 12:1–13, God's chastening is proof that He loves us and that we are genuinely His children.

What happened to David during those difficult months? For one thing, he became a physical wreck. He was probably about fifty when he disobeyed the Lord, but he began to feel and look like a sick old man. Usually robust and ready for action, David now had constant pain in his body (see 51:8) and was groaning ("roaring" KJV) because of it. The hand of God was heavy upon him, and instead of feeling fresh and full of vigor, he was dried up like a plant during a drought (see 38:2 and 39:10). Did he have a fever that dehydrated him? Whatever it was, he was miserable, for he had a defiled conscience, a worried mind ("When will I be found out?"), and a sick body. But it was worth the pain, for the experience brought him back to the Lord.

The Way of Deliverance (vv. 5–7)

The Lord sent the prophet Nathan to David to confront him with his sins and bring him God's word of forgiveness (2 Sam. 12). David's confession "I have sinned against the Lord"[21] was answered with, "The Lord also has put away your sin" (2 Sam. 12:13 NKJV). The king didn't have to do penance or go on probation; all he had to do was sincerely confess his sins, and the Lord forgave him (1 John 1:9). The burden of transgression had been carried away, the debt was canceled, the twisted was made straight, and the Lord didn't put David's sins on the record. Instead of imputing our sins, the Lord puts the righteousness of Christ on our account, and we are accepted in Him (see Rom. 4:3ff; 5:13; 2 Cor. 5:19–21; Gal. 3:6). David offered no excuses; he admitted that he had sinned and was guilty before God. Guilt is to the conscience what pain is to the body: it tells us that something is wrong and must be made right, or things will get worse. The promise is for everybody ("godly" = chosen ones, God's people; 4:3), and we must confess our sins immediately, when we find them out and while God may be found (69:14; Isa. 55:9; Prov. 1:24–33). The waters of chastening will only get deeper and the storm increase, so don't tempt the Lord!

But God's forgiveness isn't a negative thing; the Lord adds positive blessings to help us on the road to recovery. David exchanged hiding his sins for a hiding place in the Lord. God removed his troubles and put a wall of protection around him. Did David deserve these blessings? Of course not—nor do we! But this is the grace of God as found in Jesus Christ our Lord.

"God's kiss of forgiveness sucks the poison from the wound," wrote Alexander Maclaren, and that says it all. This doesn't mean that David didn't suffer because of the consequences of his sins. God in His grace forgives us, but God in His government says, "You shall reap what you have sown." Bathsheba conceived and gave birth to a son, but the baby died. David's son Amnon raped his half-sister Tamar (2 Sam. 13) and was slain by David's son Absalom. Then Absalom tried to seize the throne and was slain by Joab (2 Sam. 14–18). While David was dying, his son Adonijah tried to take the scepter from Solomon (1 Kings 1), and Adonijah was slain. However, David faced these calamities with God's help and lived to assemble what was needed for the temple so that Solomon (Bathsheba's second son) could build it.

After David was forgiven and restored, he went to the sanctuary to worship the Lord (2 Sam. 12:15–23), and there with the other worshipers, he was surrounded by "songs [shouts] of deliverance," that is, praise to God for His mercies. That's exactly what David needed to hear!

The Joy of Obedience (vv. 8–11)

God speaks to David in verses 8–9, assuring him that the joy of salvation would be restored to him (51:12) if he obeyed the Lord and walked in His way. David's wrong thinking got him into serious trouble, but the Lord would instruct him, guide him, and keep His loving eye on him (see 33:18; 34:15). David's faith (vv. 5–6) must now issue in obedience, for faith and works must go together. God doesn't forgive us so that we can go back and sin! "But there is forgiveness with You, that You may be feared" (130:4).

When he gazed at Bathsheba, lusted after her, and then committed adultery, and when he plotted to kill her husband, David saw himself acting like a free man; *but God saw him acting like an animal!* We are made in God's image, but when we choose to knowingly rebel against God's law, we descend into what the older translations call acting "brutish" (see 92:6; 94:8; Jer. 10:8,

14, 21) and modern translations "senseless." Like the horse, David rushed ahead impetuously, and like the mule, he was stubborn and tried to cover his sins. The only way to control animals is to break them and harness them, but God didn't want to do that to His beloved servant David. Instead, He would teach him His Word and keep His eye upon him, surrounding him with mercy (see 23:6).

When he joined the assembly at the sanctuary of God (vv. 1–2), David began his song with the joyful announcement that God had forgiven him. Now he closed the psalm by exhorting the other worshipers to join him in celebrating the joy of the Lord. "Be glad! Rejoice! Shout for joy!" Years later, his son Solomon would write, "He who covers his sins will not prosper, but whoever confesses and forsakes them will have mercy" (Prov. 28:13 NKJV).

Psalm 33

The verbs in this psalm are plural, which means it involved the worshiping community at the sanctuary. The leader called them to worship (vv. 1–3), the choir led the assembly in praising the Lord, and all closed with the affirmation of faith in verses 20–22. It's likely that their praise was occasioned by the nation's victory over an enemy (vv. 10–11, 16–19). Except for the prayer in verse 22, the entire psalm is devoted only to praise and forms a helpful "primer on praise."

Who Should Worship the Lord? (v. 1)

This verse parallels 32:11 and reminds us that only those who are righteous by faith and obedient in their walk ("upright") can sincerely worship the Lord (Ps. 15; Gen. 15:1–6). It's a fitting and proper thing for those who have experienced the grace of God and his forgiveness (32:1–3) to praise the Lord (147:1). He is the Creator and cares for us. He is the Lord of all and watches over us. "We are his people, and the sheep of his pasture" (100:3). He has redeemed us and we belong to Him. No wonder the worship leader exhorted the people to rejoice, praise, play instruments, and sing to the Lord. A sinner who has been saved by God's grace ought to have no problem praising the Lord.

How They Should Worship the Lord (vv. 2–4)

Both voices and instruments were used in public worship at the sanctuary (see 1 Chron. 25). According to verse 3, the voices were to be enthusiastic ("shout for joy") in the Spirit but not demonstrative in the flesh, and joyful in the Lord but not jovial and jolly. The instruments should be played with skill and the players give their very best to the Lord. The "new song" may mean new in time or new in expression. The term is used nine times in Scripture (40:3; 96:1; 98:1; 144:9; 149:1; Isa. 42:10; Rev. 5:9 and 14:3). The Spirit of God can make an old song new to us as we grow in our knowledge of God and His Word, or as we have new experiences, and He can also open our hearts to a song completely new to us. (Some people don't like to learn new songs.) Our growth in our appreciation of "psalms and hymns and spiritual songs" (Eph. 5:19) is one indication of our development in the Christian life. Of greatest importance is that the worship be Scriptural (v. 4a; and see Col. 3:16). A choir has no more right to sing a lie than a preacher has to preach a lie, and not all "religious songs" are doctrinally correct. When God works, He obeys His own Word; so any worship that is contrary to God's Word will not please the Lord.

Why They Should Worship the Lord (vv. 5–19)

The mention of God's Word in verse 4 reminds us that by knowing the Word of God, we get better acquainted with the God of the Word. Creation reveals His existence, power, wisdom, and majesty, but the revelation in Scripture tells us about His mercy and grace and His wonderful plan of salvation. He is a faithful God, a God of truth, righteousness, justice, and goodness. God's throne is built on righteousness and justice (89:14; 97:2; Isa. 9:7; 32:1, 17). To eyes of faith, the earth is full of His goodness (v. 5), His glory (Isa. 6:3; Num. 14:21–22), and His praise (Hab. 3:3), and one day will be filled with the knowledge of the Lord (Hab. 2:14). The beauty of God's character should elicit from His people songs of praise and thanksgiving. Unless our worship focuses on the character of God, we have ignored the Person who ought to be the center of true worship.

We also worship the Creator and praise Him for His wonderful works (vv. 6–9). Out of nothing, He created everything by the power of His Word (vv. 6, 9; 119:89–91; 147:15, 18; 148:5; Gen. 1:1–2:1; Heb. 11:3). The Word that created the universe is also holding it together (Heb. 1:3; 2 Peter 3:5–7). "The breath of his mouth" may refer to the Holy Spirit of God (Gen. 1:1–2), for "breath" and "spirit" are the same word in Hebrew. "Host" includes the stars and planets (Gen. 2:11), and verse 7 takes us back to Genesis 1:9–10. When you see the heavens above and the earth and seas below, you must marvel at the handiwork of God and stand in awe at the power of His Word. As we worship the Lord, we must praise the Creator and the provisions He has made for us to live on this planet. We must also resolve to be good stewards and not abuse and waste His wonderful gifts.

In our praise, we must thank God for the wisdom of His counsel (vv. 10–11). People with authority make decisions that affect the destinies of nations, and when God isn't permitted to rule, then He overrules; for His will shall be accomplished. He can turn the policies and plans of nation into nothingness (Isa. 8:10; 19:3). The will of God for His children comes from the heart of God and is an expression of His love for them, so there is no cause for us to be alarmed or afraid (Jer. 29:11). What a privilege it is for Israel to be the people of God and the Lord's treasured inheritance (v. 12; 28:9; 74:2; 78:62, 71; Deut. 4:20; 32:9). May the church never lose the wonder of being the people of God! (1 John 3:1–3).

We worship the Lord because of the assurance of His divine care (vv. 13–19). Not only does He keep His eye on His individual saints (32:8; 34:15; 1 Peter 3:12), but He watches "all the sons of men" and "all their works." He knows what the saints are doing and what the sinners are doing to the saints! The word translated "look" in verse 14 means "to gaze intently." As God watches, He sees not only the actions of the body but the "thoughts and intents of the heart" (Heb. 4:12). He made the human heart, He understands it better than we do (Jer. 17:9), and He knows our motives (11:4; 34:15; 2 Chron. 16:9). The king's heart is just like the heart of any other man, and no nation can win a war just because it has a big army and a large supply of weapons and ammunition. At The Exodus, God looked down at the great Egyptian army and destroyed it (Ex. 14:24ff). God delivers His people from danger and death, and He keeps them alive when times are difficult. He cares for us (1 Peter 5:6–7).

What Should Happen Because They Worship the Lord (vv. 20–22)

These words may have been expressed by the congregation and choir as the song came to an end, a confession of faith in the living God. Because they had worshiped the Lord, they had peace in their hearts and could quietly wait for Him to work. Their hope had been strengthened, and they looked expectantly for Him to accomplish His purposes in them, through them, and for them. They had confidence in the Lord that He would send help when they needed it (see 30:10; 40:17; 46:1; 54:4; 63:7; 70:5; 115:9–11; 146:5). On "shield," see 3:3, and note that "help" and "shield" often go together (28:7; 115:9–11; Deut. 33:29). God protects us, not to pamper us but to prepare us to go back into the battle. He is a "refuge and strength" who hides us long enough to help us.

Worship should not only strengthen our inner peace and power, increase our hope, and give us greater confidence in the Lord, but it should also increase our joy. The psalm begins and ends with the theme of joy. Along with that blessing, we find our faith strengthened as we behold the beauty and glory of the Lord in our worship. "Let your unfailing love surround us" is the closing prayer (NLT), so we have the three great Christian virtues brought together: faith (v. 21), hope, and love (v. 22). It isn't enough to leave the place of worship simply "feeling good," because feelings are temporary and sometimes deceptive. If we find ourselves loving God and His people more, having greater faith and hope in the Lord, and going forth into the battle of life with greater confidence and joy, then our worship has accomplished what God wanted it to accomplish.

Psalm 34

Like Psalm 25, this is an acrostic psalm with the Hebrew letter *waw* omitted and an extra *pe* added at the beginning of verse 22. The title connects the psalm with David's dangerous experience with the Philistines in Gath, as recorded in 1 Samuel 21:10–22:1, after which he fled to the cave of Adullum. The emphasis on fearing the Lord (vv. 7, 9, 11) and trusting His goodness (vv. 8, 10, 12) would fit into this historical context. The Philistine king is called Achish in 1 Samuel, but the dynastic title of Philistine kings was Abimelech, as in the title of the psalm. Egyptian rulers were called Pharaoh and the Amalekite kings called Agag. Verse 8 is quoted in 1 Peter 2:3 and verses 12–16 in 1 Peter 3:10–12. Out of his experience in Gath, David shared in this psalm four instructions for his own followers (1 Sam. 22:1–2), as well as for us today, to help us keep out of tight situations and live a life that pleases God.

Bless the Lord (vv. 1–3)

David was delighted to be out of enemy territory (where he probably shouldn't have gone to begin with) and back in the wilderness with his men. Note the verbs: bless, boast, magnify, exalt. The name "Lord" is used sixteen times in the psalm. If initially, David was speaking to his own men, then he was calling them to interrupt warfare and focus on worship. "In prayer, we act like men [people]," wrote Puritan preacher Thomas Watson, "in praise we act like angels." David gave thanks to the Lord by magnifying Him and exalting His name. See what He did for David: He answered prayer (vv. 4, 15), provided his needs (vv. 9–10), delivered him from trouble (v. 17), and protected him from danger (v. 7). David didn't boast about his own cleverness or skill; he boasted about the Lord—who He is and what He does. David saw God's people as nothing in themselves, for they were only the humble and the poor (vv. 2, 6); but they had everything because they belonged to the Lord. They feared the Lord (vv. 7, 9), were set-apart ("saints") as His righteous ones (vv. 10, 15, 19, 21), and were the servants of the Lord God (v. 22). Knowing who we are in Christ and who the Lord is ought to make us want to bless the Lord.

Seek the Lord (vv. 4–8)

David gave a threefold witness of what the Lord does for His own: He saves (vv. 4–8), He keeps (v. 7), and He satisfies (v. 8). He sought the Lord and was saved from the fears ("terrors"; see 31:13) within him, and he cried to the Lord and was delivered from the troubles around him. To seek the Lord is the same as to look to the Lord; and when we look to Him by faith, He looks to us and "shines upon us" (4:6; Num. 6:22–27). If we walk in unbelief, our faces will be ashamed; if we walk by faith, our faces will be aglow (Ex. 34:29; Matt. 17:2; Acts 6:15; 2 Cor. 3:18). The word "radiant" in verse 5 describes the joyful countenance of a mother who is welcoming her children home (Isa. 60:4–5). After the Lord saves us, He keeps us and sends His angels to protect us (v. 7; 35:5–6; Gen. 48:16; Ex. 14:19). The Angel of the Lord is Jesus Christ, the second Person of the Trinity (Josh. 5:13–15), the Lord of the hosts of the angels, who made pre-incarnation visits to His people during Old Testament times. When David envisioned a camp of angels around him, he may have been recalling Jacob's experience at Mahanaim ("the two camps"; Gen. 32:1–2). The angels are servants of the saints today and minister to us in ways we will never know about until we get to heaven (Heb. 1:14).

Those who seek the Lord discover that He not only saves and keeps but that He also satisfies (v. 8). "Taste" doesn't suggest a sip or a nibble; it implies feeding on the Lord through His Word and experiencing all He has for us (1 Peter 2:3; see Heb. 2:9 and 6:3). It means knowing Him better and enjoying Him more. It was a great blessing for David to be delivered from Gath, and it was a greater blessing for him to be protected by the Lord after he fled, but the greatest blessing was drawing nearer to God and enjoying His presence, not just His gifts. David found God's Word sweet (119:103), and he rejoiced in the goodness of the Lord. "Good" is an important word in this psalm (vv. 8, 10, 12, 14).

Fear the Lord (vv. 9–16)

Those who fear the Lord (vv. 7, 9, 11) need fear nothing else, for this is the fear that drives out all fear (112:1). When we fear the Lord, He provides all that we need when we need it. Verse 9 is the Old Testament equivalent of Matthew 6:33. "No good thing does he withhold from those who walk uprightly" (84:11 NASB). God promises to give us what is good for us and to cause all things to work together for good (Rom. 8:28). If we don't receive what we think we need, it means it isn't good for us and we don't need it at this time. At this point, David may have gathered the children and youths around him to teach them the secret of real living. Peter quoted verses 12–14 in 1 Peter 3:10–12, and his instructions are wise and workable.

Desire what is good (v. 12). To "love life" means to desire a full life, the abundance life Christ came to give (John 10:10). This kind of life has little to do with possessions, status, or fame, but it has a lot to do with character, faith, and a desire to honor the Lord. They seek the Lord and want nothing less than His will for their lives. Solomon had wealth, knowledge, fame, and power, yet he wrote, "Therefore, I hated life …" (Eccl. 2:17–20). To cultivate a heart that desires what is good, a heart that delights in the Lord (37:4), is the first step toward the life that overflows with the blessing of the Lord.

Speak what is true (v. 13). If we can control the tongue, we can control the body (James 3:1–12); "whoever guards his mouth and tongue keeps his soul from troubles" (Prov. 21:23 NKJV). To speak the truth in love (Eph. 4:15) and to speak nothing evil is not easy in today's competitive and corrupt society, but it can be done. Note David's prayer in 141:3–4.

Pursue what is right (v. 14). This means abandoning sin once and for all, doing good as God gives strength and opportunity, and being a peacemaker and not a troublemaker. Christians don't seek "peace at any price," for peace depends on purity (James 3:13–18; Isa. 32:17), but they do make every effort not to make enemies (Matt. 5:9; Rom. 14:19; Heb. 12:14–21). Sometimes our best efforts seem to be in vain, but at least we obeyed the Lord (Matt. 5:21–26; 18:15–35). "Pursue" means that we have to work at it, with the help of the Lord.

Expect what is best (vv. 15–16). We must live by faith, trusting the Lord to guide us, care for us, and help us do the right thing. We need not fear because His eyes are upon us (32:8) and His ears are attentive to our prayers. God's face is against those who would do evil to us. This promise is illustrated in Acts 12, when Peter was in prison awaiting execution, the church was praying, and King Herod seemed to be having his way. God saw Peter's plight, He heard the prayers of the saints, and He delivered Peter but destroyed Herod.

Trust the Lord (vv. 17–22)

Nowhere in this psalm does David suggest that the life of faith and obedience will exempt the child of God from trouble (see vv. 4, 6, 17, 19). He does promise that, if we trust Him and call on Him, the Lord can see us through our troubles and make them a blessing to us and through us to others. (See 28:7, Isa. 41:10, Heb. 13:6.) He is also able to help us with our feelings (v. 18). The assurance is that God is near us when our hearts are broken and our spirits are crushed, *whether we feel like it or not.* This is not a promise with conditions attached to it; *it is a fact.* (See 69:20; 119:151; 147:3; Isa. 50:8 and 61:1; Luke 4:18.)

The Lord will take care of our physical safety (vv. 19–20) until our work is finished. The word "keep" means "to exercise great care over," as when Adam cared for the garden (Gen. 2:15) or Jacob cared for his sheep (Gen. 30:31). The apostle John quoted verse 20 in John 19:36 and applied it to Jesus, the Lamb of God (Ex. 12:46; Num. 9:12). The Lord is able to keep our enemies in check, and their own evil deeds will destroy them, for sin is its own executioner (v. 21; see 7:14–16; 9:16; 10:2; Prov. 5:22; Rom.

12:17–21). "Desolate" in verses 21–21 (KJV) means "condemned." The wicked are condemned, but the righteous face no condemnation because they trust the Lord (Rom. 8:1, 33–34). God redeemed David, just as He had redeemed Israel from Egypt, and He is able to redeem us from our troubles.

Psalm 35

Once again, David was being hounded by Saul and slandered by Saul's men, many of whom had been David's friends. David was championing the right cause, for he was God's chosen king, while Saul was trying to destroy him so that one of his own sons would become king. Instead of managing the affairs of the kingdom, Saul was driven by his paranoia to pursue David and seek to kill him, and his zeal was fueled by the lies of his officers. (For the background, see 1 Sam. 19:5; 20:1; 23:25; 24:9–15; 25:29; 26:18–19.) This is classified as an imprecatory psalm (see Ps. 5 for discussion). David made three requests of God, and eventually He granted all of them.

Protect Me (vv. 1–10)

David merged two images in verse 1—the law court ("plead my cause"; see 43:1; 74:22; Jer. 2:9; Mic. 6:1) and the battlefield. Saul chose the battlefield, but David turned to the Lord and asked Him to be Advocate and Judge in the dispute. "The Lord is a man of war" (24:8; 45:3–5; Ex. 15:3; Josh. 5:13–15), so if Saul wanted a fight, God would accept the challenge (see 18:25–27). A soldier himself, David envisioned the Lord dressed in armor and wielding his weapons. The buckler was a large shield that covered most of the body. The enemy hated David (v. 19), lied about him (v. 11), persecuted him (v. 2), and wanted to hurt him and kill him (vv. 4, 26), so the conflict was a matter of life and death; *but there was no just cause for this opposition.* (See vv. 7, 19; 38:19; 69:4; 109:3; 119:78, 86, 161.)

David asked the Lord to block the way and stand between him and Saul and his army (v. 3), just as He had done at The Exodus (Ex. 14:19ff). Then he asked that the angel of the Lord (34:7) confuse the enemy, turn them around, and chase them (v. 4). This would lead to their disgrace, defeat, and eventual destruction (v. 8). In verse 26, he repeated the prayer of verse 4. David frequently mentioned that he was a man with a price on his head (37:32; 38:12; 40:14; 54:3; 63:9; 70:2), so it's no wonder he asked the Lord for a special word of assurance (v. 3; 27:1–3). Confronted by God's heavenly army, Saul and his men were like the chaff: weightless, worthless, defenseless, and harmless. (See 1:4; 83:13; Isa. 17:13; 29:5; Dan. 2:35; Matt. 3:12). They would try to run on the slippery mountain trails and in the darkness fall to their death or fall into one of their own traps (vv. 7–8). These traps were probably pits with nets over them, covered with branches and leaves. Saul treated David like an animal, but it was Saul and his army that were the animals (vv. 15, 17, 25).

In this psalm, David followed each of his three requests with a song of praise to the Lord (vv. 9–10, 17–18 and 27–28), showing that his great desire was to magnify Him. David's joy was in God's salvation, for which only God could receive the glory. His whole being ("all my bones"; see 51:8) would give thanks and praise to the Lord. "Who is like you?" (v. 10) reminds us of Israel's triumph song after The Exodus (Ex. 15:11). David knew that God had chosen him to be king of Israel and that his greatest task would be to unite and strengthen the kingdom and lead the people back to God. Israel had an important work to do in the world and David's leadership was essential.

Reward Me (vv. 11–18)

David stated the evidence that proved he was innocent. The enemy depended on lies, false ("malicious") witnesses who accused him of being a traitor. (See 27:12; Deut. 19:15–21; 1 Sam. 24:10.) Quite the contrary, it was Saul and his officers who were the traitors, for they returned evil for the good David did to them. On two occasions, David could have killed Saul, but instead, David returned good for evil (1 Sam. 24, 26; and see 38:20; 109:5; Jer. 18:18–23). Saul even admitted that David was the better man (1 Sam. 24:17). It pained David deeply that the men he had served with in Saul's army had betrayed him (see 41:9; 55:12–14). He had prayed for them when they were in need, but his prayers returned to him unanswered. David received a blessing because he prayed, but God couldn't send a blessing to such evil people. The only "return" David got from his prayers was evil for good, so he asked the Lord to send him good to compensate for their evil. Those who criticize David for his imprecatory prayer in verses 4–8 should remember that first he prayed for their help and healing. Saul's men "tore David apart" with their wicked words (v. 15). Like court jesters, at their meals they made him the butt of their vicious jokes (v. 16, and see 69:12). (On the question "How long?" see 6:3.) David knew that God would eventually reward him for his faithfulness, but he didn't know when. His first praise to God (vv. 9–10) was personal, but the second expression of praise (v. 18) is in the congregation with the saints.

Vindicate Me (vv. 19–28)

The trial was about to end and the enemy was confident of victory. "Aha, aha, our eyes have seen it" [David's defeat, v. 21 NASB]. In his imagination, David saw Saul's men winking at each other arrogantly (Prov. 6:13; 10:10), as if to say, "He's done for!" They would never accept a truce or even talk about peace, but this was God's way of judging Saul for his sins and eliminating him from the political equation in Israel. After Saul's death, David had seven years of trouble with Saul's son (2 Sam. 1–4), but the Lord eventually solved that problem. David prayed that God would vindicate him, because David's cause was God's cause, and the Lord's reputation was at stake (v. 24). In verse 26, he repeated his request from verse 4 and asked that the enemy be shamefully defeated. David's desire was that the Lord be magnified in His own way and His own time.

In contrast to the shame of the enemy in their defeat are the joyful shouts of the righteous in David's victory. Unlike Elijah, who felt he was fighting all alone (1 Kings 19:10–18), David knew that many people in Israel supported him, those who were living "quietly in the land" (v. 20). Even in the darkest days of Israel's history, there has always been a faithful remnant that stayed true to the Lord and prayed for His will to be done. David closed the psalm with a song of confidence and joy, witnessing to God's righteousness and power. The word translated "prosperity" (v. 27 KJV) is the familiar Hebrew word "shalom—peace," which means much more than a mere cessation of hostilities. It carries the idea of well being in every aspect of life, including peace with God, with others, with yourself, and with the circumstances of your life.

David's experience reminds us of Jesus Christ, the Son of David, who was also hated without a cause (John 15:25) and falsely accused and attacked by those for whom He had shown nothing but kindness and love. God delivered David from his enemies, but the Father "spared not his own son" (Rom. 8:32) but willingly gave Him to die for the sins of the world.

Psalm 36

The psalm is attributed to David "the servant of the Lord" (see 18, title; 35:27; Deut. 34:5; Josh. 24:29; Dan. 6:20; James 1:1; Titus 1:1). David pondered the reality of evil in God's world (vv. 1–4), he praised God's character (vv. 5–9), and then he prayed that God would protect him from evil and eventually judge the wicked. He solved the perplexing problem of evil in the world by being a worshiper, not a philosopher, and by taking personal responsibility to obey God and serve Him. If there were more salt and light in this world, there would be less decay and darkness in society.

Revelation: The Corruption of the Human Heart (vv. 1–4)

In Scripture, an oracle is usually an authoritative pronouncement from the Lord; but here it is sin that is speaking an oracle deep in the heart of the sinner. In Psalm 10, the sinner talks to himself, but here sin speaks to the sinner. Sin deceives us (Rom. 7:11) and flatters us (10:3; Deut. 29:18–19), giving us the false assurance that our rebellion will go unpunished (Gen. 3:1–5).

"Listen to your heart!" the world tells us, forgetting that "The heart is more deceitful than all else and is desperately sick; who can understand it?" (Jer.17:9 NASB).

Of course, the sinner's self-confident arrogance brings tragic consequences, starting with *an absence of the fear of God* (v. 1). This is not the word for the reverential respect of God that all believers should cultivate, but rather the word that means the dread of God and of His judgment. Paul quotes this verse in Romans 3:8, along with others Old Testament statements that reveal the wickedness of the human heart. When we don't fear God, we flatter ourselves, and that flattery gives us more confidence to sin. We don't really see ourselves as the Lord sees us, and we are blind to our own sins and what they can do to us. (On the fear of the Lord, see 34:9; 55:19; 64:4; 111:10; 119:120; Josh. 24:14; Prov. 1:7.) This kind of person doesn't hate sin (v. 2) or despise it or reject it (v. 4) but finds delight in doing it.

When they lose the fear of God, they start to lose everything else that is important to good character and conduct. Out of a sinful heart come sinful words and sinful deeds (v. 3; Matt. 12:34–35). Instead of acting wisely, they set themselves and are determined to do evil. They don't meditate on God's truth while in bed (1:2; 16:7; 42:8; 63:6) but devise evil schemes. They can't relax and go to sleep until they've hatched a new plot (Mic. 2:1). The corrupt heart has produced a defiled conscience, a confused mind, and a perverted will.

Adoration: The Character of God's Heart (vv. 5–9)

David did a wise thing when he stopped contemplating the sinners and started focusing on the glories of the Lord. Knowing the character of God is essential to a balanced Christian life, and these five verses are a concise systematic theology. *Mercy* (vv. 5, 7, 10) is translated "lovingkindness" in the *New American Standard Bible* and "love" in the *New International Version*. Some translations use "covenant love" or "steadfast love." Mercy and faithfulness are often joined (57:3; 61:7; 85:10; 86:15), as are righteousness and justice (33:5; 89:14; 97:2). God's mercy and faithfulness are as limitless as the skies, His righteousness as firm as the mountains, and His judgments (justice) as inexhaustible and mysterious as the ocean depths (see Rom. 11:33–36). Yet He takes care of people and animals on the earth! What a gracious and generous God! His mercy is priceless, for it took the death of His Son to accomplish salvation for a lost world (1 Peter 1:18–19).

The "refuge" in verse 7 is probably the Holy of Holies in the sanctuary of the Lord, for he mentions God's house in verse 8. If so, then the "wings" are those of the cherubim on the mercy seat of the ark (Ex. 37:9). (See 57:1; 61:4; 63:7; Ruth 2:12; Heb. 10:19–25.) God's "shadow" offers us better protection than the world's armies! In 90:1 and 4, the image is that of the mother hen protecting her young with her outspread wings. (See Matt. 23:37 and Luke 13:34.) The priests received portions of some sacrifices for their own use and would feast in the sanctuary (Lev. 6:14–23; 7:11–38; Deut. 18:1–5; 1 Sam. 2:12–17). But David sees all of God's people enjoying a feast in God's house where there is an abundance of food and water (63:1–5; 65:4). The image of the Lord's satisfying river is found often in Scripture: 46:4; Isaiah 8:5–8; Jeremiah 2:13–19; Ezekiel 47; John 4:1–15 and 7:37–39; Revelation 22:1. The word "pleasures" (delights) in verse 8 comes from the same Hebrew root as "Eden" in Genesis 2 and 3, and it means "delight." Man sinned and was cast out of Eden, but through faith in Christ, we have access into God's presence and can delight in His blessings. The river in verse 8 reminds us of the rivers in Eden (Gen. 2:8–14). Life and light go together (v. 9; 49:19; 56:13; John 1:4; 8:12), and the Lord is the source of both. The wicked feed on flattery (v. 2), but the righteous feed on the Lord's rich blessings.

Expectation: The Confidence of the Believer's Heart (vv. 10–12)

What a privilege it is to be God's children! We are resting safely under His wings, feasting joyfully at His table, drinking abundantly from His river, and walking confidently in His light!

In response to these blessings David prayed that the Lord would continue His blessings on His people (v. 10) and one day judge the wicked (vv. 11–12). God will continue to bless us if we love Him, get to know Him better, and walk in obedience to His will. David knew that the enemy was subtle and that he dared not become overconfident, so he prayed for the Lord's protection from their hands and feet. He didn't want to be knocked down and trampled upon and forced to leave his own land. By faith, David looked ahead and saw the enemies of the Lord completely defeated, and on this confidence, he continued to serve the Lord.

Psalm 37

David had written about the wicked in Psalm 36 (see vv. 1 and 11), and he will pick up the theme again in Psalm 39. He wrote Psalm 37 in his mature years (v. 25), and in it he discussed the age-old problem of why the righteous suffer while the wicked seem to prosper. Perhaps this psalm was part of David's preparation of Solomon for the throne (1 Kings 2:3; see Prov. 23:17–18, 24:19–20). Honest atheists and agnostics don't have to wrestle with this problem because their philosophy of relativism forbids them to use words like good, bad, righteous, and wicked. However, those who believe in God sometimes wonder why He allows the wicked to succeed while the righteous suffer. The word "wicked" is found fourteen times in the psalm (KJV). The theological foundation for the psalm is the covenant God made with Israel, recorded in Leviticus 26 and Deuteronomy 27–30. God owned the land, and if the nation obeyed Him, they could live in the land and enjoy its blessings. But if Israel disobeyed the Lord, He would first chasten them *in the land* (invasion, drought, famine), but if they continued to rebel, He would then take them *out of the land* (captivity). (See Deut. 11 and 33:28, and Lev. 26:3–10.) But it seemed that the wicked were prospering and that God wasn't doing anything about it (see Jer. 12). The righteous could fret over the problem (vv. 1, 7–8), leave the land (v. 3), or go on being faithful, trusting the Lord to keep His Word (vv. 3, 5, 7, 34, 39). Like any mature believer who had been through his own share of suffering, David took the long view of the situation and evaluated the immediate and the transient in terms of the ultimate and the eternal. He encouraged Solomon and the people to believe God's promises and wait on Him. In the psalm, he gave four encouraging assurances to believers who question how God is running His world. (See also 49 and 73.)

The Lord Can Be Trusted (vv. 1–11)

David gave one negative instruction—"Don't fret" (vv. 1, 7, 8)—and four positive instructions: trust in the Lord (v. 3), delight in the Lord (v. 4), commit yourself to the Lord (vv. 5–6), and rest in the Lord (v. 7).

Fret not (vv. 1–2). The word translated "fret" means "to burn, to get heated up." David's message was, "Cool down and keep cool!" When we see evil in the world, we ought to feel a holy anger at sin (Eph. 4:26), but to envy the wicked only leads to fretting, and fretting leads to anger (v. 8). His argument is that the wicked are temporary and will one day be gone (see vv. 9, 22, 28, 34, 38). They are like grass that either fades away or is cut down and burned. In the Middle East, vegetation is abundant during and immediately after the rainy seasons, but it quickly vanishes when the moisture is gone. (See 90:5–6; 102:11; 103:15–16; Isa. 40:6–8; James 1:10–11; 1 Peter 1:24.)

Trust in the Lord (v. 3). A fretful heart is not a trusting heart, because it lacks joy and peace (Rom. 15:13). Faith and works go together, so we should also do good as we wait on the Lord (34:14; Luke 6:35; Gal. 6:10). Some of God's people were tempted to leave the land (see Ruth 1; 1 Sam. 26:19), which was tantamount to saying that God wasn't faithful and couldn't be trusted. But David urged them to stay in the land and trust God for what they needed (v. 27). Each tribe, clan, and family in Israel had its assigned inheritance which was not to pass into other hands, and the Lord promised to care for the land of the faithful (vv. 9, 11, 22, 29, 34). The promise in verse 3 is variously translated: "enjoy safe pastures" (NIV), "feed on His faithfulness"

(NASB margin; NKJV), "enjoy security" (RSV). If we are faithful to God, He will be faithful to us. Trusting the Lord is a key theme in this psalm (vv. 4, 5, 7, 34, 39).

Delight in the Lord (v. 4). The word translated "delight" comes from a root that means "to be brought up in luxury, to be pampered." It speaks of the abundance of the blessings we have in the Lord Himself, totally apart from what He gives us. To enjoy the blessings and ignore the Blesser is to practice idolatry. In Jesus Christ, we have all God's treasures, and we need no other. If we truly delight in the Lord, then the chief desire of our heart will be to know Him better so we can delight in Him even more, and the Lord will satisfy that desire! This is not a promise for people who want "things," but for those who want more of God in their lives.

Commit your way to the Lord (vv. 5–6). The verb means "to roll off your burden" (1 Peter 5:7). God doesn't take our burdens so that we can become irresponsible, but so we can serve Him better. Sometimes less care means we become careless, and that leads to failure. One of the things He will "bring to pass" is the vindication of His servants who have been slandered by God's enemies (v. 6 NIV; see vv. 28, 32–33).

Rest in the Lord (vv. 7–11). The verb means "be silent, be still." It describes calm surrender to the Lord (62:5). Creative silence is a rare commodity today, even in church worship services. People cannot tolerate silence. A silent radio or TV screen invites listeners and viewers to switch to another station or channel. But unless we learn to wait silently before God, we will never experience His peace. For us to get upset because of the evil schemes of the ungodly is to doubt the goodness and justice of God (vv. 7, 12, 32). "Meekness" does not mean "weakness." It means force under the control of faith. Moses was meek (Num. 12:3), but he was a man of great power. Jesus quoted verse 11 (Matt. 5:5) but expanded it to include "the earth." "Inherit the land" (vv. 9, 11, 22, 29) refers to the security of future generations in the Land of Promise, according to God's covenant (Gen. 12:1–3; 13:14–18; 15:7–17), for God had a great work for His righteous remnant to do in that land, cul-minating in the coming of Messiah. Eventually, the wicked will be cut off (vv. 9, 22, 28, 34, 38), which in Israel usually meant exclusion from the covenant community (Ex. 12:15; 30:33, 38; 31:14; Lev. 7:20–21), but it could mean execution (Gen. 9:11; Lev. 20:17; Num. 15:30–31).

The Lord Understands Your Situation (vv. 12–20)

Since God can be trusted, we should not fret, and since God understands our situation, we should not fear. The wicked plot against the poor and needy (v. 12, and see 7, 32) and act like wild beasts about to devour them ("slay" in v. 14 means "to butcher an animal"), but the Lord laughs at the wicked (see 2:4) for He knows their judgment is coming. He also knows that their own weapons will turn against them (v. 15; 7:15ff; 9:15ff). God upholds the righteous (vv. 16–17) and sees to it they have what they need (Prov. 15:16; 16:8). Just as Jesus met a great need with a few loaves and fishes, so the Lord can "make a little go a long way." "Know" in verse 18 refers to much more than intellectual understanding—"God knows what's going on"—but indicates that He is involved and caring for us daily (see 1:6; 31:7, 15). "Give us this day our daily bread" (Matt. 6:11).

There is in verse 18 the suggestion of something beyond the needs of this life. The emphasis in Psalm 34 is on Israel's national life in the land, and the ancient Jew saw his "immortality" in his posterity, but occasionally in The Psalms you catch a glimpse of the eternal. (See 16:11, 17:15 and the "forever" statements in 37:18 and 27–29.) The wicked will perish like smoke at the altar (102:3; Hos. 13:3; the *New International Version* reads "like the beauty of the fields," an image used in v. 2). If the punishment of the wicked involves more than suffering and death in this life, will not the blessing of the righteous go beyond this life as well?

The Lord Blesses His People (vv. 21–31)

He blesses them first of all with *provision of their daily needs* (vv. 21–22). The wicked may succeed for a time, but eventually they have to borrow in order to survive; while the godly have what they need and can lend to others (Deut. 15:6; 28:12, 44). This isn't a promise for every believer at all times in all places, for many believers have died in poverty and hunger. Like the statements in the book of Proverbs, it's a generalization that proves true in so many cases that we can safely apply it to life. God not only gives provision, but He also gives *protection* (vv. 23–24). "Ordered" means "secured, established" (119:133), and even if believers stumble, God will pick them up and get them going again. He can keep us from stumbling (Jude 24), and He can restore us if we do stumble. Why? Because the Father delights in His children and wants them to learn to walk.

Along with the blessing of provision and protection is the blessing of the Lord's *presence with His people* (vv. 25–26). As an elder saint, David bore witness to God's faithfulness to him and his descendants. Not only did God meet every need, but He gave enough so that David could share it with others (Luke 6:38). As we pray for daily bread (Matt. 6:11), the Lord answers. God also blesses His people by enabling them to live *obedient lives* (vv. 27–29), which means righteousness in character and justice in conduct. God's blessing on the godly continues in the lives of their children, but the descendants of the wicked are cut off. Alas, the sins of ungodly fathers influence their children to disobey God, and the Lord has to punish them as well. Finally, God blesses the righteous with *His Word* (vv. 30–31). God's Word in the heart is the secret of a holy life (1:1–3; 40:8; 119:9–16; Deut. 6:6).

The Lord Judges the Wicked (vv. 32–40)

Three images illustrate God's judgment of those who reject Him and rebel against His law: the court trial (vv. 32–34), the tree (vv. 35–36), and the rescue (vv. 37–40). The wicked watched the godly and tried to find some reason for accusing them. In spite of David's integrity and Solomon's great wisdom, the judicial system in Israel was far from efficient, and it was easy for the rich to oppress the poor and take what little they possessed (Amos 2:4–8; 4:1–3). But the Lord is the highest judge, and He knows how to deliver the righteous from lying witnesses and judges who have been bribed.

The godly are pictured by the fruitful tree (1:3) and the ungodly by a luxurious ("overbearing and towering") shrub or tree, planted in its native soil where its roots can go down deep (vv. 35–36). Not only did the tree die and fall, but there was no evidence left behind that there had ever been a tree there at all! So God will do to the wicked, who appear to be successful and permanent but are destined for judgment. God not only judges the wicked but He also rescues the righteous from their clutches (vv. 37–40). The key question isn't what people look like or what they possess, but what is their final end? (See Prov. 5:4; 14:12–13; 16:25; 24:20). "There is a future for the man of peace … but the future of the wicked will be cut off" (vv. 37–38 NIV). Some see this as referring to posterity, and that may be included, but certainly it describes the final destiny of the righteous and the wicked. The Lord delivers the righteous from eternal judgment, but He also delivers them from the attacks and accusations of the wicked in this world today. Why? "Because they trust in him" (v. 40). Fretting and fear cannot stand before faith in the living God.

Psalm 38

This is the third of the penitential psalms and, as you would expect, it has things in common with its predecessors (6, 32). Compare 6:1 with 38:1; 32:3 with 38:3, 8, 13–14; and 32:5 with 38:18. The description here of David's physical condition is similar to the one in 32, so perhaps both psalms (along with 51) came out of the same sad situation. David's sins (vv. 3, 4, 18) had brought God's chastening to his life and David was a very sick man. Not all affliction comes from disobedience (John 9:1–3), but physical troubles can be a consequence of sin (John 5:14). David doesn't question the legitimacy of his suffering, for he admitted his sins (v. 18), but he wonders why his suffering is so severe. Like the prophet Habakkuk, David wanted God to remember to be merciful (Hab. 3:2). The title "to bring to remembrance" (KJV) is found also at Psalm 70. The *New American Standard Bible* reads "for a memorial" and the *New International Version* "a petition." For God to "remember" someone means that He begins to act on their behalf and meet some need (Gen. 8:1; 19:29; 30:22; 1 Sam. 1:19). David wanted God to remember him and grant forgiveness and healing. When God's people suffer the consequences of sin and feel the chastening hand of God, they must choose one of three responses.

We Can Focus on Ourselves and Experience Sin's Painfulness (vv. 1–8)

Pain hurts, and David wasn't ashamed to write about it, using a number of vivid images to convey to the Lord and to us the severity of his suffering. Like a loving Father, the Lord first rebuked David and then chastened him, both of which are evidences of His love (Prov. 3:11–12; Heb. 12:1–11). If we don't listen to the words of His heart, we will have to feel the weight of His hand (32:4; 39:10–11). Alexander Maclaren compared "hot displeasure" to "hot bubbling lava" about to erupt. God was also shooting "arrows" at David, hurling down one affliction after another with great force (see Job 6:4; 7:20; 16:12; "mark" means "target"). He was drowning in a sea of suffering (v. 4; see 42:7; 69:2, 14; 88:16; 124:4; 130:1–2), and the whole experience became a burden too heavy for him to carry.

In great detail, David described his "loathsome disease" (v. 7 KJV). This was not one isolated sickness but a collection of physical disorders that produced "searing pain" (NIV), fever, and inflammation. He had festering wounds (v. 5) that smelled foul and looked ugly, his heart wasn't functioning properly, and his eyes were getting dim (v. 10). There was no health in his body (vv. 3, 7); one minute he was burning with fever, the next minute he was numb with cold (vv. 7–8). His body was feeble and twisted with pain, and he walked about all day like a man at a funeral (vv. 6, 8). At times, his pain was so severe, he cried out like a wild beast (v. 8). All this happened because he had been foolish and had sinned against the Lord (v. 5; 107:17). We are free to disobey the Lord, *but we are not free to change the consequences.*

We Can Focus on Others and Experience Sin's Loneliness (vv. 9–14)

David opened the psalm with "LORD—JEHOVAH," and now he addressed God once more, this time as "Lord—Adonai—Master." He will use both names in verses 15 and 21–22. For a brief moment, he took his eyes off his own sufferings and looked to the Lord, knowing that God saw his heart and knew all his longings. God knows what we want, but He also knows what we need. Then why pray? Because God has commanded us to pray, and "you do not have because you do not ask" (James 4:2 NKJV). Furthermore, as we pray, God works in our hearts to give us a clearer understanding of ourselves and of His will for us. Prayer isn't a theological concept to analyze and explain; it's a privilege to cherish and a blessing to claim.

David's focus now was on the people around him, and he felt abandoned and lonely. The people who should have encouraged and comforted him—his loved ones and friends—kept their distance, along with his enemies, who wanted him to die. David expected his enemies to plot against him (v. 12), gloat over his fall (v. 16), hate him, slander him, and return evil for the good he did to them (vv. 19–20), but he didn't think his friends and relatives would turn against him. (See 31:11–12; 41:9; 69:8; 88:8, 18; Job 19:13–19.) "Sore" in verse 11 means "a stroke, a blow" and is sometimes translated "a plague," the word used to describe leprosy. David's family and closest friends were treating him like a leper and keeping their distance. They didn't want to be contaminated! But before we criticize them, have we been obeying Galatians 6:1–2 and 2 Corinthians 2:5–11?

As he grieved over his sins and over the unconcern of his loved ones, David realized that his enemies were plotting to get him out of the way (v. 12). They talked about his ruin and destruction, and he heard what they were saying; but he did not reply to their threats or their false accusations. He knew he had sinned, so why put up a feeble defense? But he also knew that his accusers were sinning and really had no cause for deposing him. But suppose he did win his defense and then fall again (v. 16)? His enemies would then have a stronger case against him. So, the wisest course was to remain silent. That being the case, he kept quiet and turned the matter over to the Lord. He followed the instructions he had given in Psalm 37.

We Can Focus on the Lord and Experience Sin's Forgiveness (vv. 15–22)

For the third time, David addressed the Lord, but this time he got down to business and dealt with his sins. He hoped in (waited for) the Lord, knowing that God would hear his prayers. He wasn't praying only for his own deliverance just so he could be comfortable; he wanted God to work so the enemy couldn't use him as an excuse for sinning (vv. 16, 19–20; 25:2; 35:19). When they slandered David's name, they also slandered the Lord (see 2 Sam. 12:14), and David wanted to honor the Lord. He felt like he was about to die (v. 17), and he confessed his sins to the Lord in true repentance and faith.

What did David mean when he described his enemies as "lively" (v. 19)? He was contrasting his own condition with their condition: he was weak, they were strong; he was about to die, they were very much alive; he was sick, they were "vigorous" (NASB, NIV). Confident that the Lord had forgiven him, he closed his prayer with three requests. *Be with me* (v. 21) is answered by Deuteronomy 4:31 and 31:6, 8, and Hebrews 13:5. *Be near me* (v. 21) finds its answer in 16:8, 34:18 and James 4:8. *Be for me and help me* (v. 22) leads us to 28:7, Isaiah 41:10 and Romans 8:33–39. These three requests cover just about everything!

Psalm 39

Both 38 and 39 record David attempting to remain silent in a time of trial, lest he say something that would offend believers or give ammunition to unbelievers (38:13–14; 39:1–3, 9; see 73:15).

(For other parallels, see 38:15–16/39:7–8; 38:1–3, 11/39:10–11.) In this psalm, David doesn't seem to be gravely ill, but he has been visited by some "stroke" from the Lord because of his sins (vv. 9–11). Also, the old problem of the prosperity of the wicked is in the picture (v. 1). It appears that the wicked ("the foolish" v. 8) were blaspheming God and maligning David in his affliction, and the king was greatly concerned lest he bring reproach on the name of the Lord. There is a dirge-like quality to the psalm, and we marvel that David gave the hymn to the chief musician to use in public worship. Jeduthun was one of three musicians David put in charge of the worship at the sanctuary; the others were Heman and Asaph (see 1 Chron. 16:37–43; 2 Chron. 5:12; 35:15). Jeduthun is mentioned in the titles to Psalms 62 and 77. Recorded in this psalm are four progressive stages in David's overcoming his difficult experience.

He Was Silent—A Burning Heart (vv. 1–3)

Seeing the prosperity of the wicked and hearing their blasphemous words so angered David that he wanted to retaliate and say something to defend God, but he deemed it best to keep quiet. But this restraint only made his heart burn with intense pain (see 32:3 and Jer. 20:9) until finally he had to speak out. The two Emmaeus disciples had "burning hearts" because of the way the Lord had expounded the Word to them, and Ezekiel had anguish in his spirit because of the difficult calling God had given him. David didn't even say good things; he just kept quiet as long as he could. There is "a time to keep silence, and a time to speak" (Eccl. 3:7), and wise is the person who knows the difference. David didn't argue with God (v. 9) or with those who reproached him, but he did pray to the Lord.

He Was Despondent—A Burdened Heart (vv. 4–6)

When we find ourselves burying our true feelings and creating physical and emotional pain for ourselves, then it's time to talk to the Lord and seek His help. David knew that life was short and that the days would pass swiftly; he also knew that he was frail and that one day would die. He began to measure his days (90:12;

119:84) and saw that they were but a handbreadth (four fingers) and his age nothing in God's sight. (See 90:1–11.) "Verily, every man at his best state [in his vigor] is altogether vanity" (v. 5) sounds like a statement from Ecclesiastes by David's son Solomon, and he repeated the thought in verse 11. The Hebrew word translated "vanity" means "a breath, emptiness" (see 62:9; 144:4; Job 14:2; Eccl. 6:12). One of my Hebrew professors described "vanity" as "what's left after you break a soap bubble." In verse 6, he compared life to an "empty show," with shadow people bustling about, trying to get rich. Busy for what? Wealthy for what? Years later, Solomon raised the same questions (Eccl. 2:18–19), and Jesus emphasized the same truth in Luke 12:16–21. If you measure the length of life, you may become despondent, but if you look around you and measure the depth of life, you are appalled. Life is swift, life is short, and for most people, life is futile. In modern vocabulary, people are living for the image and not the reality.

He Was Confident—A Believing Heart (v. 7)

This is the central verse in the psalm and the turning point in David's experience. "If life is short and goes past so swiftly," asks David, "what am I waiting for? If the world is nothing but a shadow image, let me give myself to the Lord, who is the foundation of all that is real and lasting." Today we would say, "The reality is of Christ" (Col. 2:17 NIV). The main concern is not *how long we live* but *how* we live. Life is measured, not by how rich we are in material wealth, but whether we have values that last. Are we living with eternity's values in view? "He who does the will of God abides forever" (1 John 2:17 NKJV). In turning by faith to the Lord, David moved from hopelessness to hope and from paralysis to action. The next verses describe what he did to bring about change.

He Was Repentant—A Broken Heart (vv. 8–13)

We begin with David the sinner and listen to his prayer for forgiveness (vv. 8–9). Like every truly convicted sinner, his mouth had been stopped (Rom. 3:19), and he admitted his guilt before God (see 1 Sam. 3:18; Lam. 1:21). We don't know the particular sins that had brought this stroke from the Lord, and we don't have to know. We do know that God listens to the cry of the brokenhearted (51:17) and forgives when we confess (1 John 1:9). David was especially concerned that he not give occasion to "the foolish" to ridicule his faith (14:1; 69:7; 74:22; 79:4).

Next, David the sufferer pleaded with God to remove the stroke and heal his body (vv. 10–11; see 32:4; 38:2). He used three images to get his point across: a plague or sickness, draining away his life; the blow of God's hand, like a loving parent disciplining a child; the rebuke of His Word, that cut deeply into David's heart. C. S. Lewis was correct when he wrote in *The Problem of Pain*, "God whispers to us in our pleasures, speaks in our conscience, but shouts in our pains: it is His megaphone to arouse a deaf world."[22] The human body ages, decays, and dies; and the material wealth we gather gradually loses its value, like a moth silently destroying a garment. Jim Elliot's oft-quoted statement certainly applies here: "He is no fool who gives what he cannot keep to gain that which he cannot lose."[23] Vanity of vanity, all is vanity—unless we put our faith and hope in God.

Finally, David the sojourner prays for God's direction as he makes his pilgrim way through life with its joys and sorrows. The world is a "vain show" (v. 6)—John Bunyan called it "Vanity Fair"—and God's people are aliens and strangers here (119:19; Gen. 23:4; Lev. 25:23; 1 Chron. 29:15; Heb. 11:13; 1 Peter 1:1; 2:11). We are not strangers to God, for He knows us and we know Him, but we are strangers with God as His welcomed guests (90:1; 23:6). He hears our prayers and cries, and He sees our tears. "In the world you will have tribulation," Jesus told His disciples, "but be of good cheer, I have overcome the world" (John 16:33 NKJV). His closing prayer was that God would turn away His frowning face and give him strength to return to life with its duties and burdens, and then one day enable him to pass into eternity. The phrase "no more" doesn't suggest annihilation or the absence of an afterlife, but that David would "no more" be on his earthly pilgrimage. "I will dwell in the house of the Lord forever" (23:6).

Psalm 40

Hebrews 10:5–9 quotes 40:6–8 and applies the passage to Christ, which makes this a Messianic psalm. Some see the birth of Christ in verse 7, His sinless life in verse 8, and His sacrificial death in verse 6. However, it was first of all a psalm about David and his needs and how the Lord met them, but the historical setting is obscure. David may have written it during his difficult exile years or perhaps during the early years of his reign. It's unusual for a psalm to have a prayer for mercy following praise and dedication. However, if verses 1–5 picture his deliverance during the dangerous exile years, and verses 6–10 describe his dedication as the new king, then verses 11–17 could be a record of his prayer for personal forgiveness (v. 12; see 38:3–5 and 39:8–9) and victory over his enemies following his coronation. It does seem that verse 16 is a royal prayer for God's blessing on the nation. You find verses 13–17 repeated in modified form in Psalm 70. From whatever experiences led to the writing of this psalm, David learned some valuable lessons and gave us three important instructions to follow in the difficult times of life.

Praise God for All He Has Done (vv. 1–5)

No matter what our trouble or trial, it's always good to look back and recall the goodness of the Lord. David remembered how long he had waited before the Lord delivered him from his enemies and from Saul, but the day came when God inclined His ear (31:3), heard his cries, and lifted him up from the pit. If David learned anything from his exile years, it was that ultimate success depends on faith in the Lord and patience during His providential working (5:3; 33:20; 37:34; 38:15; Heb. 6:12). We are not to take the description of the pit literally (slime, mud, mire), but figuratively, as a picture of those difficult years David endured. "The pit" is also a term for sheol, the realm of the dead, and David's life was certainly in danger. A quaint country preacher used verses 2–3 for a sermon text, and his "points" were: God brought him up, God stood him up, and God tuned him up! David had a new beginning with a new song of praise in his mouth (18:49; 22:22; 33:3). God helped David because he trusted the Lord, did not show respect to the arrogant who opposed God, and remained true to the God of Israel. "Lies" in verse 4 refers to idols. Unlike David, King Saul was a proud man who trusted in himself and made himself more important than God. In looking back on those years as an exile and a hunted man, David saw the greatness of God's works (wonders) and the wisdom of His plans (v. 5). This is his version of Romans 8:28.

Give God All That He Asks (vv. 6–10)

David has moved from the pit to the rock, and now he goes to the sanctuary of God. After all God had done for David, how could the king express to the Lord his appreciation for His mercies? He could bring sacrifices to the altar, but that wasn't God's first desire. This doesn't mean that such sacrifices were wrong, or that God didn't want His people to offer them, but that God wanted their hearts first of all. Throughout the Old Testament, the Lord made it clear that He could not accept sacrifices unless the worshiper showed sincere devotion, dedication, and obedience. No doubt David heard how Saul learned that important lesson—too late (1 Sam. 15:22). (See 50:8–15; 51:16–17; Prov. 21:3; Isa. 1:11–17; Jer. 7:22–23; Hos. 6:6; Mic. 6:6–8; Mark 12:32–33.)

In verse 6, *sacrifice* means any animal whose blood was offered at the altar, followed by a communal meal. *Offering* refers to the meal offering that could accompany the sacrifices, and the *burnt offering* symbolized total dedication to the Lord. The *sin offering* was given to cover specific offenses and bring reconciliation between the offender and God. All of these were fulfilled in Jesus Christ whose sacrifice on the cross satisfied the justice of God once and for all, for time and eternity (Lev. 1–7; Heb. 10:1–17).

The "open ears" refer to his readiness to hear and obey God's will (1 Sam. 9:15; 20:2; Isa. 48:8; 50:4–5; Matt. 3:9, 43; Acts 7:51, 57). This is not a reference to the servant in Exodus 21:1–6. The passage is paraphrased in Hebrews 10:5–10 as "a body you have prepared for me," i.e., the body in which Messiah served the Father here on earth. An open ear means a yielded will and a surrendered body. When the heart delights in God's law, the will has no problem obeying (119:11; Deut. 6:6; 11:18; Prov. 3:3, 7:3; Jer. 31:33). "Lo, I come" means "Here I am, ready to obey" (see 1 Sam. 3:4, 6, 8; Isa. 6:8). The scroll may be a reference to Deuteronomy 17:14–20, and see 2 Kings 11:12 and 22:13. The Old Testament predicts the coming of the Messiah (Luke 24:27).

David was enthusiastic about telling others what the Lord had done for him, and he is a good example for us to follow (22:25; 26:12; 35:18; 111:1; 149:1). Among the worshipers at the sanctuary, the king gave glory to the Lord. This reminds us of our Lord's resurrection praises (22:31; Heb. 2:12).

Trust God for All That Remains (vv. 11–17)

When the worship service was ended and David had returned to his royal duties, he discovered that there were new battles to fight and fresh problems to solve, so he turned again to the Lord for help. Worship is not an escape from life but the opportunity to honor God and be equipped to face life and live for His glory. David had his own personal problems to deal with (vv. 11–13), for he had a sensitive conscience and knew that he was a sinful man. He also had enemies who wanted to dethrone him (vv. 14–15) and so he prayed for victory. (See 25:4, 21–27.) Most of all, David wanted the Lord to be magnified and His people to be blessed as they served Him (vv. 16–17). David couldn't see what lay ahead (v. 12; 31:9; 38:10), but God knew the future and had everything under control. As he often did (7:1, 5; 22:19; 38:22; 71:12), David prayed for speedy deliverance. "I am—You are" (v. 17) says it all. The great I AM is adequate for every need.

Psalm 41

Sickness (vv. 8,10) and sin (v. 4) again unite to put David into distress and danger as his enemies plot against him and wait for him to die. These factors seem to place this psalm in the time of Absalom's rebellion. David's illness prevented him from leading the nation as he wanted to (2 Sam 15:1–6), and Absalom took advantage of this to promote himself as king. If the "dear friend" of verse 9 is David's counselor Ahithophel, then the matter of the historical setting is settled (2 Sam. 16:15ff). Jesus quoted verse 9 in the upper room when referring to Judas (John 13:38), so the psalm has Messianic overtones. When we find ourselves in difficulty, we may use this psalm to take an inventory of our spiritual condition by asking and answering four questions.

Integrity: How Do We Treat Others (vv. 1–4)?

Before we can claim God's promises, we must examine our own hearts to see if we have sincerely met the conditions the Lord had laid down. David no doubt based his prayer on the stipulations given in the covenant (Lev. 26:1–13; Deut. 7:13–16; 28:1–14). He knew that he had no right to claim mercy from the Lord if he himself had not shown mercy to others. But David had fully obeyed the Lord's rules and had shown mercy to King Saul, to Saul's grandson Mephibosheth, and to the needy in the land. (See Matt. 5:7 and Luke 6:37–38.) "Poor" refers to the helpless, the miserable people whose lot was difficult and who depended on the help of others. To "consider" these pitiable people meant being attentive to their needs and assisting them. It also meant not judging and blaming them, as Job's friends blamed him and the disciples blamed the blind man (John 9:1–4). We have every reason to believe that David sought to care for the poor and needy in his kingdom and therefore was praying with integrity. In verse 1, he referred to himself in the third person, a true mark of his humility before the Lord.

He listed in verses 2–3 the blessings God would send because he confessed his sins and asked God to be merciful to him (v. 4). God would protect him from his enemies and prolong his life in the land. That in itself would bear witness to his enemies that David was a man favored by God. God would also heal him of his sickness and raise him up from the sickbed. "Make all his bed" (v. 3 KJV) simply means "heal him and raise him up." This would be the gracious and merciful act of the Lord, undeserved by David but lovingly granted by Jehovah. "If I regard wickedness in my heart, the Lord will not hear" (66:18 NASB), so it's important that we confess our sins to the Lord. If we haven't been merciful to others, how can our heart be right to ask Him for mercy?

Treachery: How Do Others Treat Us (vv. 5–9)?

It wasn't enough that David was sick in bed, but he also had to deal with treachery among his own family and friends, including men like Ahithophel, his official counselor, who sided with Absalom. Ahithophel was Bathsheba's grandfather (2 Sam. 11:3 and 23:34) and hated David for what he did to her and to her husband Uriah. These false friends visited the king and lied to him ("We hope you'll get well soon"), but they really wanted David to die and even plotted against him. But if Absalom became king, that would be the end of the Davidic dynasty, for Absalom had no son (2 Sam. 18:18). God promised David that his descendants would sit on the throne of Israel forever (2 Sam. 7:11–16), a promise ultimately fulfilled in Jesus Christ (Luke 1:31–33). David was gifted at reading people (2 Sam. 14:17–20) and knew the truth.

Jesus used verse 9 when referring to the traitor Judas (John 13:18–19; and see 55:12–14; 69:25; 109:8; Matt. 26:63; Mark 14:18; Luke 22:21; Acts 1:16–20). Note that our Lord didn't quote the phrase "whom I trusted" from verse 9, for He knew that Judas had no saving faith (John 6:70–71). This psalm opens with a statement about the poor, and Judas tried to identify himself with the poor (John 12:4–6; 13:26–30). David's enemies wanted the king's name to perish, but it was Judas who destroyed a good name—"Judah," which means "praise." We call our sons David but we would never call a son Judas. (See 2 Sam. 16:15–17:23 for

Ahithophel's part in the rebellion.) The phrase "lifted up his heel" pictures a deceptive and underhanded attack, but see Joshua 10:4 and Romans 16:20.

Mercy: How Does God Treat Us (vv. 10–12)?

God in His mercy doesn't give us what we do deserve, and God in His grace gives us what we don't deserve, and He does this because of Jesus Christ His Son who died for us on the cross. David prayed for mercy, because he knew he had sinned (v. 4). He also affirmed his integrity (v. 12), for he had walked before the Lord in humility and submission (7:8; 18:19–25; 25:21; 78:72). When confronted with his sins, he confessed them and sought the face of the Lord (2 Sam. 12:13ff). David wanted mercy for himself but not for his enemies, except for his son Absalom (2 Sam. 18:5). Why? Because his enemies (especially Absalom) had committed treason against the Lord's chosen and anointed king. This was not a personal vendetta on David's part, but a concern for the future of the nation of Israel and the dynasty of David. As ruler of the land, David wielded the sword of justice (Rom. 13:1–4), and nations today punish treason with death.

More than anything else, David wanted to please God (v. 11; 18:19; 22:8; 35:27; 2 Sam. 15:26). He had confidence that the Lord would heal him, restore him to the throne, and deal with those who opposed him. Even more, he was certain that one day he would be in the presence of the Lord and serve in His holy courts in heaven forever (v. 12; 16:11; 17:15; 21:6; 101:7; 2 Sam. 7:16).

Glory: How Do We Treat God (v. 13)?

This verse was probably added later by an editor to mark the end of book one of the Psalms. Each of the first four books ends with a similar doxology (72:18–20; 89:52; 106:48), and Book Five ends with a praise psalm (150). But the verse reminds us that the main thing in our lives must be the eternal praise and glory of the Lord. "Hallowed be thy name" is the first request in the Disciple's Prayer (Matt. 6:9), and it governs all the other requests. God answers prayer, not to make His people more comfortable, but to bring glory to His name. The Lord still had more work for David to do, particularly the preparation for the building of the temple, and His glory would one day move into that holy sanctuary (1 Kings 8:1-11).

Can we honestly say "Amen and amen!" to the prayer in verse 13?

THREE

PSALMS 42 – 72

Book II

Psalms 42 and 43

The repeated refrain (42:5, 11; 43:5) and the general theme of these two psalms would indicate that the two psalms were no doubt originally one, but nobody seems to know why they were separated. Korah was a grandson of Kohath and was killed for rebelling against the Lord (Num. 16). However, his sons escaped judgment (Num. 16:11) and became worship leaders in the sanctuary (1 Chron. 9:19ff; 26:1–19). They are also named in the titles to 44–49, 84 and 87–88, and see the introduction to Psalm 39. Some associate these psalms with Absalom's rebellion, but the geography in verse 6 seems to put the stetting too far north for that, since David camped over the Jordan at Mahanaim. The author was evidently a Levite exiled among Gentiles (43:1) who oppressed him and questioned his faith (42:3, 10; 43:2). He was a worship leader who had led groups of pilgrims to Jerusalem for the assigned festivals (84:7; Ex. 23:14–17; 34:18–26; Deut. 16:1–17). It was time for such a journey but he wasn't able to go, and this grieved his heart because he felt that the Lord had forgotten him (42:9; 43:2). In the psalm, he uses *El* or *Elohim* twenty times and *Jehovah* only once

(42:8). The psalms are intensely personal, containing over fifty personal pronouns; and the writer fluctuated between faith and despair as he wrestled with the Lord. He questions the Lord eleven times as he wonders why God doesn't do something for him. We see him passing through three stages before he comes to victory and peace.

Longing for God (42:1–5)

During a drought, the writer saw a female deer (hind) panting and struggling to reach water to quench her thirst (Joel 1:20), and this reminded him that he thirsted for the Lord and wanted to go on pilgrimage to Jerusalem. The living God was the God of his life (v. 8; see 84:2), and he could not live without Him. Note that the essentials for physical life are mentioned here: air (panting), water (v. 2), and food (v. 3), but without worship (v. 4), life to him was meaningless. Hunger and thirst are familiar images of the quest for fellowship with God and the satisfaction it brings (36:8–9; 63:1; Matt. 5:6; John 4:10–14; 7:37–39; Rev. 21:6; 22:17). Day and night (vv. 3, 8) he felt the pain caused by separation from God's sanctuary and by the constant ridicule of the people around him. He "fed" on his grief (not a wise thing to do) as his tears became his bread. His weeping was as regular as his eating had been.

"Where is your God?" (vv. 3, 10) was a standard question the Gentile idolaters asked the Jews (79:10; 115:2; Joel 2:17; Mic. 7:10; see Matt. 27:43). However, the question indicates that the writer must have been a devout believer who wasn't ashamed of his faith; otherwise, his tormentors wouldn't have questioned him. He remembered better days when he used to lead processions of pilgrims to Jerusalem to celebrate the feasts. Memory can be either a blessed medicine for the troubled heart or it can open new wounds and keep the pain fresh. The writer poured out his soul in prayer (v. 4; 62:8; 104 title), pleading for the Lord to set him free and take him back to Jerusalem. But then he confronted himself (v. 5) and admonished himself not to be downcast but to hope in the Lord and wait on Him. The repetition of this admonition (v. 11; 43:5) suggests that the writer was having his "ups and downs" as he struggled with his circumstances and himself. He would find his consolation and peace only in the Lord, and not in nature (vv. 1, 6–7), memories (v. 4), or nursing grief (v. 3). His hopes had been shattered, his prayers were unanswered, his enemies were vocal, and his feelings were more than he could handle, *but God was still on the throne*. God's presence was with him and he would yet have the joy of worshiping God in Jerusalem. That was God's promise in His covenant (Deut. 30).

Remembering God (42:6–11)

The emotional and spiritual landscape changes from drought to a storm, with the writer feeling like he was drowning in sorrow and pain (vv. 6–7). The Jordan River has its source in the Hermon range, and the rains and melting snow would turn the rivulets into cascades of water and dangerous cataracts, a picture of intense suffering (69:1–2; 88:7; Jonah 2:4). "Mizar" means "littleness," and certainly the writer felt very small in the midst of that storm. But he made a wise decision when he decided to remember God and not "the good old days" (v. 6). The cascades, cataracts, and waves were *His* and the psalmist had nothing to fear. This reminds us of the night Jesus walked on the water and frightened His disciples, yet He was in full command of the situation (Matt. 14:22–33). God was in command (v. 8; see 33:9; 44:4; 71:3; 91:11), a new day would dawn, and the situation would look different. Like David's storm experience recorded in Psalm 29, see God on His throne and anticipate the glory and peace after the storm. Believers today remember that the waves of God's wrath went over Jesus on the cross when He experienced His Calvary "baptism" (Matt. 20:22; Luke 12:50). Meanwhile, God can give us "songs in the night" as we wait for the dawning of a new day (77:4–6; Job 35:10; Matt. 26:30; Acts 16:25).

In verse 8, the writer used *Jehovah* instead of *Elohim*, and this was a turning point in his difficult experience. Jehovah is the God of the covenant, the faithful God who cares for His people. He is the God who showers His people with lovingkindness, gives them promises they can claim when they pray, and hears them when they praise and worship. The writer didn't have to go to Jerusalem to worship; he could worship God right where he was! The hand of God was with him in the daytime and the song of the Lord in the long hours of the night. Everything might be changing, but the Lord was still his Rock—stable, strong, and unchanging. (See 18:2, 31, 46; Ex. 33:22; Deut. 32:4; 1 Sam. 2:2.)

Trusting God (43:1–5)

The landscape changes a third time as the dawn announces the morning and reminds the psalmist of God's light and truth (v. 3). The Lord had led Israel from Egypt to the Promised Land by a pillar of cloud by day and a pillar of fire by night, and so His light and truth (faithfulness) would bring him back to Jerusalem. The innocent exile would be vindicated before his accusers and be rescued from an ungodly nation. His strength was in the Lord alone, the Rock of his salvation (42:9), and soon his despair would be replaced by joy. As they trust in the Lord, God's people must remember that His goodness and mercy follow them (23:6), and His light and truth lead them (43:3; see 27:1; 26:3; 30:9; 40:10). God's "holy hill" is Mt. Zion, where God's sanctuary was located, the dwelling place of God.

But the writer wasn't exulting simply in freedom from his enemies and a return to his native home, but in the privilege of visiting God's altar, offering his sacrifices, and praising the Lord. He has made great progress since he watched the hind seeking for water. The "living God" (42:2) became "the God of my life" (42:8), and now He is "God my exceeding joy … God, my God (43:8 NASB). His focus is no longer on himself, his disappointments, or his circumstances, but on the Lord his God, and that makes all the difference. The refrain in 43:5 must not be read with the same dejected voice as 42:5 and 11, for faith in Jehovah has changed everything. The *New American Standard Bible* and the *New King James Version* translate verse 5, "Hope in God, for I shall yet praise Him, the help of my countenance, and my

God." The word "help" can be translated "health." When by faith we see the face of God smiling upon us (Num. 6:22–27), our own countenance brightens up and becomes spiritually healthy. We know God is for us, that God will set us free and guide us to His holy city, where we shall worship Him and sing His praises. "Weeping may endure for a night, but joy comes in the morning" (30:5 NKJV).

Psalm 44

The Jewish people sang praises to God after their great victories (Ex. 15; Judg, 5), but this psalm was sung after a humiliating defeat (vv. 9–14, 22). The parallels between Psalms 44 and 60 suggest that Edom and the Arameans were the enemies involved (44:3/60:5; 44:5/60:12; 44:9, 23/60:1, 10). (See 2 Sam. 8 and 10; 1 Chron. 18.) Although Israel finally won great victories over their enemies, there must have been some defeats along the way that greatly disturbed the people. After all, Jehovah was their King (v. 4) and had enabled Israel to conquer the land; so why would He desert His people as they sought to protect their inheritance? Perhaps this psalm was used at a national "day of prayer" with a worship leader speaking the "I/my" verses and the people the "we/our" verses. The four stanzas that make up this psalm reveal four different attitudes on the part of the people.

Boasting in God: "You Have Helped Us" (vv. 1–8)

Reviewing Israel's history since the exodus from Egypt, the writer glorified God for all He did to defeat the Canaanite nations and enable Israel to claim their inheritance (v. 8). The Jewish parents were faithful to obey God and tell their children and grandchildren what the Lord had done (see 78:3; Ex. 12:26–27; 13:8, 14; Deut. 6:1ff; 32:7; Josh. 4:6, 21). God had rooted out the godless nations, planted Israel in the land, and enabled the nation to take root and grow (80:8–11; Ex. 15:17; Isa. 5). All of this was done, not because Israel deserved it, but because of God's love and grace (Deut. 4:34–37; 7:7–9, 19; 8:17; 9:4–6; 26:8–9). God's power gave the victory and His countenance smiled upon His people (4:6; 31:16; 80:3, 7, 19). The psalmist affirmed that Jehovah was still their King (v. 4; 10:16; 29:10; 47:6; 74:12) and could easily command (decree) victories for His people. The nation wanted no glory for itself; they wanted the Lord to receive all the glory.

Forsaken by God: "You Are Not Helping Us" (vv. 9–16)

But the people were perplexed. If God gave them the land in His grace, and enabled them to defeat their enemies, why was He now forsaking them and allowing the idolatrous nations to win the victories? For many years, the Lord had been the "invisible warrior" who went before the Jewish armies and led them to victory (Josh. 5:13–15; 6:6; Num. 10:35; 2 Sam. 11:11), but now He seemed to have forsaken His people and abandoned His covenant. Israel was God's precious flock (74:1; 77:20; 80:1; 100:3; Num. 27:17; Ezek. 34), but He was permitting them to be slaughtered by the enemy and treated as worthless (Judg. 2:14; 3:8; 4:2, 9). Those prisoners of war that weren't slain were sold as slaves and scattered among the neighboring pagan nations. These nations rejoiced that Israel had been humiliated by defeat, and they taunted and ridiculed the Jews. It was a dark day for the people of God, and they could not understand what the Lord was accomplishing. (See 42:10; 74:10, 18, 22; 79:4, 12.) Dishonor and disgrace brought the people to the place of submission and intercession.

Faithful to God: "You Should Help Us" (vv. 17–22)

Whenever there was trouble in Israel, the first explanation was usually, "Somebody has sinned." Certainly this was true when Israel was defeated at Ai (Josh. 7), when there was a three-year famine in David's time (2 Sam. 21), and when David numbered the people (2 Sam. 24). But as far as the psalmist knew, there was no sin to be confessed because the people were faithful to the Lord. God could search their minds and hearts and not find any breach of the covenant. They were faithful to God, they had not turned to the idols for help, and now they were giving their lives to protect the land that He had so graciously given them.

Paul quoted verse 11 in Romans 8:36 as part of his magnificent argument that nothing could separate God's people from His love, *not even defeat after a record of victories!* The principle is the same for both God's old covenant people and His new covenant people: those who give their lives in His cause are conquerors, not victims, and God can be glorified even in seeming defeat. When the five young men gave their lives in Ecuador to help reach the Auca Indians, many people asked, "Why this waste?" But what looked like terrible defeat turned out to be glorious victory as many young people around the world felt the call of God and surrendered to serve Him. Israel's defeat didn't mean that God loved them less; it meant that He was permitting this to happen so that He could carry out a purpose known only to Him. Like the martyrdom of Stephen (Acts 6:9–8:3), Israel's defeat gave their enemies further opportunity to come to know the Lord. Saul of Tarsus was greatly moved by Stephen's death (Acts 22:17–21), and this undoubtedly helped to prepare him for his meeting with Christ on the Damascus Road. No matter how their lives may end, God's servants never die like beasts, for "Precious in the sight of the Lord is the death of His saints" (116:15 NKJV).

Trusting in God: "You Will Help Us" (vv. 23–26)

In verse 23, the writer used the name "Adonai" (Lord) when speaking to God. This is the name that declares that He is Owner and Master of all, including the nations of the world. It is sometimes translated "Sovereign LORD" (Adonai Jehovah; 2 Sam. 7:18–20 NIV). He is "Lord [Adonai] of all the earth" (97:5), and the earth should tremble "at the presence of the Lord [Adonai]" (114:7). The psalmist came to the place where he knew he could trust God to handle the defeats of life and ultimately turn them into victories. Yes, it seemed like God was asleep, and the nation had to awaken Him (7:6; 78:65), but "He who keeps Israel shall neither slumber nor sleep" (121:4 NKJV). The people of Israel had come to the place that Job reached when he said, "Though he slay me, yet will I trust him" (Job 13:15).

We can't always explain the so-called "tragedies" of life, especially those that happen to God's people, but Romans 8:28 is still in the Bible. The prophet Isaiah gives us wise counsel in 50:10—"Who is among you that fears the Lord and obeys the voice of His servant, that walks in darkness and has no light? Let him trust in the name of the Lord and rely on his God" (NASB). We may look like sheep for the slaughter, but in God's sight we are "more than conquerors through him that loved us" (Rom. 8:37).

Psalm 45

"A song of loves" identifies this as a marriage song, and "Shoshannim" (lilies) identifies the tune to which it was to be sung (see 60, 69, 80). The wedding was obviously that of a king (vv. 1, 11, 14; and note the mention of throne, scepter and majesty), and some have identified him with Solomon, who married an Egyptian princess (1 Kings 3:1; 9:24). Of all David's sons, only Solomon was anointed king (v. 7). Solomon was noted for his wealth in gold (vv. 9, 13; 1 Kings 9:28), and he had a close association with the great city of Tyre (v. 12; 1 Kings 9:10–14). But it's clear that one "greater than Solomon" (Matt. 12:42) is present in this beautiful psalm, and that one is Jesus Christ, the King of kings. If this were merely a secular love song, why would it be given to the chief musician to be used in the worship of the Lord at His sanctuary? That would be blasphemy. Solomon was not a warrior (vv. 3–5), and certainly an inspired writer would not address Solomon as "God" (v. 6). Hebrews 1:8–9 marks it as a Messianic psalm, so whatever may have been the historical use of this psalm, the ultimate message is about Jesus Christ and His bride, the church (Eph. 5:23ff; Rev. 19:6–21; 22:17). The writer presents four pictures of our Lord and in so doing also described His bride.

The Gracious Son of Man (vv. 1–2)

This is a song for the heart from the heart of an inspired and excited writer. His heart was "bubbling over" with his theme, for it is the greatest theme in the universe: the glories of the Son of

God. Jesus endured the cross "for the joy that was set before him" (Heb. 12:2), which was the joy of presenting His bride to the Father in glory (Judg. 24; John 17:24). It is the work of the Holy Spirit to glorify Jesus Christ in this world (John 16:14), and He inspired this writer to do just that. The King described in this psalm is both God (v. 6) and man (v. 2), and that can only be Jesus.

The writer began with the beauty of the King (v. 2), "fairer than the children of men," literally, "beautified with beauty." King Saul was known as a handsome man (1 Sam. 9:2; 10:23) and so was David (1 Sam. 16:12), but none surpasses Jesus. When He ministered on earth, our Lord had no special physical beauty (Isa. 53:2), and when His persecutors were through with Him, He didn't even look human (Isa. 52:14). But today, Jesus Christ is the center of heaven's glory and the focus of heaven's worship (Rev. 4—5). We love Jesus even though we have never seen Him, but one day we shall behold the King in His beauty (Isa. 33:17), and we shall be like Him (1 John 3:1–3). The writer also marveled at His gracious speech, but so did the people who heard Him preach and teach on earth (Luke 4:18, 22, 32; John 7:46; see Mark 1:22; 6:2; 11:18). Visitors from distant lands came to hear Solomon's wisdom (1 Kings 4:29–34), but the Father has hidden all the treasures of divine wisdom in Jesus Christ (Col. 2:3). Solomon died, and except for what he wrote in Scripture, his wisdom died with him, but Jesus is blessed forever (v. 2), has a throne forever (v. 6), and His name will be praised forever (v. 17). In the Bible, "forever" can mean "as long as you live" (Ex. 21:6), but here it means "for eternity." He is "King forever" (29:10).

The Victorious Warrior (vv. 3–5)

We live in a day when the militant side of the Christian faith is criticized and even eliminated, an attitude that is both unbiblical and dangerous. Since Genesis 3:15, God has been at war with Satan and sin, for the Lamb of God is also "the Lion of the tribe of Judah" (Rev. 5:5). Jesus suffered and died on the cross, not only to save sinners but also to defeat Satan (Col. 2:13–15), and one day He will return as a warrior and defeat His enemies and establish His righteous kingdom (Rev. 19:11ff). Indeed, His right hand will accomplish "awesome things." The church of Jesus Christ doesn't use human weapons to accomplish His will (John 18:10–11, 36–37) but instead uses the sword of the Spirit, the Word of God (Heb. 4:12; Eph. 6:17; see Rev. 1:16 and 19:15). Jesus is fighting on behalf of "truth and meekness and righteousness" (v. 4 NASB), and it's difficult to believe that anyone would want to oppose that kind of war. As God's people share His love, serve others, and declare the Word, they are "waging peace" and seeking to reconcile men and women with God (2 Cor. 5:14–21). The Father has promised to give His Son the nations of the earth for His inheritance (2:8–9), and He will keep that promise.

The Righteous King (vv. 6–7a)

Those who deny the deity of Christ refuse to accept the translation "Thy throne, O God," because they want to make the psalm only Jewish history and not Messianic prophecy. However, "Thy throne, O God" is the plain sense of the text and is supported by Hebrews 1:8–9 and Luke 1:30–33. "He shall reign forever and ever" (Rev. 11:15). While it is true that Scripture uses *elohim* to refer to human rulers (82:6–7; Ex. 21:6; John 10:35), that is not the meaning here. The writer clearly affirmed the eternal reign of the eternal Son of God. His reign would also be righteous and all evil would be removed. Jesus Christ is reigning now in heaven, seated at the right hand of the Father (110:1–2; Matt. 26:64; Acts 2:33, 5:31, 7:55–56; Rom. 8:34; Eph. 1:20; Col. 3:1; Heb. 1:3). He is the King-Priest "after the order of Melchizedek" (Heb. 7–9). One day, His people will reign with Him and share His glory (Rev. 5:10; 20:6).

The Glorious Bridegroom (vv. 7b–17)

These verses describe the royal wedding, beginning with *the preparation of the Bridegroom* (*vv. 7b–9*). The anointing in verse 7b is not His anointing as King but as the honored guest at the wedding feast. It is the "oil of gladness" representing the eternal joy that belongs to the happy bride and Bridegroom (Isa. 61:3). The soldiers gambled for our Lord's garments when He hung on the cross (John 19:23–24), but at the wedding feast, His garments will be fragrant and glorious. To have ivory inlay on the walls of your house was the height of prosperity (Amos 3:15; 1 Kings 22:39), but the King's palace is made of ivory. As the King prepares to meet the bride, the musicians play beautiful music. In ancient times, a Jewish bridegroom went to the bride's house to claim her and then took her to his own home, and Jesus will do that when He returns to claim His church (1 Thess. 4:13–18). The "king's daughters" (v. 9) are princesses who accompany the bride; we would call them bridesmaids. In verse 14 they are called "virgin companions" (NIV), so they must not be confused with harem women, who certainly would not be in a wedding procession.

Next comes *the preparation of the bride (vv. 10–13)*. Today, the church of Jesus Christ is spotted by the world and looking old and wrinkled because of inner decay, but one day it shall be a glorious bride, spotless, blameless, and without spot or wrinkle (Eph. 5:27). Though criticized today, the church in that day will be beautiful and bring great glory to Christ (Eph. 1:6–12, 18). As the queen waits within her palace chamber (v. 13), she is dressed in the finest garments, embroidered with the finest gold (1 Kings 9:28), and she is given counsel as she enters this new relationship. She must forget the past, submit to her Husband the King, and seek only to please Him. What a word for the church in the world today—"forgetting those things which are behind" (Phil. 3:13). Our Lord loves us and sees beauty in His bride, and we must acknowledge that He is Lord and worship Him, showing respect and homage to Him (1 Peter 3:6; Gen. 18:12). It would be idolatry to worship a human king, but this is the King of Glory (24:7–10). "The daughter of Tyre" means "the people of Tyre," just as "the daughter of Zion" means "the inhabitants of Jerusalem" (Matt. 21:5; Isa. 4:4). Tyre was a powerful and wealthy city in David's day, and its king was the first foreign ruler to recognize the kingship of David (2 Sam. 5:11). There will come a time when the kings of the earth will bring their wealth and glory into the city of the great King (Rev. 21:24–26).

In the next stage of the wedding, *the bride is brought to the King* (*vv. 14–15*), and her companions are with her. It is a time of beauty and joy as the wedding party enters the banquet hall in the palace and shares in the wedding feast. (See Rev. 19:1–10.) As the King and His queen leave, the writer pronounces *a benediction* (vv. 16–17), speaking especially to the King. (The pronouns are masculine.) We may paraphrase it: "No matter how great your ancestors were, your descendants will be even greater. They will be princes in all the earth, not just government officers in the kingdom. You will reign forever and ever and your name will never be forgotten. The people will praise you forever." Words like these spoken at an ancient eastern wedding would be considered polite exaggeration, but when applied to Jesus Christ, they aren't strong enough! He is bringing many children to glory (Heb. 2:10, 13), and His family will share His glory and His reign.

Hallelujah, what a Savior!

Psalm 46

Most people recognize this psalm as the basis for Martin Luther's hymn "A Mighty Fortress Is Our God." The historical background is probably God's deliverance of Jerusalem from the Assyrians in the time of King Hezekiah (2 Kings 18–19; 2 Chron. 32; Isa. 36–37). It would be helpful for you to read these accounts before examining the psalm. King Hezekiah was a poet and may have written not only this psalm but also 47 and 48, which probably came out of the same historical context and celebrate God's victory over the enemy. The personal pronouns in 46 are plural (our, we, us), so this is a song for communal encouragement and worship. "Alamoth" means "young women" and is a musical direction we can't define. No female choir was used in the sanctuary liturgy, although 68:25 indicates that the women did participate (see Ex. 15:20–21). The emphasis in this psalm is on the presence of the Lord with His people (vv. 1, 5,

7, 11) and the difference it makes when we trust Him in the changes and difficulties of life. The psalm focuses on the Lord and what He is to His trusting people.

God Is Our Tower of Strength (vv. 1–3)

The word translated "refuge" in verse 1 means "a shelter, a rock of refuge," while the word in verses 7 and 11 means "a stronghold, a high tower, a fortress." Both words declare that God is a dependable refuge for His people when everything around them seems to be falling apart. See 61:3; 62:7–8; 142:5. But He doesn't protect us in order to pamper us. He shelters us so He can strengthen us to go back to life with its duties and dangers (29:11; 68:35; Isa. 40:31). Both concepts are found in 71:7. In times of crisis, the Jewish leaders were too prone to turn to Egypt for help (Isa. 30:1–2) when they should have turned to the Lord and trusted Him. He is an "ever-present help," but He cannot work for us unless we trust Him (Matt. 13:58).

The word "trouble" describes people in tight places, in a corner and unable to get out; and when that occurs, the admonition is, "Don't be afraid!" When the Assyrian officials threatened Jerusalem, Isaiah told the king, "Do not be afraid because of the words that you have heard" (2 Kings 19:7 NASB). The earth may change, the mountains may be hurled violently into the sea, there may come earthquakes and tidal waves, but all things are in the control of our sovereign Lord. The "waters" in verse 3 may also symbolize the unrest of the nations, mentioned in verse 6 (Dan. 7:2–3; Luke 21:25; Rev. 13:1; 17:15). Circumstances may change, but God's covenant with His people will never change (Isa. 54:10). He is our high tower and our refuge in the uncertainties of life.

God Is Our River of Joy (vv. 4–7)

The scene shifts into the city of Jerusalem where the people are confined because of the Assyrian army camped around them. Water was a precious commodity in Palestine and especially in Jerusalem, one of the few ancient cities not built on a river. Wisely, Hezekiah had built an underground water system that connected the Spring of Gihon in Kidron with the Pool of

Siloam within the city, so water was available (2 Kings 20:20; 2 Chron. 32:30). But the psalmist knew that God was their river and provided them with the water of life (36:8; 65:9; 87:7; and see John 7:37–39). In the days of King Ahaz, Isaiah compared an Assyrian invasion to an overflowing river, but he reminded the Jews that their God was like a quiet river (Shiloah) and would bring them peace (Isa. 8:1–10). God's people have always depended on the hidden spiritual resources that come from God alone. Whenever Israel turned to a pagan nation for help, they ended up in worse trouble.

Jerusalem was indeed the holy city, set apart by God, and His sanctuary was there, but these things were no guarantee of victory (Jer. 7:1–8). The king and the people needed to turn to the Lord in confession and faith, and He would hear and save them, and this is what they did. God did help Jerusalem when the morning dawned (v. 5 "right early" KJV), for the angel of the Lord killed 185,000 Assyrian soldiers and sent Sennacherib home (Isa. 37:36).

Indeed, Jehovah is God Most High! (v. 4). All He had to do was speak the word (v. 6), and the enemy was defeated. He is the "Lord of Hosts—the Lord of the armies of heaven and earth." This name for God is found first in Scripture when Hannah asked God to give her a son (1 Sam. 1:11). The Commander of the armies of the Lord is always with us (Josh. 5:13–15), for He is "Immanuel, God with us" (Matt. 1:23; Isa. 7:14; 8:8). No matter what the circumstances, we may drink at the river of His joy and blessing and find the peace and strength we need.

God Is Our God! He Will Be Glorified! (vv. 8–11)

The third scene is on the fields surrounding Jerusalem where the Assyrian soldiers lay dead, their weapons and equipment scattered and broken. There had been no battle, but the angel of the Lord left this evidence behind to encourage the faith of the people. "Come and see the amazing things (desolations) the Lord has made!" The Lord defeated and disarmed His enemies and destroyed their weapons, and they could attack no more.

"Be still" literally means "Take your hands off! Relax!" We like to be "hands-on" people and manage our own lives, but God is God, and we are but His servants. *Because Hezekiah and his leaders allowed God to be God, He delivered them from their enemies.* That was the way King Hezekiah had prayed: "Now therefore, O Lord our God, I pray, save us from his hand, that all the kingdoms of the earth may know You are the Lord God, You alone" (2 Kings 19:19 NKJV). The Lord calls Himself "the God of Jacob," and we remember how often Jacob got into trouble because he got his hands on circumstances and tried to play God. There is a time to obey God and act, but until then, we had better take our hands off and allow Him to work in His own time and His own way. If we seize His promises by faith with both hands, we won't be able to meddle!

God allows us to get into "tight places" so our faith will grow and He will be exalted. (See 22:27; 64:9; 86:9; 102:15.) The theme of the next psalm is the exaltation of God in all the earth (47:9), and it's likely Hezekiah wrote it. People boast of the great things they have done and never give God credit for anything, not even the strength and breath He gives them freely. But that will change. "The lofty looks of man shall be humbled, the haughtiness of men shall be bowed down, and the Lord alone shall be exalted in that day" (Isa. 2:11 NKJV).

Psalm 47

The promise of 46:10 is fulfilled in 47, "I will be exalted among the nations, I will be exalted in the earth" (NASB). Five times the people are commanded to "sing praises" to the Lord who "reigns over the nations" (v. 8 NASB). If this psalm was written to celebrate the defeat of Sennacherib (see 46), then it describes the people of Israel proclaiming to the surrounding Gentile nations the glorious victory of their God, a victory won without their having to fight a battle! The psalm is used in the synagogues on Rosh Hashana, the Jewish New Year's Day, and in the church, it is used on Ascension Day (see v. 5, 68:18 and Eph. 4:8–10). This also makes it a Messianic psalm, with an emphasis on the coming kingdom. As the people of Israel praise their God to the Gentiles around them, they make three affirmations about Him.

Our God Is an Awesome King (vv. 1–4)

We have moved from "Be still" (46:10) to shouting, clapping, and the blowing of trumpets. Jewish worship was enthusiastic, but they also knew how to be quiet before the Lord and wait upon Him (Lam. 2:10; Hab. 2:4; Zeph. 1:7; Zech. 2:13). Since the theme of the psalm is the kingship of the Lord, they worshiped Him the way they welcomed a new king (1 Sam. 10:24; 2 Kings 11:12–13, 20). "The shout of a king is among them" (Num. 23:21). The early church patterned its worship after the synagogue and emphasized prayer, the reading and expounding of Scripture, and the singing of psalms, hymns, and spiritual songs. When the Jewish people clapped their hands and shouted, it was to the Lord in response to His marvelous works. They did not do it to praise the people who participated in the worship service.

To know God is to know One who is awesome in all that He is, says, and does (65:8; 76:7, 12). Jerusalem's deliverance from Sennacherib proved once more that the God of Israel was greater than all gods and deserved all the praise His people could bring to Him. He gave them victory over the nations in Canaan and gave them the land for their inheritance (135:4; Ex. 15:17; 19:5; Deut. 4:21, 37–38; 32:8). Since God chose the Jews in His love and gave them their land in His grace, what right did the Assyrians have to try to take it from them? (See 2 Chron. 20:10–12.) The land of Israel is very special to the Lord and He watches over it (Deut. 8:7–20; 11:10–12).

Our God Is a Triumphant King (v. 5)

God fills heaven and earth, but when He acts on earth on behalf of His people, the Scriptures sometimes describe Him as "coming down." He came down to visit the tower of Babel and judged the people building it (Gen. 11:5), and He also came down to investigate the wicked city of Sodom and destroyed it (Gen. 18:21). The night 185,000 Assyrian soldiers were slain by the angel, God came down and brought judgment (Isa. 37:28–29,

36) and then "went up" in great glory to His holy throne (v. 8). David gave a similar description of victory in 68:18, a verse Paul quoted in Ephesians 4:8–10, applying it to the ascension of Jesus Christ. From the human viewpoint, the crucifixion of Jesus Christ was a great defeat and tragedy, but not from God's viewpoint. In His sacrifice on the cross, Jesus won the victory over the world and the devil (John 12:31–32; Col. 2:15) and satisfied the claims of God's holy law so that sinners could believe and be saved. What a victory! He then ascended to heaven, far above every enemy (Eph. 1:19–22), where He sits at the right hand of the Majesty on high (Heb. 1:3).

Our God Is King of Kings (vv. 6–9)

A remarkable thing occurs: the rulers and peoples of the Gentile nations join Israel in praising the Lord Jehovah! He is not simply the God and King of Israel, but He is the "king of all the earth." It was God's plan when He called Abraham that Israel would be a blessing to all the earth (Gen. 12:1–3; John 12:32; Gal. 3:7–9), for "salvation is of the Jews" (John 4:22). Throughout their history, Israel has been persecuted by many nations of the world, yet it is Israel that has blessed the world. Israel brought us the knowledge of the one true and living God, they gave us the Scriptures, and they gave us Jesus Christ, the Savior of the world. Today, Jews and Gentiles in the church are praising God together (Eph. 2:11ff), and one day in the glorious kingdom, Jews and Gentiles will glorify and praise Him (67:1–7; 72:8–11; Rom. 15:8–13).

The psalmist saw God's defeat of the Assyrians as a sign of His defeat of all the nations and the establishment of His glorious kingdom. The prophets announced that the Gentiles would turn to the Lord and share the kingdom with Israel (Isa. 2:1–5; 11:1–10; Mic. 4:1–5), and the psalmist looked down the ages and saw this fulfilled. The Gentile leaders, representing their people, will come and give their allegiance and their praise to Jesus Christ, "[a]nd the Lord shall be king over all the earth" (Zech. 14:9). Paul alludes to verse 7 in 1 Cor. 14:15 when he admonishes us to "sing with the understanding." The word "shields" can refer to kings since they are the protectors of the people (89:18). The kings of the earth belong to the Lord because He is the King of Kings (Rev. 19:16). The image of God sitting upon His holy throne is used often in the book of Revelation (4:2, 9–10; 5:1, 7, 13; 6:16; 7:10, 15; 19:4; 21:5).

For God's people, everyday is Ascension Day as we praise and worship the exalted and ascended Lord.

Psalm 48

This is the third of the psalms celebrating Jehovah's victory in delivering Jerusalem from the Assyrians (see 46 and 47). The emphasis is on the Lord and Mount Zion. Other psalms about Zion are 76, 84, 87, 122, and 132. Believers today are citizens of the Zion that is above (Gal. 4:21–31; Heb. 12:18–24; Phil. 3:20) and rejoice that the Lord cares for us even as He cared for His ancient people Israel. The various speakers in this psalm deal with four important topics.

God and Their City (vv. 1–3)

In this first section, the people of Jerusalem speak about their city with pride and gratitude. David took Mount Zion from the Jebusites (2 Sam. 5:6–9; 2 Chron. 11:4–7) and made Jerusalem the capital of his kingdom. Ideally situated 2500 feet above sea level, the city was almost impregnable. Not far away was the juncture of the north-south and east-west trade routes, important for the economy and for communications. David brought the ark of the covenant to Jerusalem, and this made Zion a "holy mountain," for the Lord dwelt there (2:6; 3:4; 15:11 43:3; 99:9). Jerusalem thus became "the city of God" (vv. 1, 8) and the "city of the Great King" (v. 2; 47:2; see Matt. 5:35). The greatness belongs to the Lord and not to the city (47:9), for in His grace, the Lord chose Zion (78:68; 132:13). The Jews saw Jerusalem as a beautiful city (50:2), a safe fortress, and "the joy of all the earth" (but see Lam. 2:15). Spiritually speaking, the city has brought joy to all the earth because outside its walls Jesus died for the sins of the world, and from Jerusalem first sounded out the Gospel of Jesus Christ. One day in the future, Jerusalem will be the center of Christ's glorious kingdom (Isa. 2:2ff and 60:1ff). Zaphron (NIV) refers to the north, a mountain in northern Syria where the god Baal was supposed to dwell. (See Ex. 14:1 and 9 and Num. 33:7.) The safety of Jerusalem was not in her location or her walls (vv. 14–15) but in her God; for He was their fortress (v. 3; see 46:1, 7). It was in the defeat of Sennacherib's army that God "made himself known as a stronghold" (v. 3 NASB).

God and Their Enemies (vv. 4–7)

The citizens had been speaking *about* the Lord, but now they speak *to* the Lord about what He did to the Assyrians. Sennacherib and his huge army, plus the vassal kings of his empire (v. 4; Isa. 10:8), surrounded Jerusalem and hoped to capture it, but godly King Hezekiah, with the help of Isaiah the prophet (Isa. 14:24–27), turned to the Lord for help, and He came to their rescue (Isa. 36–37). The Lord fought for Israel just as He had fought against the Egyptians (Ex. 14:25). God sent His angel to the Assyrian camp and he killed 185,000 men. The judgment came suddenly, like the pain of a woman in labor, and the destruction was like that of a storm shattering a fleet of ships (Ezek. 27:26). Note the shattered weapons in 46:8–9. The overconfident Assyrians and their allies found themselves defeated and disgraced and had to go home.

God and Their Worship (vv. 8–11)

The speakers in this section appear to be a group of pilgrims going to Jerusalem after the great victory. They had heard about Assyria's defeat, but now they could see with their own eyes the great things that the Lord had done for His people. (It's likely that Ps. 126 also fits into this event.) The pilgrims immediately went to the temple to worship the Lord, to meditate on His faithfulness, and joyfully praise Him. Worship is the proper human response to divine mercies. Note how the fame of the Lord spread from the city itself (v. 11a) to the towns of Judah that Sennacherib had plundered (v. 11b; Isa. 36:1) and then to the ends of the earth (v. 10). So may it be with the message of the Gospel! (Acts 1:8). When the Lord Jesus Christ returns to defeat His enemies and establish His kingdom, His glory and dominion will be from sea to sea (Zech. 9:9–10), and the city of Jerusalem will be named "The Lord our Righteousness" (Jer. 23:6; 33:16).

God and Their Future (vv. 12–14)

After the worship was completed, perhaps one of the sons of Korah (see title) became "tour guide" for the pilgrims and led them around the city. He showed them the towers and the outer walls (ramparts), but he was careful to remind them that the city's protection was the Lord Jehovah and not stone and mortar. The Assyrian officers had counted the towers (Isa. 33:18) and calculated how to capture the city, but they hadn't taken the Lord into consideration. The guide told the visiting Israelites that it was their responsibility to teach the coming generation about the Lord, lest the nation abandon the God of Abraham and Isaac and Jacob. The greatest danger a nation faces is not the invading enemy on the outside but the eroding enemy on the inside—a people gradually turning away from the faith of their fathers. Each generation must pass along to the next generation who the Lord is, what He has done, and what they must do in response to His goodness and faithfulness (71:18; 78:4, 6; 79:13; 109:13; 145:4; 2 Tim. 2:2). God's plan is to make Jerusalem a joy to many generations (Isa. 60:15). To trust and obey a Lord who is "our God" and "our Guide" is to have a future that is secured and blessed.

Psalm 49

The psalmist had a message for everybody in the world, the important people and the nobodies, the rich and the poor (vv. 1–2). The word "world" is the translation of an unusual Hebrew word that means "the total human scene, the whole sphere of passing life," not unlike "world" in 1 John 2:15–17. The writer spoke from his heart (v. 3; see 45:1) the wisdom and understanding that the Lord gave him, and he dealt with an enigma that only the Lord could explain (v. 4). The enigma was life itself and its puzzling relationship to the distribution of wealth and the power that wealth brings. How should believers respond when they see the rich get richer? Should they be afraid that the wealthy will abuse the poor? Should they be impressed by the wealth that others possess and seek to imitate them? The writer gives us three reminders to help us keep our perspective in a world obsessed with wealth and the power it brings.

Wealth Cannot Prevent Death (vv. 5–12)

It isn't a sin to be wealthy if we acknowledge God as the Giver and use what He gives to help others and glorify His name (1 Tim. 6:7–19; Matt. 6:33). But an increase in wealth often leads to an increase in evil. It's good to have things that money can buy, if we don't lose the things money can't buy. It's sad when people start to confuse prices with values. Jesus concluded a sermon on riches by saying, "For what is highly esteemed among men is an abomination in the sight of God" (Luke 16:15 NKJV). The psalmist feared that the wealthy in the land would start to take advantage of poorer people. It was easy for the rich to bribe judges and rob the poor of their rights. (See James 2:1–9; 5:1–6; Amos 4:1–3; 5:10–15.)

Those who boast of their wealth have a false sense of security, because their wealth can't protect them from "the last enemy"—death (1 Cor. 15:26). Jesus had this truth in mind when He spoke about the rich farmer in Luke 12:13–21. If a relative was poor, a Jew could redeem him by paying his debts (Lev. 25:23ff), but if a relative was dying, no amount of money could come to the rescue—and to whom would you give the money? A murderer could not be redeemed (Num. 35:31), even if you could calculate the worth of a human life. So, money can't rescue you on this side of the grave, nor can it rescue you on the other side of the grave, because you can't take your money with you (vv. 10–12 and 17; Eccl. 2:18, 21; 7:2; 9:5). Whether you are rich or poor, wise or foolish, you leave everything behind. Many wealthy people think they will go on forever and enjoy their houses and lands, only to discover that death is a great leveler. After death, the rich and the poor stand equal before God. The rich may call their lands after their own names, but the names engraved in stone will outlast the owners. The phrase "he is like the beasts that perish" (v. 12 KJV and see Eccl. 3:10, 19, and 7:2) doesn't suggest that humans are on the same level as brute beasts, but only that both face ultimate death and decay.

Wealth Will Not Determine Your Destiny (vv. 13–15)

When Jesus told His disciples that it was hard for a rich person to enter the kingdom of heaven, they were astonished; for most Jews believed that the possession of wealth was a mark of God's blessing (Matt. 19:23–30). If wealthy people have a hard time getting into the kingdom, what hope is there for the rest of us? But people with wealth tend to trust themselves and their money and to believe the nice things people say about them (v. 13). The writer pictured wealthy lost people as dumb sheep being led to the slaughterhouse by Death, the shepherd, who would devour them. (See Luke 16:14, 19–31.)

For the believer, death is only a valley of temporary shadows, and Jesus is the Shepherd (23:4). There is coming a "morning" when the dead in Christ will be raised and share the glory of the Lord (1 Thess. 4:13–18; see Ps. 16:10–11; Isa. 26:19; Dan. 12:3). We can't ransom someone who is about to die (vv. 7–8), but the Lord has already ransomed us from sin and the power of the grave (v. 15; 1 Cor. 15:20ff). When we die, God will receive us to Himself (73:24; 2 Cor. 5:1–8; Gen. 5:24), and when Jesus returns, He will raise our bodies from the grave. Decision for Christ, not the possession of great wealth, determines our eternal destiny.

Wealth Must Not Increase Your Desires (vv. 16–20)

Don't be impressed and "over-awed" (NIV) when you see others getting wealthy and buying bigger houses and cars. All their wealth will be left behind when they die and ultimately lose its value. They won't be able to praise themselves, nor will they be able to hear others praise them. We take nothing with us when we die (Job 1:21; Eccl. 5:14; 1 Tim. 6:7). If we have been faithful stewards of what God has given us, we possess eternal riches that will never fade (Matt. 6:19–34). We can't take wealth with us, but we can send it ahead.

The statement in verse 12 is repeated in verse 20 with the addition of the phrase "without understanding." The writer penned this psalm so we would have understanding! We need to understand that wealth cannot prevent death or determine our destiny, and that we must not become covetous when we see others prospering in this world. It isn't a sin to have wealth, provided we earned it honestly, spend it wisely, and invest it faithfully in that which pleases the Lord.

Psalm 50

Every seventh year, during the Feast of Tabernacles, the priests were obligated to read the law to the people and explain its meaning (Deut. 31:9–18; Neh. 8), and this psalm may have been written for such an occasion. The emphasis is on the consistent godly living that should result from true spiritual worship. Asaph was one of David's worship leaders (see Ps. 39 introduction and 1 Chron. 15:17ff and 16:4ff). A group of eleven psalms attributed to Asaph is found in 73–83. God the Judge summons the court (vv. 1–6) and confronts two offenders: the formalist, to whom worship is a ritual to follow (vv. 7–15), and the hypocrite, to whom worship is a disguise to cover sin (vv. 16–21). The psalm closes with a call to all worshipers to be faithful to God (vv. 22–23).

The Holy Judge (vv. 1–6)

Human judges are called "The Honorable," but this Judge is called "The Mighty One" (El), "God" (Elohim), "the LORD" (Jehovah), "the Most High" (Elyon, v. 14), and "God" (Eloah). He is Judge (vv. 4, 6), Prosecutor, and Jury—and He knows all about those who are on trial! He calls heaven and earth to witness the proceedings (vv. 1, 4, 6; see Deut. 4:26, 32; 31:28; 32:1; Isa. 1:2; Mic. 1:2 and 6:1–2). When a judge enters a courtroom, everybody stands respectfully; but God's entrance into this assembly is accompanied by the shining of His glory (80:1; 94:2) and a fiery tempest, not unlike the scene at Mount Sinai when He gave His law (Ex. 19:18; 24:17; Deut. 4:11–12; 33:2; Heb. 12:18, 29). When we forget the transcendence of God, we find it easier to sin. The ark was with the people on Mount Zion ("Immanual, God with us"), but the nation must not forget Mount Sinai where their God revealed His holiness and greatness. The psalmist praised Zion for its beauty (v. 2; 48:2; Lam. 2:15), but he also wants us to remember "the beauty of holiness" (27:4; 90:17; 110:3).

God is Judge (vv. 4, 6; 7:11; 9:8; 11:4–7; 75:2; 96:10, 13; 98:9), and judgment begins with His own people (1 Peter 4:17). They are "godly ones," that is, a people set apart exclusively for the Lord because of the holy covenant (vv. 5, 16; Ex. 19:1–9; 24:4–8; Amos 2:3). Some of His people had sinned, and He had been longsuffering with them and silent about the matter (vv. 3, 21). They have interpreted His silence as consent (Eccl. 8:11; Isa. 42:14; 57:11), but now the time had come for the Holy God to speak. The purpose of this "trial" was not to judge and condemn the sinners but to expose their sins and give them opportunity to repent and return to the Lord.

The Heartless Worshipers (vv. 7–15)

"Hear, O my people" has a majestic ring to it (Deut. 4:1; 5:6; 6:3–4; 9:1; 20:3; 27:9). The Lord speaks first to those who are indeed His people, but their hearts are not in their worship. Their devotion is faithful but only routine. Like the church at Ephesus, they had "left their first love" (Rev. 2:4) and were worshiping the Lord out of habit and not from the heart. Outwardly, they were doing what the Lord commanded and honoring the daily sacrifices (Ex. 29:38–42), but inwardly they lacked love and fellowship with God. They forgot that God wanted their hearts before He wanted their sacrifices (Isa. 1:11–15; Jer. 7:21–23; Hos. 6:6; 8:13; Amos 5:21–26; Mic. 6:6–8; Mark 12:28–34).

The sacrifices that the Lord commanded were indeed important to the spiritual life of the nation, but they did no good to the worshipers unless there was faith in the heart and a desire to honor the Lord. The animals they brought belonged to Him long before the worshipers ever saw them! The world and everything in it belongs to Him (v. 12; 24:1; 89:11; Acts 17:24–25; 1 Cor. 10:26), and there is nothing we can give to God. Some of the pagan religions of that day taught that their gods and goddesses "ate" the animals that people sacrificed, but this was not a part of the Hebrew religion (Deut. 32:37–40). What the Lord wanted from His people was thanksgiving from their hearts, obedience to His Word, prayer, and a desire to honor Him in everything (vv. 14–15). But the Lord doesn't want ritualism or formalism. He wants our worship to come from the heart.

The Hypocritical Sinners (vv. 16–21)

This message was addressed to "the wicked," the Israelites in the covenant community who were reciting the creed with their lips but deliberately disobeying God's law. After breaking God's law, they would go to the sanctuary and act very religious so they could cover up their sins. They helped to make the sanctuary a "den of thieves"—the place where thieves go to hide after they have committed their wicked deeds (Jer. 7:11; Matt. 21:13). They had no respect for God's Word (v. 17) and not only consented to the sins of others but participated in them and enjoyed doing so (vv. 18–20). To "hate instruction" means to reject an ordered way of life patterned after God's Word, to reject a responsible life. The Lord specifically named stealing (the eighth commandment, Ex. 20:15), adultery (the seventh commandment, Ex. 20:14) and deceitful speech and slander (the nineth commandment, Ex. 20:16). These are not "old covenant sins," for believers today who live under the new covenant can be just as guilty of committing them.

Once again, the silence of God is mentioned (v. 21; see v. 3). God is longsuffering with sinners, but these wicked people interpreted God's silence as His approval. (See Isa. 42:14; 57:11; 64:12; 65:6; Mal. 2:17; 3:14–14.) Their thinking was so confused that they ended up creating a god in their own image (v. 21).

God was in the hands of ignorant sinners! They had forgotten God (Rom. 1:22–28) and didn't want Him to interfere with their lifestyle. They had a false confidence that they could sin and get away with it.

The Honest Worshiper (vv. 22–23)

In the two closing verses, the writer succinctly summarized the characteristics of the kind of worshiper God is seeking (John 4:23–24). The true worshiper has a proper fear of the Lord and seeks only to honor Him in his worship. He obeys God's will ("orders his way aright" NASB) and is able to experience ("see") the salvation of the Lord. When you combine these characteristics with verses 14–15—gratitude to God, obedience, prayer, and a desire to glorify God—you have a description of worshipers who bring joy to the heart of God.

Psalm 51

During his lifetime, King David did what had pleased the Lord, "except in the case of Uriah the Hittite" (1 Kings 15:5 NASB). This is the fourth of the Penitential Psalms (see 6) and is David's prayer of confession after Nathan the prophet confronted him with his sins (see 32; 2 Sam. 11–12). This is also the first of fifteen consecutive psalms in Book II attributed to David. In his prayer, David expressed three major requests.

"Cleanse Me" (vv. 1–7)

What dirt is to the body, sin is to the inner person, so it was right for David to feel defiled because of what he had done. By committing adultery and murder, he had crossed over the line God had drawn in His law ("transgression"); he had missed the mark God had set for him ("sin") and had yielded to his twisted sinful nature ("iniquity"). He had willfully rebelled against God, and no atonement was provided in the law for such deliberate sins (Lev. 20:10; Num. 35:31–32). David could appeal only to God's mercy, grace, and love (v. 1; Ex. 34:6–7; 2 Sam. 12:22). "Blot out" refers to a debt that must be paid (130:3; Isa.

43:25), and "cleanse" refers to defilement caused by touching something unclean (Lev. 11:32) or from disease (Lev. 13:1–3). "Wash" (vv. 2, 7) refers to the cleansing of dirty clothing (Isa. 1:18; 64:6). In the Jewish society of that day, to wash and change clothes marked a new beginning in life (Gen. 35:2; 41:14; 45:22; Ex. 19:10, 14), and David made such a new start (2 Sam. 12:20).

David had certainly sinned against Bathsheba and Uriah, but his greatest responsibility was to the Lord who had given the law to His people (2 Sam. 12:13; Ex. 20:13–14). Godly Jews saw all sins primarily as offenses against the Lord (Gen. 39:9). David openly acknowledged his sins and vindicated the Lord (v. 4; 1 John 1:9–10). Paul quoted verse 4 in Romans 3:4 as part of his argument that the whole world is guilty before God. He also confessed that he was not only a sinner by choice but also by nature (v. 5; 1 John 1:8). His statement doesn't suggest that sex in marriage is sinful, or that his inherited fallen nature was an excuse for disobedience, but only that he was no better than any other man in the nation. (See Gen. 6:5; 8:21; Jer. 17:9; Matt. 15:19; Rom. 1:19ff.) The sinfulness of humans doesn't mean that people can't do anything good (Luke 11:13) but that their "goodness" can't earn them entrance into God's family (Eph. 2:8–10; Titus 3:3–7).

David knew the truth of God's Word and loved it (19:7–11), but he had deliberately lied to himself ("I can get away with this") and to the people, and he tried to lie to God. For nearly a year he attempted to cover up his sins, but God does not allow His children to sin successfully. Now he asked God for truth and wisdom in his innermost being (v. 6).

"Hyssop" (v. 7) was a shrub with hairy stems that could be dipped into liquid, and the priests used hyssop to sprinkle blood or water on people needing ceremonial cleansing (Lev. 14:4, 6; Num. 19:6, 18; see Ex. 12:22). Today's believers find their cleansing in the work Jesus accomplished on the cross (1 John 1:5–10; Heb. 10:19–25).

"Restore Me" (vv. 8–12)

David's sins had affected his whole person: his eyes (v. 3), mind (v. 6), ears and bones (v. 8; see 32:3–4; 35:9–10; 38:8), heart and spirit (v. 10), hands (v. 14), and lips (vv. 13–15). Such is the high cost of committing sin. David knew this, so he asked for more than cleansing, as important as that is; he wanted his entire being to be restored so he could serve the Lord acceptably. He wanted the joy of the Lord within him (see v. 12) and the face of the Lord smiling upon him (10:1; 44:24; 88:14; 104:29). "Joy and gladness" is a Hebrew phrase meaning "deep joy." David asked the Lord to create a new heart within him and to give him a steadfast spirit that would not vacillate. Verse 10 is the central verse of the psalm and it expresses the heart of David's concern. David knew that the inner person—the heart—was the source of his trouble as well as the seat of his joy and blessing, and he was incapable of changing his own heart. Only God could work the miracle (Jer. 24:7; Ezek. 11:19; 36:25–27).

The Lord gave the Holy Spirit to David when Samuel anointed him (1 Sam. 16:13), and David didn't want to lose the blessing and help of the Spirit, as had happened to Saul when he sinned (1 Sam. 16:1, 14; see 2 Sam. 7:15). Today the Spirit abides with believers forever (John 14:15–18), but God's children can lose His effective ministry by grieving the Spirit (Eph. 4:30–32), lying to Him (Acts 5:1–3), and quenching Him by deliberate disobedience (1 Thess. 5:19). The phrase "willing spirit" in verse 12 refers to David's own spirit, as in verse 10. A "willing spirit" is one that is not in bondage but is free and yielded to the Spirit of God, who ministers to and through our own spirit (Rom. 8:14–17). It isn't enough simply to confess sin and experience God's cleansing; we must also let Him renew us within so that we will conquer sin and not succumb to temptation. The Lord did forgive David but permitted him to suffer the tragic consequences of his sins (2 Sam. 12:13–14).

"Use Me" (vv. 13–19)

David was God's servant, and he wanted to regain his ministry and lead his people. He especially wanted to make careful preparations for the building of the temple. It's interesting that Solomon, the child eventually born to Bathsheba, was chosen to be David's successor and the one to supervise the temple construction. "But where sin abounded, grace abounded much more" (Rom. 5:20 NKJV). David wanted to witness to the lost and wandering and bring them back to the Lord (v. 13), and he wanted to sing the Lord's praises (vv. 14–15). "Bloodguiltiness" refers to Uriah's blood on David's hands, for it was David who ordered his death (2 Sam. 11:6ff; see Ezek. 3:18–20; 18:13; Acts 20:26).

David was wealthy enough to bring many sacrifices to the Lord, but he knew that this would not please the Lord (50:8–15; see 1 Sam. 15:22) and that their blood could not wash away his sins. David wasn't denying the importance or the validity of the Jewish sacrificial system; he was affirming the importance of a repentant heart and a spirit yielded to the Lord (Isa. 57:15). God could not receive broken animals as sacrifices (Mal. 1:6–8), but He would receive a broken heart!

Some students believe that verses 18–19 were added later to adapt this very personal psalm for corporate worship, but there's no reason why David could not have written these words. As king, he was certainly burdened for the welfare of Jerusalem and the kingdom, and he knew that his sins had weakened Israel's position among the nations (2 Sam. 12:14). David must have begun building and repairing the walls, otherwise Solomon couldn't have completed the work early in his reign (1 Kings 3:1). David destroyed much good when he sinned, but he also did much good during his lifetime and served the Lord faithfully.

Psalm 52

When David wrote this psalm, he was angry and rightly so. (For the reason, see 1 Sam. 21:1–9 and 22:6–23.) Doeg was one of many men around Saul who catered to his whims and inflated his ego in order to gain power and wealth. He typifies all who promote themselves at the expense of truth and justice. Doeg was an Edomite, which means he was descended from Esau, the enemy of Jacob (Gen. 27–28; Heb. 12:16–17). The battle between the flesh and the Spirit still goes on. However, it's possible that David was also writing about Saul, who certainly fits the description given of the proud powerful tyrant. There has always been a certain amount of evil in high places, and God's people must learn to handle it in a godly manner. David paints for us three contrasting scenes.

The Sinners Are Boasting (vv. 1–4)

The phrase "mighty man" is the equivalent of our "big shot" and was spoken derisively. Doeg and Saul were mighty in their own eyes but insignificant in God's eyes; David was insignificant in their eyes but important to God. David depended on the mercy of the Lord (vv. 1, 8) while Saul and his men depended on themselves and their own resources. With tongues like honed razors, they issued orders and told lies without considering the consequences (see 5:9; 55:21; 57:4; 59:7; 64:3). Even when they told the truth—as Doeg did about David—they did it with evil intent because they were possessed by a malignant spirit. Their words devoured people and destroyed them (see 35:25). It isn't difficult to find people like Doeg and Saul in our twenty-first century world.

The Saints Are Laughing (vv. 5–7)

Verse 5 is the central verse of the psalm and marks the turning point in David's experience as he contemplated the wickedness of the human heart. He was confident that God would one day judge Saul, Doeg, and all who follow their evil philosophy of life. Note the powerful verbs: "break you down ... snatch you up ... tear you away ... uproot you ... ." (NASB). (See Job 18 for a similar description.) The righteous would only *see* but not experience this devastation (91:8), and they would stand in awe of the holy wrath of God (40:3). Then they would laugh in derision at the humiliating fall of these pompous leaders (2:4). What Saul and Doeg did to the priestly community at

Nob (1 Sam. 22:6ff), the Lord would do to them, for sinners ultimately fall into the pits they dig for others (9:15; Prov. 26:24–28; 29:6).

The Faithful Are Serving (vv. 8–9)

The contrast is clear: the wicked are like uprooted trees, but the godly are like flourishing olive trees that are fruitful and beautiful. Saul and Doeg would perish, rejected by the Lord, but David and his dynasty would be safe in the house of the Lord! It's possible that the tabernacle at Nob had olive trees growing around it and David would have seen them. The olive tree lives for many years and keeps bearing fruit (1:3; 92:12–15; see Jer. 17:7–8, and note 37:35–36), and certainly David was a blessing to the nation while he lived and long after he died—and he is a blessing to us today. He trusted God's lovingkindness and the Lord did not fail him, and he never failed to give God the glory. The phrase "wait on thy name" (v. 9 KJV) means to hope and depend on the character of God as expressed in His great name. The psalm ends with David vowing to praise the Lord in the congregation as soon as God established him in his kingdom. The private victories God gives us should be announced publicly for the encouragement of God's people. Meanwhile, though evil may seem to triumph, we must continue to obey and serve the Lord and not get discouraged. The "last laugh" belongs to the Lord's people.

Psalm 53

This is Psalm 14 with some minor revisions and the addition of the last two lines in verse 5. One of the sanctuary musicians revised the original psalm to fit a new occasion, perhaps the defeat of the Assyrian army in the days of King Hezekiah (v. 5; Isa. 37). It's a good thing to adapt older songs to celebrate new experiences with the Lord. The major change is the use of Elohim ("God") instead of Jehovah, the God of the covenant. The psalm still exposes and refutes the foolish unbelief of those who reject God. The boasting of the Assyrians is a good example.

Verse 5b describes the scattered corpses of a defeated army after God's great victory. For a body to remain unburied was a great disgrace in the ancient Near East, even an executed criminal was supposed to have a decent burial (Deut. 21:23; see 2 Kings 23:14; Ezek. 6:5). The Lord despised the arrogance of the Assyrians and put them to open shame. So will He do to the armies of the world that oppose Him (Rev. 19:11–21).

Psalm 54

The Ziphites lived about fifteen miles southeast of Hebron (see 1 Sam. 23:13–24 for the background). Twice they betrayed David to Saul (see 1 Sam. 26:1) and both times the Lord delivered him. This psalm reveals three stages in David's experience as he turned to God for help.

The Starting Point—Danger from the Enemy (vv. 1–3)

David's life was in danger (v. 3; see 1 Sam. 23:15), and he called on God to save him and vindicate his cause (1 Sam. 24:15). David was the rightful king of Israel, and the future of the nation and the dynasty lay with him. This included the promise of Messiah, who would come from David's line (2 Sam. 7). "By your name" means "on the basis of your character," especially His strength (v. 1) and faithfulness (v. 5). David promised to praise God's name after the great victory (v. 6). He used three different names of God in this brief psalm: Elohim (vv. 1, 2, 3, 4), Adonai (Lord, v. 4), and Jehovah (LORD, v. 6). "Hear my prayer" (v. 2) is a favorite approach with David (4:1; 39:12; 143:1).

"Strangers" (v. 3) doesn't suggest that his enemies were Gentiles, for the Ziphites belonged to the tribe of Judah, David's own tribe. The word is used in Job 19:13 to describe Job's family and friends, and David used it in a similar way in 69:8. It can describe anybody who has turned his or her back on someone, which the Ziphites certainly did to David, their king. Why did they do it? Because they disregarded the Lord and His will for the nation of Israel. Unlike David (16:8), they did not set God before them (see 10:4–5; 36:1; 86:14).

The Turning Point—Confidence in the Lord (v. 4)

This is the central verse of the psalm, and it records the turning point in David's experience. The word translated "help" or "helper" is related to "Ebenezer" in 1 Samuel 7:12, "Thus far the Lord has helped us" (NASB) and is a word David often used in his prayers (10:14; 30:10; 33:20; 79:9; 86:17; 115:9–11). It's worth noting that Jonathan visited David about this time, and the Lord used him to encourage His servant (1 Sam. 23:16–18). The Lord doesn't always send angels to encourage us; sometimes He uses other believers to minister to us (see Acts 9:26–28; 11:19–26). Every Christian ought to be a Barnabas, a "son of encouragement."

The Finishing Point—Praise to the Lord (vv. 5–7)

Twice David had opportunity to slay Saul but refrained from doing so, for He knew that God would one day deal with the rebellious king (see 1 Sam. 26:8–11). "He will pay back evil to my enemies" (v. 5 AMP). (See 7:15–16, 35:7–8, Prov. 26:27, 28:10, 29:6.) David was away from the sanctuary, but he lifted his voice in praise to God, and his words were like a freewill offering to the Lord (Heb. 13:15). In verses 1–6, David spoke directly to the Lord, but in verse 7, he spoke to those around him and gave witness to the blessing of the Lord. His words revealed his faith, for he spoke of his deliverance as already completed as he looked calmly at his enemies (22:17; 59:10; 92:11; 118:7). David had more suffering and peril to experience before he would ascend the throne, but he was confident that the Lord would see him through—and He did!

Psalm 55

It's likely that this psalm was written early in Absalom's rebellion (2 Sam. 15–17), when David was still in Jerusalem (vv. 9–11) and the revolt was gathering momentum. If so, then the "friend" of verses 12–14 and 20–21 had to be David's counselor Ahithophel who had sided with Absalom. Many commentators claim that the king and his officers didn't know about

Ahithophel's treachery until after David had fled the city (2 Sam. 15:31), but this isn't clearly stated in Scripture. David was a man with keen discernment, and it is difficult to believe that his closest advisor's treachery was hidden from him. If this psalm was David's prayer while still in Jerusalem, then his prayer in 2 Samuel 15:31 is simply a repetition of verse 9. The psalm reveals four possible approaches to handling the painful problems and battles of life.

We Can Look Within at Our Feelings (vv. 1–5)

David opened with a plea to the Lord that He would not hide His face from his supplications. "Don't ignore my prayer!" (See 10:1; 13:1; 27:9; 44:24; 69:17; 143:7.) David knew that his own negligence as a father had turned Absalom against his father, the Lord, and the nation. He also knew that the revolt was part of the discipline that Nathan the prophet promised because of David's adultery and the murder of Uriah (2 Sam. 12:9–12). What David heard and saw in the city distressed him greatly (vv. 2, 17), and he realized that his own life was in danger. The opposition was bringing trouble upon him the way soldiers fling stones at the enemy or roll down rocks upon them (v. 3). But David's concern was for the safety of his people and the future of the Lord's promises to his own dynasty (2 Sam. 7). He felt like everything was falling apart and there was no hope. It's natural to look at our feelings and express our fears, but that isn't the way to solve the problems.

We Can Look Beyond for a Safe Refuge (vv. 6–8)

When we find ourselves in the midst of trouble, our first thought is, "How can I get out of this?" But the dedicated believer needs to ask, "*What* can I get out of this?" David had learned some strategic lessons while hiding in the wilderness from Saul, but in his later years, he had some more important lessons to learn. The human heart longs for a safe and peaceful refuge, far from the problems and burdens of life. Elijah fled from the place of ministry and hid in a cave (1 Kings 19). Jeremiah longed for a quiet lodge where he might get away from the wicked people around him (Jer. 9:2–6), but when given the opportunity to leave Judah, like a true shepherd, he remained with the people (Jer. 40:1–6). Doves can fly long distances and they seek for safe refuges in the high rocks (Jer. 48:28). But we don't need wings like a dove so we can fly away from the storm. We need wings like an eagle so we can fly *above* the storm (Isa. 40:30–31). More than once David had prayed that the Lord would "hide him," and He answered his prayers (17:8; 27:5; 64:2). David did flee Jerusalem (2 Sam. 15:14ff) and lodged in the wilderness across the Jordan River at Mahanaim.

We Can Look Around at the Circumstances (vv. 9–15; 20–21)

David wasn't living in denial; he knew what was going on around him, and he directed operations in a masterful manner, worthy of his reputation. But he also prayed that God would bring confusion to Absalom's ranks (v. 9; 2 Sam. 15:31), and that's just what happened. The Lord used Hushai to influence Absalom to reject Ahithophel's counsel, and this led to the defeat of Absalom's forces (2 Sam. 16:15–17:31).

While still in Jerusalem, David witnessed violence and strife as people took sides and many followed Absalom (2 Sam. 15:10–14). "They" in verse 10 refers to violence and strife, which are personified as walking the walls along with mischief (malice) and sorrow (abuse). Among the rebels, David singled out one person who broke his heart, and that was Ahithophel, "a man like myself." As David's counselor, Ahithophel was not equal to the king in rank or authority, but he was very close to David. They had worshiped the Lord together, but now Ahithophel was counseling David's son to rebel against his father! In verses 20–21, David again mentioned Ahithophel, his violation of the covenant of friendship with David, and his deceptive persuasive speech. (See 5:9; 7:4; 12:2; 28:3; 41:9; Prov. 5:3) But God used Hushai to overrule Ahithophel's plans so that Absalom was defeated and David spared (2 Sam. 17). The picture in verse 15 reminds us of God's judgment on Korah, Dathan, and Abiram because of their rebellion against

Moses (Num. 16:28–33). David was God's anointed king, and the Lord protected him.

We Can Look up to God and Trust Him (vv. 16–19, 22–23)

While it's normal for us to hope for a quick way of escape, and important for us to understand our feelings and circumstances, it's far more important to look up to God and ask for His help. David could no longer lead an army into battle, but he was able to pray that God would defeat the rebel forces, and God answered his prayers. David used Jehovah, the covenant name of God, when he said, "The LORD will save me" (v. 16 NASB). The Jews did have stated hours of prayer (Dan. 6:10; Acts 3:1), but "evening, morning, and at noon" (v. 17) means that David was praying all day long! He no doubt also prayed at night (v. 10). David was certain that the Lord would hear him and rescue him because He was enthroned in heaven and in complete control. David's throne was in danger, but God's throne was secure (9:7–8; 29:10; 74:12).

During his difficult years of preparation, David had experienced many changes, and this taught him to trust the God who never changes (Mal. 3:6; James 1:17). Absalom and his friends had lived in luxury and ease and knew very little about the challenge of changing circumstances, so they had no faith in God or fear of God. A prosperous life is an easy life until you find yourself in the midst of the storm, and then you discover how ill–prepared you are; for what life does to us depends on what life finds in us.

The pronouns "you" and "your" in verse 22 are singular, but who is speaking and to whom? Did God speak to David through Nathan or another prophet and then David speak to the person reading the psalm? That's probably the correct answer. This promise is repeated in 1 Peter 5:7. The word translated "burden" ("cares" NIV) means "that which he has given you," reminding us that even the burdens of life come from the loving heart and hand of God (Ps. 33:11; Rom. 8:28). When David's lot was a happy one, it came from the Lord (16:5–6), and when he experienced times of pain and sorrow, the Lord was still in control.

He closed the psalm by speaking to the Lord and affirming his faith (7:1; 10:1), confident that God would judge his enemies. Was he anticipating the suicide of Ahithophel (2 Sam. 17:23)?

We must remind ourselves that our Lord Jesus Christ also had a traitor who hanged himself (Matt. 27:1–10), that Jesus also crossed the Kidron Valley (2 Sam. 15:23; John 18:1), and that He wept on the Mount of Olives (2 Sam. 15:30; Luke 22:39–44; Heb. 5:7). Rejected by His own people, today He is enthroned in heaven and will one day return to Jerusalem to establish His kingdom (Zech. 14:4ff).

Psalm 56

In an hour of deep despair and doubt, David left Judah and fled to Gath, the Philistine city identified with the giant Goliath whom David had slain (1 Sam. 17). David was alone and didn't get a very good reception. (The second time he went to Gath, he was accompanied by his men and was accepted. See 1 Sam. 27–30.) This psalm reveals that his life was in great danger, and history tells us that he had to pretend to be insane in order to escape (1 Sam. 21:10–22:1). Psalm 34 also came out of this experience in Gath. The musical inscription is translated variously: "the silent dove among those far away," "the silent dove among the strangers," "the dove on the distant oaks (or terebinths)." Some connect this inscription with 55:6–8 and see David as the dove (innocence), silent under attack while far from home. In the midst of peril and fear (vv. 3, 4, 11), David lifted three requests to the Lord, and the Lord answered.

Deliver Me from Death (vv. 1–4)

"All day long" David was harassed by the Philistines, who remembered that Israel sang his praises as a great military leader. They pursued him like hungry panting animals, and David cried out for mercy (see 51:1, 57:1). The record in 1 Samuel doesn't record any physical attacks on David, but he heard a great deal of slander and his life was in danger. David manifested both fear and faith as he cried out to God (Matt. 8:26; 14:30; Mark 5:6). The refrain in verses 3–4 is repeated in verses 10–11 as David affirms that God alone gives him the power to praise Him and trust Him. "So then faith comes by hearing, and hearing by the Word of God" (Rom. 10:17 NKJV). Faith and praise cannot be "manufactured"; they must be received as God's gift. "Mortal man" is "mere man, man who is flesh." This phrase is quoted in 118:6 and Hebrews 13:6. What Scripture says about fallen human nature is negative (John 6:63; Rom. 7:18; Phil. 3:3).

Deliver Me from Stumbling (vv. 5–11)

David literally had to "watch his step" in Gath, not only in what he did but also what he said, because he was a man under suspicion and was being watched. He had a target on his back and only the Lord could protect him. David chose Gath because he thought it was the last place Saul would expect to find him, but when he made that choice, he was walking by sight and not by faith. Faith is living without scheming. David prayed that God would judge Israel's enemies.

In verses 8–9, David reminded the Lord of the sufferings he had endured in exile, and then suggested that these sufferings qualified him to have his prayers answered and his enemies defeated. That would assure David that God is behind his cause (Rom. 8:31–39). God knew about David's wanderings and numbered them (121:8), and He had preserved his tears as well (see 2 Kings 20;1–6). God listed his tears on His scroll (v. 8 NIV), or put them in His bottle or wineskin (KJV, NASB). Archaeologists have unearthed small "tear bottles" in which mourners collected their tears and then deposited the bottle at the gravesite. The point is simply that God is aware of what we feel and how we suffer, and His records are accurate (69:28; 87:6; 130:3; 139:16; Ex. 32:32; Neh. 13:14; Ezek. 13:9; Dan. 7:10; Mal. 3:16; Rev. 20:12; 21:27). David repeated the refrain in verses 10–11, but he used the covenant name "Jehovah" this time.

Deliver Me so I Can Praise You (vv. 12–13)

David's greatest desire was to glorify the Lord, and this is why he wrote this psalm. He had vowed to serve the Lord and he meant to keep his vow. He had also vowed to present thank offerings to the Lord when his days of wandering were ended. Part of the thank offering was retained by the worshiper so he could enjoy a fellowship meal with his family and friends, and David looked forward to that blessing.

According to verse 13, God answered David's prayers. He delivered him from death; He kept him from stumbling; and He enabled him to walk in a godly way and praise the Lord. "Light of the living" can also be translated "light of life," as the phrase used by Jesus in John 8:12. As we follow the Lord Jesus today, we enjoy fullness of life and the glorious light of His presence. We walk in the light.

Psalm 57

After his deliverance from Gath, recorded in 56, David fled for protection to the cave of Adullam (1 Sam. 22:1ff), and later he would move to a cave in Engedi (1 Sam. 24; see Ps. 142). Better to be in the will of God in a cave than out of His will in a king's palace. The melody "Destroy not" was also assigned to 58, 59, and 75. This psalm covers one day in David's life as a fugitive, for verse 4 records his lying down and verse 8 his waking up to greet the dawn. God quieted his heart and gave him the sleep he needed (see 4:8 and 5:3). Note the repetition of *mercy* and *refuge* (v. 1), *sends* (v. 3), *steadfast* (v. 7) and *awake* (v. 8), and refrain in verses 5 and 11. From his difficult experience in Gath, David shares with us some responsibilities (and privileges) believers have every day.

Each Day Is a Day of Prayer (vv. 1–5)

As in 56:1, he began with a cry for mercy, for David depended on the grace of God to see him through his trials. His worship and prayer turned the cave into a Holy of Holies where he could hide under the wings of the cherubim on the mercy seat of the ark (Ex. 25:17–20, and note the verb "overshadowing"). This image is found frequently in Scripture and must not be confused with the wings of the bird as in 91:4, Deuteronomy 32:11, Matthew 23:37, and Luke 13:34. (See 17:8; 36:7–8; 61:4; Ruth 2:12.) David wanted the wings of a dove to fly away (55:6), when what he needed was the wings of the cherubim in "the secret place of the Most High" where he could safely hide (Heb. 10:19–25). David had taken refuge in the Lord many times in the past, and he knew the Lord was faithful. The word "calamities" means "a destructive storm that could engulf me."

Saul and his men were like panting animals pursuing their prey (vv. 3–4; see 7:2; 10:9; 17:12; 57:4; Dan. 6; 1 Peter 5:8), but God would protect David with His love and faithfulness. If David lay down in the cave to sleep, perhaps Saul's men would find him. But David's God is "God Most High" (7:17; 57:2; 78:56) and "possessor of heaven and earth" (Gen. 14:19), and He would fulfill His great purposes for David (138:8). David included a song of praise in his evening prayer (v. 5) and lay down and went to sleep. David didn't pray only at bedtime, as too many people do, but all day long; however, he closed the day with a special time of worship and commitment.

Each Day Is a Day of Praise (vv. 6–11)

In verses 1–5, the order is prayer (v. 1), witness (vv. 2–3), and a description of the enemy (v. 4), followed by the refrain, but in this section the order is the enemy (v. 6), witness to the Lord (vv. 7–8), and praise (vv. 9–11), with praise as the emphasis. David now compared his enemies to hunters who dug pits and set traps for their prey, an image frequently used in biblical poetry (7:15; 9:15ff; 35:7). However, David trusts God and has good reason to sing and praise the Lord. A steadfast heart is one that is fixed on the Lord's promises and not wavering between doubt and faith (51:10; 108:1; 112:7; 119:5). This same word is used to describe the constancy of the heavenly bodies (8:3; 74:16). Note that verses 7–11 are found also in 108:1–5. David praised the Lord all day long, but he opened the day with special praise and even anticipated the sunrise. Instead of the dawn awakening him, his voice awakened the dawn. (See 30:5; Lam. 3:22–23.)

David wanted his victory in the Lord to be a witness to the other nations, for as king, he knew that Israel was to be a light to the Gentiles. His psalms bear witness today of the great things God did for him. In verse 3, God sent His mercy and truth *down* from heaven, but in verse 10, mercy and truth *reach up* to the clouds! There is plenty for everybody!

Each Day Is a Day of Exalting the Lord (vv. 5, 11)

This refrain calls upon the Lord to manifest His greatness in such a way that people had to say, "This is the Lord's doing; it is marvelous in our eyes" (118:23 KJV). In his other psalm from Gath, David called on people to exalt the Lord (34:3; and see 18:46; 21:13; 30:1; 35:27; 40:16; 99:5, 9; 107:32; 145:1; 108:5; Matt. 5:16). If we are praying, trusting, and praising the Lord, we should have no problem exalting His name in all that we say, do, and suffer. We're commanded to do everything to the glory of God (1 Cor. 10:31), and if "everything" includes hiding in caves, then may the Lord be magnified! The elements of prayer, praise, and a desire for God to be magnified will transform any cave into a Holy of Holies to the glory of God.

Psalm 58

During David's exile years, Saul led the nation down a path of political and spiritual ruin as he disobeyed God's law and opposed God's anointed king. Saul was surrounded by a group of fawning flatterers who fed his ego and catered to his foolish whims (1 Sam. 22:6ff), and he put into places of authority people who used their offices for personal gain and not for the national good. They wanted to get as much as they could before the kingdom collapsed. David himself had been treated illegally, and it's likely that many of his men lost all they had because they followed David (1 Sam. 22:1–2). This psalm was probably written late in David's exile, or very early in his reign in Hebron, and may have grown out of his pondering the mess he had inherited from his father-in-law. (See 82 for a parallel psalm by Asaph.) The prophets often preached against the lawlessness of the leaders in Israel (Isa. 1:23–28; 5:22–25; 10:1–4; Amos 5:7–13; Mic. 3:1–4, 9–12; 7:1–6). Certainly nations, corporations, and even churches today need to take this kind of leadership crisis seriously. This is an imprecatory psalm (see 6).

Accusation—Lawlessness Practiced (vv. 1–5)

David addressed the lawless leaders and asked them if their words were just, their decisions legal, their sentences fair, and their silences honest. Were they upholding the law and defending the righteous or twisting the law and benefiting the wicked? He knew the answer, and so do we. When they should have spoken, they were silent, and when they spoke, they ignored God's law. The problem? They had evil hearts, for they were born in sin just like the rest of us (51:5; Gen. 8:21). However, they made no effort to seek God's help in controlling that sinful nature but gave in to its evil impulses. It's because humans are sinners that God established government and law, for without law, society would be in chaos. It's from the heart that evil words come out of our mouth and evil deeds are done by our hands.

These unjust judges were liars. Their words were like venom that poisoned society instead of like medicine that brought health (Prov. 12:18; 15:4). David compared them to snakes (vv. 4–5) and lions (v. 6), both of which are images of the devil (Gen. 3; 2 Cor. 11:3; 1 Peter 5:8). Like the cobra, they obeyed the charmer only when they got something out of it, but they had a mind of their own. Snakes have no visible ears or internal eardrums, but they do have small bones in the head that conduct sound vibrations. The cobra responds more to the movements of the charmer than to the tune he plays.

Condemnation—Lawlessness Punished (vv. 6–8)

Seeing innocent people suffer because of unjust judges made David angry, and rightly so. There is a righteous anger that ought to show itself whenever innocent people are condemned or helpless people are abused. David didn't do any of the things he mentioned but instead asked the Lord to do them. He knew that vengeance belongs to the Lord (Deut. 32:35; Heb. 10:30; Rom. 12:19). A lion without teeth is severely limited in his attacks; water that has soaked into the ground has lost the power to destroy (2 Sam. 14:14); and arrows without points won't penetrate the body. The snail doesn't actually "melt away" while moving along the rock, but the trail of slime left behind makes it look that way. The stillborn child is dead and can't function at all. "Let these unjust leaders be gone!" said David.

Vindication—Righteousness Praised (vv. 9–11)

David added a sixth image to describe their ultimate judgment, which would happen suddenly and without warning. A desperate traveler in the wilderness could cook a meal over a fire of thorns, but the fire might suddenly go out because the fuel burned quickly—or a whirlwind might come up and scatter fuel, fire, and cooking pots. To use a modern colloquial expression, these godless leaders are only "a flash in the pan." There is coming a day of judgment and they will not escape (118:12; 2 Sam. 23:6).

David's second picture comes from the battlefield and is even more vivid (v. 10). When victorious soldiers walked around the field and picked up the spoils of battle, their feet were stained by the blood of their enemies. Walking in cream and oil was a picture of wealth (Job 29:6), and walking in blood was a picture of great victory (see 68:23; Isa. 63:1–6; Rev. 14:17–20). The fact that the righteous rejoice at this is no more sinful than that prisoners of war rejoice at their release from a death camp or that downtrodden citizens are set free from a cruel dictator. After all, heaven rejoices at the fall of Babylon (Rev. 18:20–19:6). God vindicates Himself, His law, and His people, and He does it justly. So effective is His judgment that outsiders will say, "Surely there is a God who judges on earth" (v. 11 NASB).

Psalm 59

King Saul's fear and hatred of David became so compulsive that he finally gave orders to kill his son-in-law, and twice Saul tried to do it himself (1 Sam. 19:1–10). Then he plotted to have David murdered in his bed at home (1 Sam. 19:11–18), but his wife helped David escape by letting him out a window (see Acts 9:23–25). Before this attempt, Saul sent out search parties to spy on David (vv. 6, 14), and David wrote this psalm to ask God for the help he needed. The focus of the psalm is on God—the Deliverer (vv. 1–9) and the Judge (vv. 10–17). Note David's repeated "statement of faith" in verses 9 and 17. David waited and watched for God to work, and then he sang praises to the Lord for His mercies.

God the Deliverer (vv. 1–9)

God's people can always turn to the Lord in times of danger and testing because *He hears our prayers* (vv. 1–2). "Defend me" means "set me on high," for David saw the Lord as his fortress and high tower (18:2; 20:1; 46:7, 11; 91:14). However, David's prayer wasn't a substitute for action, for "faith without works is dead" (James 2:26). Michel's warning and immediate action saved his life, and her use of the "dummy" in the bed helped to buy time for her husband to get to Samuel in Ramah. But it was the Lord who answered prayer and orchestrated the escape. The Lord also *knows our hearts* (vv. 3–4) and recognized that David was innocent of the charges Saul's men were making against him (7:1–5; see 1 Sam. 20:1 and 24:11). David was not a traitor, but Saul had to have some excuse for hunting him down. David addressed the Lord as if He had been sleeping (vv. 4–5; see 7:6 and 44:23). In times of great danger, we sometimes feel that God needs to start acting on our behalf and doing it very soon!

The Lord *sees and hears our enemies* (vv. 5–7) and knows what they are saying and doing. David addressed Him as Jehovah (the God of the covenant), the Lord of Hosts (armies), and the God of Israel. David was Israel's anointed king and a son of the covenant God made with His people, so he had every right to seek God's help. Jehovah is the Lord of the Armies (Lord Sabaoth) and can defeat anyone who challenges His will. Since Saul and his men were the immediate problem, to whom was

David referring when he spoke of "the nations" (vv. 5 and 8)? The nations around Israel were usually poised and ready to attack their old foe, and Saul's mismanagement of the kingdom would make such a move even easier. He was so obsessed with destroying David that he neglected his duties as king and made the nation vulnerable. But David was God's anointed king, and Saul's attacks were exactly what the Gentile nations would do if they could. Unlike Saul, David understood the unique position of Israel among the nations and sought to maintain it (Gen. 12:1–3; Num. 23:9; 24:8–9).

David's graphic description of Saul's men (vv. 6–7 and 12–15) reveals how much he held them in disdain. They were nothing but prowling, snarling dogs, frothing at the mouth, spewing out evil words, and rummaging in the garbage dumps of the city. The Jews usually referred to *the Gentiles* as dogs! Finally, as our great Deliverer, the Lord *defends our cause* (vv. 8–9). The "dogs" were prowling and growling, but the Lord was laughing (see 2:4 and 37:13). The spies were watching David, but David was "on watch" looking for the Lord to act (vv. 9, 17; see 121:3–5, 7–8). God was his strength and fortress (46:1), and he had no reason to be afraid.

God the Judge (vv. 10–17)

God would not only take care of David, but He would also confront David's enemies and deal with them. If David's requests seem brutal and not in the spirit of Christ, keep in mind that Israel's future and the future of David's chosen dynasty were both at stake. This was not a personal crusade on David's part, for he asked God to fight the enemy for him (Rom. 12:17–21).

When it comes to facing and fighting the enemy, *the Lord goes before us* (v. 10). The mercy (lovingkindness) of the Lord would go before David and prepare the way for victory, just as when David killed the giant Goliath. The Lord also *fights for us* (vv. 11–13a) by scattering the enemy, causing them to wander and bringing their attack to a halt. The Lord is our Shield who can protect us in any battle (3:3; 18:2; Gen. 15:1; Deut. 33:29), but we must make a distinction here. David was willing that God destroy the Gentile nations and thus reveal His great power (v. 13), for God's victories bear witness to those who don't know Him. However, he asked God not to kill Saul and his men with some sudden judgment, but to allow their own sins to catch up with them and consume them gradually. This would be a strong witness and a warning to the people of Israel and teach them lessons they could learn no other way. God's victories *glorify His great name* (v. 13b) and magnify the name of the Lord to the ends of the earth (Ex. 9:16; Deut. 28:9–10; Josh. 4:23–24; 1 Sam. 17:46; 1 Kings 8:42–43). Finally, the Lord *gives us a song* (vv. 16–17) *and even before the victory*, we praise Him for who He is and what He does! The night of danger is never enjoyable, but we have His "mercy in the morning" (v. 16 KJV) because His love and compassion are "new every morning" (Lam. 3:22–23).

Psalm 60

According to the superscription, this psalm is a part of the history recorded in 2 Samuel 8:1–14 and 10:6–18 and 1 Chronicles 18:1–13 and 19:6–19, when David was winning battles and getting a name for himself (2 Sam. 8:13). While he was up north fighting the Arameans (Syrians), the Edomites attacked Israel from the south, doing a great deal of damage. David dispatched Joab with part of the army, and Joab and Abishai (1 Chron. 18:12) defeated Edom in the Valley of Salt, south of the Dead Sea. David must have written the psalm shortly after hearing the bad news of the invasion by Edom, but the psalm manifests a spirit of trust and confidence that the Lord would give Israel the victory, and He did. The musical direction means "Lily of the testimony [covenant]." (See 45, 69 and 80.)

Abandonment—A Troubled People (vv. 1–5)

The plural pronouns indicate that David was speaking to the Lord for the Israelites who felt themselves abandoned by God. The initial victory of Edom hit Israel like water bursting through a broken dam (v. 1; 2 Sam. 5:20) or an earthquake shaking the entire country (v. 2). The people acted like they were drunk on wine, staggering in bewilderment from place to place (v. 3; 75:8; Isa. 51:17, 22). David interpreted Israel's defeat as a sign that God had rejected His people (44:9–16; 89:38–45). However, being a man of faith, he didn't give up but rallied the people around the Lord's banner (v. 4; 20:5). Israel's God is "Jehovah Nissi—the Lord our Banner" (Ex. 17:15). David knew that Israel was God's own people, His beloved people ("David" means "beloved") who feared Him, and that God had covenanted to give them success against their enemies (2 Sam. 7:9–11). In David's heart, faith was conquering fear.

Encouragement—A Triumphant Message (vv. 6–8)

How David received this message from the Lord isn't explained to us, but he was quick to believe it and pass it along to the people. The message describes Jehovah as a Warrior who defeated the nations in Canaan and divided the land among His people (vv. 6–7; see Ex.15:3, 13–18; Josh. 18:10). Shechem was the chief city in Ephraim, and with Succoth, was located west of the Jordan River, while Gilead and Manasseh (the half tribe) were east of the Jordan River. The patriarch Jacob was connected with both Succoth and Shechem (Gen. 33:17–18). Ephraim was a strong tribe, called to defend Israel ("helmet"); and Judah was chosen to be the royal tribe, bearing the scepter (Gen. 49:10). The Lord didn't give the land to His people so they might lose it to their enemies! The Lord spoke with disdain of the enemies who attacked Israel, for both Edom and Moab were known for their arrogance (Isa. 16:6–14; Obad.; and see Ex. 15:14–15 and Num. 20:14–21). In God's eyes, Moab was nothing but a basin used for washing dirty feet, and Edom was a servant who cleaned dirty shoes! (David was related to the Moabites. See Ruth 4:13–22.) As for Israel's perpetual enemies, the Philistines, over them God would "raise the shout of victory" (v. 8 AMP). David claimed these promises by faith, sent part of the army led by Joab and Abishai to the south to fight

Moab, and later David joined them for a great victory. Fighting on two fronts isn't easy, but God gave the victory.

Enablement—A Trustworthy Lord (vv. 9–12).

David earnestly prayed that the Lord would honor His Word and give His beloved people victory over their enemies, and the Lord answered. David made it clear that he wasn't looking back at the defeat (vv. 9–10). He was the kind of leader who looked to the future and trusted the Lord. The "fortified city" was probably Petra (or Sela), the capital of Edom. David didn't interpret one setback as the sign of total defeat. He was making a great name for himself by his many victories, so perhaps he needed this one defeat to humble him and drive him closer to the Lord. David didn't trust in himself or in his capable officers or his valiant soldiers (v. 11). He trusted fully in the Lord, and the Lord honored his faith. The enemy would be completely defeated—trampled into the dirt—and Israel would triumph. Israel rallied to the "banner of God's truth" (v. 4), and the Lord gave them victory (1 John 5:4). "Edom will be conquered; Seir [Edom], his enemy, will be conquered, but Israel will grow strong" (Num. 24:18 NIV).

Psalm 61

David could have written this psalm during any of the many times he was in danger, but perhaps the best context is the rebellion under Absalom (2 Sam. 15–18). David prayed about a foe (v. 3), protection for his life (v. 6), and the security of his throne (v. 7, where "abide" means "be enthroned"). The psalm opens with David crying out in distress but closes with him singing praises to God.

"Hear Me"—A Cry to the Lord (vv. 1–4)

There was an urgency in David's cry because he was overwhelmed by what was happening and fainting under the pressure. (See Ps. 142.) He was obviously not at "the ends of the earth," but he felt that way, for he was away from home and away from the sanctuary of God. He was describing "spiritual geography" and his need to know the presence of God in what was going on. The image of the Lord as "rock" is a familiar one in David's writings (18:2, 31, 46; 62:2, 6, 7; etc.). David was unable to "climb" higher by himself; he needed the Lord to help him and sustain him (see 62:2, 6, 7). We are never so far away that we can't pray to God, or, as in the case of Jonah, so far down (Jonah 2). David looked back at his life and was encouraged to remember that God had never failed him in any crisis (v. 3), and He would not fail him now. To David, God's home was the tabernacle, the place where His glory dwelt; and David longed to be back in Jerusalem to worship and adore his Lord (v. 4). "Wings" probably refers to the cherubim on the mercy seat that covered the ark of the covenant in the Holy of Holies (36:7–8; 57:1; 63:2, 7). David was not a priest, so he couldn't enter the Holy of Holies, but he could abide in the Lord and find refuge in Him (46:1; 90:1). God's "wings" provided safety right where David was, so he didn't need his own "wings" to fly away (55:6–8). "Forever" in verse 4 carries the meaning of "all my life" (1 Sam. 1:22).

"You Have Heard Me"—Confidence in the Lord (vv. 5–8)

When David became king, he made some promises to the Lord and to the people, and he intended to keep those promises. All during his wilderness exile, while hiding from Saul, David obeyed the Lord (18:19–27), and he sought to be a shepherd to the nation. Why would the Lord care for David all those years, give him his throne, and then allow him to be replaced by his wicked son? His throne was his heritage from the Lord (16:5–6), just as the land of Israel was the heritage (possession) of God's people (37:9, 11, 22, 29, 34).

His requests in verses 6–7 relate to God's gracious covenant with David (2 Sam. 7). The Lord promised David a throne forever and a dynasty forever (89:36), and this has been fulfilled in Jesus Christ (Luke 1:30–37; Acts 2:22–36). David's concern was not for his own name or family but for the future of Israel and God's great plan of redemption. His own throne was in jeopardy at that time, but he had confidence that God would keep His promises. "May he sit enthroned forever" (v. 7 AMP) meant "May King David live out his full life," protected by God's mercy and truth, but to believers today it means, "May Jesus Christ reign forever!" The throne of glory is secure, for God has set His King on His holy hill of Zion! (2:6). In view of this, let's follow David's example and trust the Lord, call on Him, obey Him "day after day," and sing His praises.

Psalm 62

This psalm may have come out of David's time of trial when his son Absalom sought the throne (vv. 3–4), but it also may have been written while David was ruling over Judah in Hebron (2 Sam. 1–4). Those were difficult years as the forces of Saul tried to continue his dynasty and dethrone God's anointed king. (For "Jeduthun," see Ps. 39, and note how the two psalms parallel each other in a number of ways.) In this psalm, David shows remarkable faith as he rests in God alone (vv. 1, 2, 5, 6) and trusts Him to defeat the enemy and restore peace to the land. Three powerful truths emerge from his experience.

God Alone Saves Us (vv. 1–4)

The word translated "only" or "alone" in verses 1, 2, 4, 5, and 6, and "surely" in verse 9 (all KJV) is a Hebrew adverb that is also translated "indeed, verily, but" and is even ignored completely. David wants us to know that his faith isn't in God plus something else, but in God alone. Yes, God uses means to accomplish His work, and the same God who ordains the end also ordains the means, but our faith is in Him and not in the means. David didn't argue with the enemy or try to tell God what to do; he simply prayed, trusted and waited, knowing that God would give him the kingdom in His good time. The images of God as "rock" and "fortress" remind us of Psalm 18:1–2. A humble man, David saw himself as a bowing stone wall about to collapse and a tottering fence ready to fall down (see 1 Sam. 24:14 and 26:20). But God was his strong tower! The enemy could threaten him, lie about him, and even assault him, and he would not lose the peace God put in his heart. To wait in silence before the Lord is not idleness or inactivity. It is calm worship and faith, resting in His greatness and submitting to His will. It is preparation for the time when God gives the orders to act (18:30–45).

God Alone Encourages Us (vv. 5–8)

David has moved from "I shall not be greatly shaken" (v. 2 NASB) to "I shall not be shaken" (v. 6 NASB). The greater the realization that God was his fortress, the greater the calmness in his heart. He was not depending on himself or his own resources but on the Lord God Almighty. His throne, his reputation, and his very life depended only on the faithfulness of the Lord. In verse 8, David exhorted the people with him to see God as their refuge, to trust Him always, and to pour out their hearts in prayer (42:4; 142:2). David depended on the prayers of others and, like Paul, wasn't afraid to say, "Pray for us" (1 Thess. 5:25; 2 Thess. 3:1). Times of waiting can be difficult if we don't depend wholly on the Lord. God's delays are not God's denials, but our impatience can be used by the devil to lead us on dangerous and destructive detours.

God Alone Rewards Us (vv. 9–12)

When David looked to the Lord, he saw himself as a weak tottering fence and wall (v. 3). Now, when he looked at the enemy, he saw them as—nothing! No matter how high socially or how powerful economically, all men are but vanity ("a breath"—102:3; James 4:14; Job 7:7). Put them on the scales and nothing will register, because they weigh nothing (Job 6:2; Isa. 40:15; Dan. 5:27). David's enemies had acquired their power and wealth by oppressing and abusing others, and David warned his own people not to adopt their philosophy of life. How tragic when God's people today put their trust in their wealth, positions, and human abilities and not in the God who alone can give blessing.

The phrase "once ... twice" in verse 11 is a Hebrew way of saying "many times, repeatedly" (Amos 1:3, 6, 9, 11, 13; Job 33:14). David had often heard these words and the lesson they carried was written on his heart: God is powerful and God is merciful. God's strength and lovingkindness are sufficient for every crisis of life, for we are in the hands of a God whose omnipotent love can never fail. "Let us fall now into the hand of the Lord, for his mercies are great" (2 Sam. 24:14). God did vindicate David and give him his throne, and he reigned with great distinction. No matter what people may say about us or do to us, God keeps the books and one day will give sinners and saints the rewards they deserve. "And each one will receive his own reward according to his own labor" (2 Cor. 3:8).

Psalm 63

The superscription informs us that David was in "the wilderness of Judah" when he wrote this psalm, suggesting that it was probably during Absalom's rebellion (2 Sam. 15:23). However, he didn't look back in regret at the mistakes he had made as a father, nor did he look around in fear or complaint at the discomforts and dangers of the wilderness. Instead, he looked up to the Lord and reaffirmed his faith and love. In an hour when David might have been discouraged, he was excited about God, and in a place where there was no sanctuary or priestly ministry, David reached out by faith and received new strength from the Lord. Note the progressive experiences he had as he sought for the Lord's guidance and help at a difficult time in his life.

Desiring God (vv. 1–2)

To be able to say "my God" by faith transformed David's wilderness experience into a worship experience. There in the desert, he was hungry and thirsty, but his deepest desires were spiritual, not physical. With his whole being, body and soul, he yearned for God's satisfying presence (v. 5; 42:1–2). Just as we have physical senses that are satisfied by God's creation, so we have spiritual senses (Heb. 5:14) that can be satisfied only by Christ. He is the bread of life (John 6), and He gives us the water of life by His Spirit (John 4:1–14; 7:37–39; Rev. 22:17). Those who hunger and thirst for spiritual food and drink shall be filled (Matt. 5:6). David could say with Jesus, "I have food to eat of which you do not know" (John 4:32 NKJV).

How did David acquire this wonderful spiritual appetite? By worshiping God at the sanctuary (v. 2; see 27:4; 84:1–2). He had erected the tent on Mt. Zion and returned the ark to its rightful place, and he had found great delight in going there and contemplating God (36:8–9; 46:4). Because he didn't belong to the tribe of Levi, David couldn't enter the sanctuary proper, but from his study of the Books of Moses, he knew the design and the assigned rituals, and he understood their deeper meaning. *It is our regular worship that prepares us for the crisis experiences of life.* What life does to us depends on what life finds in us, and David had in him a deep love for the Lord and a desire to please Him. Because David had seen God's power and glory in His house, he was able to see it in the wilderness as well!

Praising God (vv. 3–5)

David didn't depend on the tabernacle or its furnishings—in fact, he sent the ark back to Jerusalem (2 Sam. 15:24–29)—but on the living God whose character and works were declared in those furnishings. Unlike the superstitious people of Judah in Jeremiah's day (Jer. 3:16; 7:1–16), David looked beyond material objects and saw spiritual realities. He had no priest or altar there, but he could lift his hands like the priests and bless the Lord and His people (Num. 6:22–27). His uplifted hands, though holding no sacrifice, signified his prayers and the love of his uplifted heart (see 28:2; 141:2; 1 Tim. 2:8). By faith, he was under the wings of the cherubim in the Holy of Holies, protected from his foes (v. 7; 36:7). There in the wilderness, he had no sacrificial meal to enjoy, but his soul feasted on spiritual delicacies that even the priests were not permitted to eat (v. 5; Lev. 3:16–17). "Marrow and fatness" typify the very finest of food (81:16; 147:14; Deut. 32:14; Isa. 25:6). Instead of complaining, as we are prone to do when things go wrong, David sang praises to the Lord.

Remembering God (vv. 6–8)

David's heart was at peace, and he was able to go to bed and calmly worship the Lord and meditate on Him (3:5–6; 42:8). The phrase "earnestly seek" in verse 1 can mean "early will I seek," so we see David at both morning and evening. The phrase "remember God" means to recall what He has said and done in the past and apply it to our present situation (42:6; 77:1–11; 105:1–5; 119:55). It was because Israel forgot what God did that they rebelled and disobeyed Him (78:40–43; 106:6ff). Our God is I AM, not "I was," and He must always be recognized in our present situation. The Jews had three night watches, from sunset to ten o'clock, from ten to two o'clock, and from two to sunrise, so whenever David awakened during the night, he immediately remembered the Lord. (Or it could mean he was awake all night, but not tossing and turning.) His bed was under the wings of the cherubim and he felt secure as he meditated on the Lord (16:7; 119:148; Deut. 6:4–9).

But David wasn't passive in his devotion, for he continued to cling to the Lord and rest in the safety of His right hand (17:7; 18:35; 41:12). Faith without works is dead. Believers are safe in the hands of the Father and the Son (John 10:27–29), but that doesn't give us license to do foolish things that would endanger us. "My soul cleaves after you" is a literal translation of verse 8, including both submissive faith in God and active pursuit of God. Jesus described this experience in John 14:21–27.

Rejoicing in God (vv. 9–11).

Some people criticize David for wanting his enemies destroyed and their bodies left for the scavengers to devour. But they should remember that these rebels were the enemies of God and God's purposes for Israel, and that those purposes included the coming of Messiah into the world. (See at Ps. 55.) David didn't execute the enemy himself but asked God to deal with them, and He did (2 Sam. 18:6–8). David only wanted the God of truth to triumph over the liars (31:5; 40:11; 43:3; 45:4). David didn't rejoice in the destruction of his enemies; he rejoiced in the God of Israel. Furthermore, he encouraged all the people to praise God with him. Often David's personal praise became communal praise as he publicly glorified the Lord for His mercies, and so it should be with us today.

Psalm 64

"The first quality for a commander-in-chief is a cool head to receive a correct impression of things," said Napoleon I. "He should not allow himself to be confused by either good or bad news." David was probably serving in Saul's court when he wrote this psalm (1 Sam. 18–20). He knew that Saul was his enemy and wanted to kill him and that most of Saul's officers were in a conspiracy against him. Though he was the anointed king, David had no authority to oppose Saul, and eventually he had to flee and hide in the wilderness. People give us all kinds of trouble, but our battle is not against flesh and blood, but against Satan and his hosts (Eph. 6:10ff). This psalm instructs us what to do in the battles of life.

Seek the Lord's Protection (vv. 1–2)

Frequently David addressed the Lord by saying, "Hear my voice" or "Hear me when I call," not because God wasn't paying attention but because David was in earnest (4:1; 5:3; 27:7; 28:2; 39:12; 54:2; 55:17; 61:1; 64:1; 140:6; 143:1). The word translated "prayer" (v. 1 KJV) also means "complaint" or "trouble" (see 142:2). David didn't ask God to change the circumstances but to fortify his own heart and deliver him from fear. The fear of the Lord mobilizes us, but the fear of man paralyzes us. As a young courtier, loved by the people but envied and hated by the king, David faced two problems: the secret conspiracy of Saul and his officers, and the open "tumult" (v. 2 NASB) of those who wanted to please Saul by oppressing David. "Insurrection" in verse 2 (KJV) doesn't suggest Absalom's rebellion, but rather what is described in 2:1–2 and 31:13. Lies about David were being passed from person to person and David knew he wasn't safe in Saul's court. Both his life and his reputation were being attacked, and only the Lord could rescue him.

Ask for the Lord's Wisdom (vv. 3–6)

David knew exactly what the enemy was saying and doing, and we need to know the strategy of Satan when he attacks us (2 Cor. 2:11). As a lion, he comes to devour (1 Peter 5:8), and as a serpent, he comes to deceive (2 Cor. 11:1–4), and one of his chief weapons is accusation (Rev. 12:10; Zech. 3). David compared his enemies' tongues to swords (55:21; 57:4; 59:7) and their words to poisoned arrows (57:4; Prov. 25:18; 26:18–19; Jer. 9:8). But they also set traps for him, confident that nobody knew what they were doing, not even the Lord (10:11, 13; 12:4; 59:7). (For some of Saul's traps and how the Lord frustrated them, see 1 Sam. 18–19.) David knew that the human heart is "deep" ("cunning" NIV; see Jer. 17:9) and that there are always new dangers to avoid, so he constantly sought the Lord's wisdom as he made decisions. James 1:5 is a great promise to claim!

Trust the Lord for Victory (vv. 7–8)

By depending on the Lord and obeying His directions, David was confident that God would defeat his enemies. "Be strong in the Lord, and in the power of his might" (Eph. 6:10). David's enemies shot arrows at him suddenly (vv. 3–4), so the Lord suddenly shot arrows at them (v. 7). They tried to trip him and trap him (v. 5), so the Lord caused David's enemies to stumble and fall (v. 8 AMP). God would use their own sword-like tongues to fight against them, and they would end up in shame and disgrace (v. 8). The very weapons that the enemy uses against us, the Lord uses to defeat them.

Give Glory to the Lord (vv. 9–10)

As the nation watched the defeat of David's enemies and his exaltation as king, it all brought great glory to the Lord. Some people stood and shook their heads in disbelief (v. 8a). Dr. Bob Cook used to say, "If you can explain what's going on, the Lord didn't do it." Faith expects to see God do the impossible! The nation had a new fear of the Lord as they saw sin judged and their godly king vindicated (59:9–13). The people praised the Lord for what He had done, and as they worshiped, they meditated on His character and His purposes. It isn't enough to know the works of the Lord; we must also seek to understand His way and learn how to please Him (103:6–7). David's great concern was that the Lord be glorified, and that was why God blessed Him. Rejoice!

Psalm 65

This is the first of four psalms (65–68) that focus on praising the Lord for His manifold blessings in nature and for His gracious dealings with His people. He is the God of creation and the God of the covenant. The psalm acknowledges our total dependence on the Lord to provide both our spiritual and material needs. The phrase "crown the year" (v. 11) suggests a harvest festival in October, the first month of Israel's civil year. (The religious calendar opened with Passover; Ex. 12:2.) Perhaps verse 3 suggests the annual Day of Atonement that ushered in the Feast of Tabernacles, a harvest festival (Lev. 17; 23:26–44). The early rains usually began in late October, softening the hard soil and enabling the farmers to plow the ground and sow their seed (vv. 9–13). Perhaps God had disciplined His people by sending drought and famine (Lev. 26:3–6; Deut. 11:8–17) and by allowing other nations to threaten Israel (v. 7). This discipline brought them to repentance and they anticipated the promised rains and a blessed harvest from the Lord. David's unusual experience involving the Gibeonites might have been the occasion (2 Sam. 21:1–14). Whatever the historical setting, the psalm helps us to worship our great God and glorify Him for who He is and what He does for us.

He Is the Savior of Sinners (vv. 1–4)

The opening phrase is literally, "To you praise is silence," which doesn't convey very much. The *New American Standard Bible* combines both: "There will be silence before Thee, and praise in Zion, O God." The Hebrew word for "silence" is very similar to the word for "fitting, proper," so some translate it, "Praise is fitting for you," that is, "It is fitting that your people praise you." But silence is also a part of worship, and we must learn to wait quietly before the Lord (62:1). Israel has no sanctuary today, but one day the temple will be rebuilt (Ezek. 40–48; Dan. 9:20–27), and the Gentile nations will come and worship the true and living God (v. 2; Isa. 2:1–3; 56:7; Mic. 4:1–5; Mark 11:17).

Before we approach the Lord, we must confess our sins and trust Him for forgiveness (1 John 1:9, and see Ps. 15 and Isa. 6). The priests were chosen by God to serve in the sanctuary (Num. 16:5), but God wanted all of His "chosen people" to live like priests (Ex. 19:3–8; Deut. 7:6–11; Ps. 33:12). Believers today are "a kingdom of priests" (1 Peter 2:9–10; Rev. 1:5–6), chosen by the Lord, offering Him their praise and worship. What the Jewish worshipers had in their sanctuary, believers today have in Jesus Christ, and we find our complete satisfaction in Him. We have all these blessings only because of the grace of God, for He chose us (John 15:16).

He Is the Ruler of All Nations (vv. 5–8)

We move now from the people of Israel to all the nations of the world, and from God's grace to the Jews to God's government of the Gentiles. God performed "awesome deeds" for Israel (47:2–4; 66:1–7; 68:35; 89:5–10), and these gave witness to the pagan nations around them that Jehovah alone is the true and living God and the Lord of all nations (Rom. 9:17; Josh. 2:1–14; Acts 14:15–17; 17:26–28; Amos 1–2 and 9:7). He chose Israel to be a light to the Gentiles (Isa. 42:6; 49:6), and this was ultimately fulfilled in the coming of Christ to the world (Luke 2:32; Acts 13:47). Day and night, God's creation witnesses to the nations and they are without excuse (19:1–6; Rom. 1:18–25; 10:14–18). Jesus Christ is the only hope of the world. The "roaring seas" are a symbol of the nations in tumult and confusion (v. 7; Isa. 17:12–13; 60:5; Dan. 7:2–3; Rev. 13:1; 17:15). From the east to the west (sunrise to sunset), His name will be reverenced. What a missionary text! The nations of the earth need to know the Gospel of Jesus Christ so they can sings songs of joy to the Lord.

He Is the Provider of All We Need (vv. 9–13)

The psalm opened in the tiny land of Israel (God's grace) and moved from there to the nations of the earth (God's government). Now the entire universe comes into the picture, for the Creator of the universe provides the sunshine and rain in their times and seasons so that people can plow the earth, plant seeds, and eventually harvest food. (See Gen. 1, 8:20–9:17.) The emphasis is on God's goodness and generosity to His people. The rains come in abundance; the rivers and streams overflow; the harvest is plenteous; the grain wagons are full; and the grain spills into the wagon ruts. Why? Because God covenanted to care for the land of Israel and visit it with His blessing if His people honored and obeyed Him (Deut. 11:8–15; Lev. 26:3–5).

This blessing was promised all during the year and year after year, even during the Sabbatical years when the people didn't cultivate the land (Lev. 25:1–22). According to verses 12–13, the "pastures of the wilderness" (uncultivated land) would produce vegetation and the hills would be clothed with beauty. The meadows would feed the flocks and herds, and the valleys would produce the grain. All of them would unite as one voiceless choir shouting for joy to the God of the universe, the Creator of every good and perfect gift. We can't read these verses without expressing appreciation and adoration to our God for His goodness and vowing not to waste food (John 6:12) or waste the precious land and resources He has given us. One day God will destroy those who destroy the earth (Rev. 11:18), who fail to see that we are stewards of His precious gifts.

Psalm 66

At the close of the previous psalm, you hear nature praising the Lord, and this psalm exhorts all mankind to join creation in celebrating God's greatness. It appears that Israel had gone through severe trials (vv. 8–12) and yet won a great victory with the Lord's help. Some students believe this event was the Lord's miraculous defeat of Assyria (Isa. 36–37) and that the individual speaking in verses 13–20 was King Hezekiah, whose prayer the Lord answered (37:14–20). The exhortation to praise the Lord begins with the Gentile nations (vv. 1–7), moves to Israel (vv. 8–12), and concludes with the individual believer (vv. 13–20).

A Global Invitation: "All Nations, Praise the Lord!"
(vv. 1–7)

The psalmist invited all the Gentile nations to praise God for *what He had done for Israel!* Why? Because through Israel, the Lord brought truth and salvation to the Gentiles. "Salvation is of the Jews" (John 4:22). This is a missionary psalm showing the importance of taking the good news of Jesus Christ into all the world. God's purpose is that all the nations shall praise Him (98:4; 100:1; Rom. 15:9–12), but they can't do that until they trust Him (Rom. 10:1ff). It's tragic that the nations today attack and persecute Israel instead of thanking God for her spiritual contribution to them. But the nations don't know the Lord, and Israel has been blinded and hardened by her unbelief (Rom. 11:25ff). When Israel sees her Messiah and trusts Him, then the world situation will change (Zech. 13–14), and all the nations will worship the Lord. One day there shall be universal praise lifted for Jesus Christ (Phil. 2:10–11; Rev. 11:15–18).

The nations are invited to "come and see what the Lord has done," and the writer reviews some of the miraculous history of Israel: the Exodus from Egypt, the crossing of the Jordan, and the defeat of the nations in Canaan (vv. 5–7; see Ex. 15:18). The Exodus was the "birthday" of the Jewish nation and has always been Israel's main exhibition of the glorious power of the Lord (77:14–20; 78:12ff; 106:7–12; 114; 136:13; Isa. 63:10–14). What the resurrection of Jesus Christ is to believers today, the Exodus was to Israel (Eph. 1:15–23). The Jews remember the Exodus at Passover, and the church remembers the death and resurrection of Christ at the Lord's Supper. "God's work is never antiquated," wrote Alexander Maclaren. "It is all a revelation of eternal activities. What He has been, He is. What He did, He does. Therefore faith may feed on all the records of old time and expect the repetition of all that they contain." (*Expositor's Bible* [Eerdmans, six vol. edition], vol. 3, p. 170).

A National Proclamation: "Israel, Praise the Lord!" (vv. 8–12)

If any nation has reason to praise the Lord, it is Israel; for He rescued them from slavery, guided them through the wilderness, took them into their land, and enabled them to defeat their enemies and claim their inheritance. He gave them His law, His sanctuary, and His priests and prophets, and He blessed them with all they needed. When they disobeyed, He disciplined them. Like a careful craftsman, He put them through the furnace and removed the impurities. (See 17:3; 26:2; Jer. 9:7; Mal. 3:2–3; 1 Peter 1:6–7; 4:12.) When they turned to the Lord, He transformed their sufferings into blessings and enlarged them (v. 12; see 4:1; 18:19, 36; 25:17). So it has been with the church. When the Lord has permitted persecution, this has invariably led to growth and blessing. We can go through fire and water and be the better for it (Isa. 43:2).

A Personal Affirmation: "Praise God with Me!" (vv. 13–20)

The change from "we/our" to "I/my" is significant, for corporate worship is the ministry of many individuals, and God sees each heart. During his times of trial, the psalmist had made vows to God, and now he hastened to fulfill them. He brought many burnt offerings to the altar, the very best he had, and they symbolized his total dedication to the Lord. We today obey Romans 12:1–2 and present ourselves as living sacrifices. When the Lord does something wonderful for us, we ought to share this with other believers and help to strengthen their faith. The entire Bible is a record of God's gracious dealings with His people, and while our words are not inspired, our witness can bring glory to the Lord. Prayer and praise go together (v. 17).

The verb "regard" (v. 18) means "to recognize and to cherish, to be unwilling to confess and forsake known sins." It means approving that which God condemns. When we recognize sin in our hearts, we must immediately judge it, confess it, and forsake it (1 John 1:5–10); otherwise, the Lord can't work on our behalf

(Isa. 59:1–2). To cover sin is to invite trouble and discipline (Prov. 28:13; Josh. 7).

Psalm 67

Except for verses 1 and 6, each verse in this brief psalm mentions "all nations" or "all peoples," and in that respect fits in with Psalms 65 and 66. It's a psalm of praise to God for all His blessings, as well as a prayer to God that His blessings will flow out to the Gentiles, especially His salvation. This was part of God's covenant with Abraham (Gen. 12:1–3). A blessing is a gift from God that glorifies His name, helps His people, and through them reaches out to help others who will glorify His name. God blesses us that we might be a blessing to others. The psalm describes the stages in this sequence.

Israel Blesses the Nations (vv. 1–2)

This prayer asks God to bless Israel so that His ways (laws) and His salvation might be known ("experienced personally") throughout the world. It's adapted from the High Priestly prayer in Numbers 6:24–26, with the psalmist using Elohim instead of Jehovah. (Other references to this prayer are 4:6; 29:11; 31:16; 80:3, 7, 19.) The glory of God was an important part of Israel's heritage (Rom. 9:1–5), for God's glory led Israel through the wilderness and rested over the tabernacle wherever the nation camped. To have the light of God's countenance smile upon them was the height of Israel's blessing, and to lose that glory meant judgment (1 Sam. 4, especially vv. 21–22). The prophet Ezekiel watched the glory depart before the temple was destroyed (Ezek. 8:4; 9:3; 10:4, 18; 11:22–23). God's people today have God's glory within (1 Cor. 6:19–20; 2 Cor. 4:6), and in our good works, godly character, and loving ministry we should reveal that glory to the world (Matt. 5:16; Phil. 2:14–16). In the same manner, Israel was to be a light and a blessing to the nations (Isa. 42:6; 49:6–7; Acts 13:47). Israel gave us the knowledge of the true and living God, the Word of God and the Son of God, Jesus Christ, the Savior of the world.

The Nations Praise the Lord (vv. 3–5)

These three verses form the heart of the psalm and focus on the Gentile nations worshiping and praising the God of Israel. Today, the nations have conspired to dethrone the Lord, and they want nothing of "his ways" (2:1–3), but the day will come when all the nations will come to the mountain of the Lord and worship the God of Jacob (Isa. 2:1–5). The *New International Version* translates these verses as a prayer, "May the peoples praise you … ." When will this occur? When Jesus Christ establishes His kingdom, judges the peoples with justice, and guides ("shepherds"—Mic. 5:2; Matt. 2:6) the nations in the ways of the Lord. The prayer in these verses is the Old Testament equivalent of "Thy kingdom come" in the Lord's Prayer (Matt. 6:9–13). Because there is no king in Israel today, the nations of the world are doing as they please (Judg. 17:6; 18:11; 19:1; 21:25), but that will all change when the kingdoms of the world belong to Jesus Christ (Rev. 11:15).

The Lord Sends the Harvest (vv. 6–7)

What does the harvest have to do with the conversion of the nations of the world? The phrase "Then the land shall yield her increase" (v. 6) is a quotation from Leviticus 26:4, and Leviticus 26 is a summary of God's covenant with Israel. (See also Deut. 28–30.) God made it clear that His blessing on the land depended on Israel's obedience to His law (Lev. 26:1–13). The blessings He would send Israel would be a witness to the pagan nations that Jehovah alone is the true and living God, and this would give the Jews opportunity to share the Word with them (Deut. 28:1–14). But if Israel disobeyed the Lord, He would withhold the rain and their fields would yield no harvest (Lev. 26:14–39), and this would put Israel to shame before the Gentile nations (Jer. 33:1–9; Joel 2:17–19; Deut. 9:26–29). Why would "all the ends of the earth" fear a God who didn't provide food for His own people? The application to the church today is obvious: as we obey the Lord, pray and trust Him, He provides what we need, and the unsaved around us see that He cares for us. This gives us opportunity to tell them about Jesus. While verse 6 speaks of a literal harvest, it also reminds us of the "spiritual harvest" that comes as we witness for the Lord (John 4:34–38).

God blesses the nations through His people Israel and through His church, and all the nations should trust Him, obey Him, and fear Him.

Psalm 68

Read the "Song of Deborah" (Judg. 5) as preparation for studying this psalm, and compare the parallels: Ps. 68:4/Judg. 5:3, 7–8/4–5, 12/30, 13/16, 18/12, and 27/14, 18. The emphasis is on God's mighty acts on behalf of Israel resulting in His decision to dwell on Mount Zion. Several names of God are used, including Elohim (23 times), Jehovah, Jah (short for Jehovah, as in hallelujah, Elijah, etc.), Adonai (6 times), and Shaddai. The psalm is Messianic; Paul quotes verse 18 in Ephesians 4:8 and applies it to the ascension of Christ. The use of "temple" in verse 29 doesn't prohibit Davidic authorship since the word *hekal* was applied to the tabernacle as well (1 Sam. 1:9; 3:3; and see Pss. 5:7; 41:4; 18:6; 27:4; 65:4). The psalm is a jubilant hymn of praise to Jehovah in which the nation of Israel gives four expressions of triumph through their God.

Our God Is Coming to Us (vv. 1–6)

Verse 1 is a quotation from Numbers 10:33–35, Israel's "marching cry" whenever they set out on their journeys. The quotation is fitting because the psalm pictures the Lord "on the march" on behalf of His people. He fights their battles, leads them into the land of their inheritance, and takes up residence in the sanctuary on Mt. Zion. The enemies of Israel are blown away like smoke (37:20) and melted like wax (97:5), while the righteous (Israel) rejoice at God's works and sing His praises. The phrase "extol him who rides upon the heavens" or "upon the clouds" (v. 4 KJV, NIV) should probably read "cast up a highway for him who rides through the deserts" (AMP). It's the picture of an oriental monarch and his entourage approaching a town, and the citizens clearing away the obstacles on the road (Isa. 40:3; 57:14; 62:10; Matt. 3:1–3). The coming of the King encourages the helpless people, especially the orphans and widows, the lonely, and those imprisoned unjustly (vv. 5–6; see Deut. 10:18–19; 27:17–19; Luke 4:16–19). But the rebels had better be careful! They might be cast out of the Promised Land that flows with milk and honey!

Our God Is Marching Before Us (vv. 7–18)

David reviewed the triumphant march of Israel, beginning with their exodus from Egypt and the journey to Sinai (vv. 7–8). (See Ex. 12–19, especially 19:9 and 16.) The rain can be taken literally, but it might also refer to the manna that came down six days a week (Ps. 78:24, 27; Ex. 16:4; Deut. 11:10–12). Then Israel entered the land and conquered it (vv. 9–14) because the Lord spoke the Word of victory (v. 11; see 33:11). He had promised Israel they would take the land, and they did (Ex. 23:20–33; Deut. 11:22–32). As at the Exodus (Ex. 15:20–21), it was the women who sang the praises of the Lord. (See also v. 25, Judg. 5 and 1 Sam. 18:6–7.) Students have long been puzzled by verses 13–14 and don't always agree on either their translations or their interpretations. There appears to be a reference to the "Song of Deborah" in Judges 5:15–18 where she shamed Reuben for staying home and not fighting the enemy, but praised Benjamin, Zebulun, and Naphtali for joining in the battle. These three tribes are commended in 68:27, but we don't know of any tribes that failed to participate in the conquering of Canaan. The *New Living Translation* interprets verses 12–14: "Enemy kings and their armies flee, while the women of Israel divide the plunder. Though they lived among the sheepfolds, now they are covered with silver and gold, as a dove is covered by its wings. The Almighty scattered the enemy kings like a blowing snowstorm on Mount Zalmon." Israel is compared to a turtledove in 74:19.

But God conquered Canaan, not only to give His people a home but also to secure a "home" for Himself. He chose Mount Zion, though it was much smaller and less imposing than Mount

Hermon, which is over 9,000 feet high, perhaps the highest mountain in Palestine. David pictured the other mountains showing jealousy because they weren't selected. God made a temporary visit to His people when He came down on Mount Sinai (Ex. 23:16), but Zion was to be His permanent dwelling place (132:13–14; 1 Kings 8:12–13). The "chariots of God" make up His heavenly army, for He is the Lord of Hosts (46:7, 11; 2 Kings 2:11; 6:17; Dan. 7:10; Matt. 26:53). To "ascend on high" means to win the victory and return in triumph (47:1–6). Some think this refers to a time when the ark was "in the field" with the army and then brought back to the sanctuary on Zion (2 Sam. 11:11; 12:26–31). Paul quoted verse 18 in Ephesians 4:8 when referring to the ascension of Christ (see also Acts 2:30–36; Col. 2:15). A king ascending the throne both receives and gives gifts, and even those who reject him will honor him outwardly.

Our God Is Dwelling with Us (vv. 19–27)

David saw the Lord's presence on Zion as a blessing first of all to those who were burdened and in danger. Jehovah our King bears our burdens and defeats our enemies. Certainly David saw the Lord win great victories for Israel so that the borders of the kingdom were greatly enlarged. "Hairy crowns" (v. 21) signifies the virile enemy warriors who trusted in their youth and strength. The enemy may flee, but the Lord will chase them down and bring them back from the tops of the mountains and the depths of the sea, from the east (Bashan) and the west (the sea). (See Amos 9:1–3.) The picture in verse 23 isn't a pretty one, but "dogs licking blood" was a common phrase for the most complete kind of judgment and humiliation (58:10; 1 Kings 21:17–24; 2 Kings 9:30–37).

The King now receives the homage of His people who gladly say, "My God, My King." (vv. 24–27). Both men and women, lay people and priests, join in praising the Lord. Zion was situated at the border of Judah and Benjamin; David came from Judah and King Saul from Benjamin. As the youngest of the sons of Jacob, and perhaps as the tribe of Israel's first king, Benjamin leads the procession along with the leaders of Judah (representing the southern tribes), and the leaders of Zebulun and Naphtali (the northern tribes). Israel is a united people, praising the Lord. "Fountain of Israel" (v. 26) refers to the Lord (NASB, and see 36:9) or the patriarchs, especially Jacob (AMP).

Our God Receives Universal Tribute (vv. 28–35)

This closing section has prophetic overtones as it describes the Gentile nations submitting to Jehovah, the God of Israel, and bringing Him their worship (Isa. 2:1–4; Rev. 21:24). Until the Lord reigns in Jerusalem, there can be no peace on earth (Isa. 9:6–7; 11:1–9). God will defeat Israel's old enemy Egypt, along with her allies (see Ezek. 29), and they will send envoys to Jerusalem with tribute. The Gentile nations will join Israel in singing praises to the Lord and extolling His majesty and power. Perhaps the sanctuary of verse 35 is the one described in Ezekiel 40–48. It certainly is awesome!

Psalm 69

This is a Messianic psalm, an imprecatory psalm, and after 22 and 110, the most frequently quoted psalm in the New Testament. It is attributed to David and has definite affinities with 35, 40, and 109, which are also Davidic psalms. But what about verses 35–36? When during David's reign did the cities of Judah need to be rebuilt and the people brought back home? When were the drunkards singing about him in the gates (v. 12) and his enemies about to destroy him (vv. 4, 18–19)? Selected data from the psalm fits the times of both Jeremiah and Hezekiah, but it is difficult to fit everything into the times of David. Perhaps David's original psalm ended at verse 29 and the Holy Spirit directed the prophet Jeremiah to add verses 30–36 after the fall of Judah and Jerusalem to the Babylonians. The collection of psalms was a "living heritage" and some of the psalms were adapted to new occasions. Whatever the answer, when you read the psalm, you find the author confronting the Lord with three important concerns.

Deliverance: "Save Me!" (vv. 1–18)

He begins by asking for deliverance for *his own sake (vv. 1–5)* and describes his dangerous situation with the metaphor of a drowning man. (See 18:4–6; 30:1; 32:6; 42:7; 88:7, 17; 130:1–2.) His cries to God show how desperate the situation was: "Save me" (v. 1); "deliver me" (v. 14); "hear [answer] me" (vv. 16–17); "redeem [rescue] me" (v. 18); "set me up on high [protect me]" (v. 29). He had prayed to the Lord, but the Lord had not yet answered (v. 3), and he wanted an answer now! (v. 17). Though he was not sinless (v. 5), he was innocent of the charges his enemies were making, and yet he was being treated as though he were guilty (v. 4). This reminds us of our Savior, who was sinless yet treated like a transgressor (Isa. 53:5–6, 9, 12). (See also 35:11–19; 38:19; 109:3; 119:78, 86, 161.) Jesus quoted verse 4 in the upper room discourse (John 15:25). Referring to verses 1–2, Amy Carmichael wrote, "Our waters are shallow because His were deep." How true!

His second reason for praying for deliverance was *for the Lord's sake (vv. 6–12)*, because those who lied about David were blaspheming the name of the Lord. David did not want God's people to suffer shame because of him (v. 6; see 25:3; 38:15–16). The word "reproach" (scorn, insults) is used six times in the psalm (vv. 7, 9, 10, 19,20). He was scorned because he stood up for the Lord (v. 7) and because he was zealous for God's house (v. 9). He even alienated his own family (v. 8; see John 7:5; Mark 3:31–35), and the insults that people threw at the Lord also fell on him (v. 9; John 2:17; Rom. 15:3; and see Isa. 56:7 and Jer. 7:11). When they blasphemed God, they blasphemed David, and their attacks against David were attacks against God, and David felt them. David had a great zeal for God's house and received the plans for the temple from the Lord and gathered the materials for its construction. It takes no special gift to discover Jesus in this psalm and to see the way people treated Him when He was ministering on earth.

His third argument for deliverance is based on *the character of God (vv. 13–18)*. What the Lord said to Moses in Exodus 34:5–9 is reflected here. In verses 14 and 15, David repeats the metaphor from verses 1–2, but he sees hope in God's lovingkindness and compassion, for the Lord is merciful and gracious. His truth endures and He will always keep His promises.

Vindication: "Judge My Enemies!" (vv. 19–29)

David told the Lord that his foes had dishonored and insulted him to the point that he was physically ill (vv. 19–21). When he looked for sympathy, none was to be found (Matt. 26:37), and his food and drink were unfit for human consumption (v. 21; Matt. 27:34, 48; Mark 15:23, 36; Luke 23:36; John 19:29). Then David prayed that the Lord would judge his enemies and give them what they deserved (vv. 22–29). (For a discussion of this type of prayer, see the comments on Ps. 5.) The enemy had put gall and vinegar on David's table, so he prayed that their tables would turn into traps. This meant that judgment would catch them unprepared in their careless hours of feasting (1 Thess. 5:3). It could also apply to the feasts associated with the sacrifices. While rejoicing after worship, they would experience God's judgment. In Romans 11:9–10, Paul applied verses 22–23 to Israel whose religious complacency ("We just sacrificed to the Lord!") only led to spiritual blindness. In verses 22–25, David prayed that some of the basic blessings of life would be taken away from his enemies—eating, seeing, walking, and having descendants—and then that life itself would be snatched from them! (vv. 27–28). In Acts 1:20, Peter applied verse 25 to Judas.

David asked in verse 28 that his enemies be slain, blotted out of the book of the living. Even more, he didn't want them identified with the righteous after they died, which meant they were destined for eternal judgment. While this kind of prayer is hardly an example for God's people today (Matt. 6:12; Luke 23:34), we can understand David's hatred of their sins and his desire to protect Israel and its mission in the world.

Praise: "Be Glorified, O Lord!" (vv. 30–36)

Perhaps this is a promise David made to the Lord, and no doubt he fulfilled it. He wanted the Lord to be glorified in his worship (vv. 30–31), his witness to the needy (vv. 32–33), in all of creation (v. 34), and in all of Israel (vv. 35–36). He asked the Lord to protect and provide for the poor whom the sinners were abusing and exploiting. He saw a day coming when the land would be united and healed and the cities populated again. "Pray for the peace of Jerusalem" (122:6). "Even so, come, Lord Jesus!" (Rev. 22:21).

Psalm 70
With a few minor changes, this is a duplicate of 40:13–16.

Psalm 71
The psalm is anonymous, written by a believer who had enemies and needed the Lord's help and protection (vv. 4, 10, 13, 24). He was probably past middle age and was greatly concerned about the burdens of old age (vv. 9, 18). He wanted to end well. From birth he had been sustained by the Lord (v. 6), and in his youth he had been taught by the Lord (v. 17). He may have been one of the many temple musicians assigned to praise God in the sanctuary day and night (vv. 22–24; 134:1). Whoever he was, he made four affirmations about the Lord and the help He gives to those who call on him and trust him.

"The Lord Helps Me Now" (vv. 1–4)
The first three verses are adapted from 31:1–3, a perfectly legitimate practice among psalmists. This writer borrowed from 22, 31, 35, and 40, to name just a few of his sources. On verse 1, see 7:1, 11:1, 16:1, 22:5, 25:2 and 20, and 31:17. (On the image of the rock, see 18:2.) If the author was indeed a temple musician, his mind and heart would have been filled with the psalms that he had sung in the sanctuary day after day. He asked the Lord to protect and deliver him so that he might remain true to the faith and not be ashamed (1 John 2:28). During the decadent years of the kingdom of Judah, some of the rulers promoted worshiping idols along with the worship of Jehovah and pressured the Levites to compromise. The writer didn't want to run away and hide from life but receive the strength needed to face life

with its challenges. The Lord was his habitation (90:1) and his help. "Righteousness" is mentioned five times in the psalm (vv. 2, 15, 16, 19, 24) and refers not only to one of God's attributes but also to His faithfulness in keeping His word. A righteous God is active in helping His people in their times of need. He issues the command and the deed is done (v. 3; 33:9; 44:4; 68:28). His people can always come to Him (v. 3; Heb. 10:19–25), always praise Him (vv. 6, 8, 15, 24), and always hope in Him (v. 14). He never fails. Perhaps verse 4 describes evil people who exploited the poor and helpless, which could include the Levites, who had no inheritance in Israel but lived by the gifts of God's people (Deut. 10:8–9; Num. 18:20–24). They served from age twenty-five to age fifty (Num. 8:23–26), so perhaps our psalmist was approaching retirement age and was concerned about his future.

"The Lord Helped Me in the Past" (vv. 5–13)

When you are discouraged and worried, look back and count your blessings. Remind yourself of the faithfulness of the Lord. Like Samuel erect your own "Ebenezer" and say, "Thus far the Lord has helped us" (1 Sam. 7:12 NASB). From conception to birth, and from birth to young manhood, the Lord had been with the psalmist, and He was not about to abandon him now or in his old age (22:9–10; 37:25; 92:14; 139:13–16). Hope doesn't end with retirement! (vv. 5, 15). (See 1 Tim. 1:1; Col. 1:27; Heb. 6:18–19; 1 Peter 1:3.)

The word "portent" means a sign or wonder, a special display of God's power, such as the plagues of Egypt. Sometimes the Lord selected special people to be signs to the nation (Isa. 8:18; Zech. 3:8), and sometimes those portents were messengers of warning (Deut. 28:45–48). Paul saw himself and the other apostles as "portents" to honor the Lord and shame the worldly believers (1 Cor. 4:8–13). The writer of this psalm must have been a high profile person because people knew him well and saw the things that happened to him. Apparently he had endured many troubles during his life but didn't falter or deny the Lord. His entire life was a wonder, a testimony to others of the goodness and faithfulness of the Lord (vv. 20–2 1). His enemies were sure the Lord would forsake him, but he was sure the Lord would *never* forsake him (Heb. 13:5). His enemies tried to bring reproach on him, but he trusted the Lord to uphold him and to turn their reproach back upon them.

"The Lord Will Help Me in the Future" (vv. 14–21)

The psalmist looked to the future and moved from "You are my hope" (v. 8) to "I will hope continually" (v. 14; see 36:5; 47:10). The future is secure when Jesus is your Lord. The word translated "hope" in verse 14 means a long and patient waiting in spite of delays and disappointments. If we trust God, then the trials of life will work for us and not against us and will lead to glory (2 Cor. 4:16–18; Rom. 5:1–5). We admire the psalmist's "But as for me" in verse 14 (NIV, NASB) because it reveals his courage and commitment. Others may drift with the crowd and deny the Lord, but he would continue to be faithful and bear witness of God's mercies. He couldn't begin to measure or count the Lord's righteous acts or "deeds of salvation" (v. 15 AMP), but he would never stop praising the Lord, especially in old age. Why? Because he wanted to tell the next generation what the Lord could do for them (v. 18; see 48:13; 78:4, 6; 79:13; 102:18; 145:4; 2 Tim. 2:2).

He was even certain that death would not separate him from his God (vv. 19–21). Some believe that the phrase "depths of the earth" is a metaphor for the troubles he had experienced ("buried under trouble"), but his trials were pictured in verses 1–2 as floods of water. Also, some texts read "us" instead of "me," which could refer to the future "resurrection" and restoration of the nation of Israel (80:3, 19; 85:4; Ezek. 37). Perhaps both personal (16:8–11; 17:15; 49:15) and national resurrection are involved. No matter what his enemies had said about him, the day would come when God would honor him and reward him.

"The Lord Be Praised for His Help!" (vv. 22–24)

The writer was a poet, a singer, and an instrumentalist, and he used all his gifts to praise the Lord. The divine name "Holy One of Israel" is used thirty times in Isaiah but only three times in the

Psalms (71:22; 78:41; 89:18). The name connects with the emphasis in the psalm on God's righteousness. "Shall not the judge of all the earth do right?" (Gen. 18:25). The psalmist sang and shouted all day long (vv. 24, 8), not just during the stated services at the temple. He opened the psalm with a request that he would never be put to shame and confusion, and now he closed the psalm with the assurance that *his enemies* would be put to shame and confusion! He had looked back at a life of trials and blessings from the Lord; he had looked around at his enemies; he had looked ahead at old age and its problems; and he had even looked down into the depths of the earth (v. 20). But it was when he looked up and realized that God's righteousness "reaches to the heavens" (v. 19 NASB; see 36:5; 57:10; 108:4) that he grew in confidence and left his worries with the Lord. This is a good example for us to follow.

Psalm 72

Solomon is connected with this psalm and 127. If the inscription is translated "of Solomon," then he was the author and wrote of himself in the third person. This would make it a prayer for God's help as he sought to rule over the people of Israel. But if the inscription is translated "for Solomon," David may have been the author (v. 20), and the psalm would be a prayer for the people to use to ask God's blessing upon their new king. If Solomon did write the psalm, then it had to be in the early years of his reign, for in his later years, he turned from the Lord (1 Kings 11; Prov. 14:34). But beyond both David and Solomon is the Son of David and the one "greater than Solomon" (Matt. 12:42), Jesus Christ, the Messiah of Israel. The psalm is quoted nowhere in the New Testament as referring to Jesus, but certainly it describes the elements that will make up the promised kingdom when Jesus returns.

A Righteous King (vv. 1–7)

The Lord was King over His people, and the man on the throne in Jerusalem was His representative, obligated to lead the people according to the law of God (Deut. 17:14–20). He had to be impartial in his dealings (Ex. 23:3, 6; Deut. 1:17; Isa. 16:5) and make sure that his throne was founded on righteousness and justice (89:14; 92:2). When the Lord asked Solomon what coronation gift he wanted, the inexperienced young man asked for wisdom, and God granted His request (1 Kings 3:1–15). One of his first judgmental decisions revealed this wisdom (1 Kings 3:16–28). Note that righteousness is mentioned four times in verses 1–3 and 7, and see Proverbs 16:12. Messiah will one day reign in righteousness and execute justice throughout the world (Isa. 9:7 and 11:4–5; Jer. 23:5–6; Zech. 9:9). In the whole land of Israel, from the mountains to the hills, Solomon's reign would bring peace and prosperity, for both of these blessings depend on righteousness (Isa. 32:17). It is because Jesus fulfilled God's righteousness in His life and death that sinners can be forgiven and have peace with God (Rom. 5:1–8), and He is our "King of righteousness" and "King of peace" (Heb. 7:1–3). Solomon's name is related to the Hebrew word *shalom* which means "peace, prosperity, well-being." The king's ministry to the poor and afflicted reminds us of the ministry of Jesus (vv. 2, 4, 12–14; Matt. 9:35–38). Early in his reign, Solomon had that kind of concern, but in his later life, his values changed, and he burdened the people with heavy taxes (1 Kings 12:1–16; 4:7; 5:13–15).

"Long live the king!" is the burden of verses 5 and 15, as long as the sun and moon endure (89:29, 36–37; 1 Sam. 10:24; 1 Kings 1:31, 34, 39; Dan. 2:4). God promised David an endless dynasty (2 Sam. 7:16, 19,26), and this was fulfilled in Jesus, the Son of David (Luke 1:31–33). The image of the rain (vv. 6–7) reminds us that a righteous king would encourage righteousness in the people, and a righteous people would receive God's promised blessings, according to His covenant (Lev. 26:1–13; Deut. 11:11–17; 28:8–14). David used a similar metaphor in 2 Samuel 23:34. Godly leaders are like the refreshing rain that makes the land fruitful and beautiful, so that even the newly mown fields will produce a second crop. They are also like lamps that light the way (2 Sam. 21:17), shields that protect (84:9;

89:16), and the very breath of life that sustains us (Lam. 4:20). Alas, very few of the kings who reigned after David were models of godliness.

A Universal Dominion (vv. 8–11)

God promised Abraham that he would give his descendants all the land from the River of Egypt in the south to the Euphrates in the north (Gen. 15:18), and He reaffirmed this promise through Moses (Ex. 23:31). Both David and Solomon ruled over great kingdoms (1 Kings 4:21, 24; 1 Chron. 9:26), but neither of them ruled "from the river [Euphrates] to the ends of the earth" (v. 8). This privilege is reserved for Jesus Christ (2:8; Zech. 9:9–10; Mic. 4:1–5; Luke 1:33). David gained the kingdom through conquest, and left it to his son who strengthened it by means of treaties. His marriages to the daughters of neighboring kings were guarantees that these nations would cooperate with Solomon's foreign policy. Even Sheba and the nomadic tribes in Arabia would pay tribute to Solomon, and so would Seba in Upper Egypt; and kings as far away as Tarshish in Spain would submit to him. (See 1 Kings 4:21, 34; 10:14–15, 24–25; 2 Chron. 9:23–24.) But there is only one King of kings, and that is Jesus Christ, the Son of God (Isa. 2:1–4; Dan. 7:13–14; Rev. 17:14; 19:16). There can be no peace on earth until the Prince of Peace is reigning, and the nations have submitted to Him.

A Compassionate Reign (vv. 12–14).

The king of Israel was looked upon as God's shepherd who lovingly cared for God's flock (78:70–72; 100:3; Ezek. 34). Any citizen had access to the king to get help in solving legal problems, and the king was to make certain that the local judges were being fair and honest in their decisions. Solomon didn't reach this ideal even though he had a vast bureaucracy, but unfortunately his officers didn't always aid the people (Eccl. 4:1). The picture here is surely that of our Savior who had such great compassion for the needy and met their needs (Matt. 9:3 6). Not only does He hold their blood (life) precious to Him (v. 14; 116:15), but He shed His own precious blood for the salvation of the world (1 Peter 1:19). The word "redeem" ("rescue" NASB, NIV) is used for the "kinsman redeemer" illustrated by Boaz in the book of Ruth.

A Prosperous Nation (vv. 15–17)

God's covenant with Israel assured them of prosperity so long as the rulers and the people obeyed His commandments. The Lord also assured David that he would always have an heir to his throne if he and his descendants obeyed God's will (2 Sam. 7:11–12, 16). Because of the promise of the coming Savior, it was important that the Davidic dynasty continue. But in the case of Jesus, He reigns "according to the power of an endless life" (Heb. 7:16). He is the life (John 14:6) and He is alive forever (Rev. 1:18). He is King forever!

Israel's prosperity would be not only political (the king), but also economic (gold), spiritual (prayer), and commercial (thriving crops). In fulfillment of His covenant with Abraham (Gen. 12:1–3), God would bless all the nations through Israel, as He has done in sending Jesus Christ (Gal. 3). The prophets wrote of this glorious kingdom and their prophecies will be fulfilled (Isa. 35 and 60–62; Ezek. 40–48; Amos 9:11–15; Mic. 4; Zech. 10 and 14). There will be abundant grain even on top of the hills in the most unproductive land. The grain fields will look like the forests of the cedars in Lebanon (1 Kings 4:33).

The closing benediction (vv. 18–19) is not a part of the psalm proper but forms the conclusion to Book II of the book of Psalms (see 41:13; 89:52; 106:48). A fitting conclusion it is, for it focuses on the glory of the Lord. Solomon's kingdom had its share of glory, but the glory did not last. When Jesus reigns on earth, the glory of God will be revealed as never before (Num. 14:21; Isa. 6:3; 11:9; 40:5; Hab. 2:14).

Isaac Watts used Psalm 72 as the basis for his great hymn "Jesus Shall Reign." Read it—or sing it—and never stop praying, "Thy kingdom come!"

FOUR

Book III

Psalm 73

Asaph, Heman, and Ethan (Jeduthun) were Levites who served as musicians and worship leaders at the sanctuary during David's reign (1 Chron. 15:16–19; 16:4–7, 37–42; 2 Chron. 5:12–14; 29:13; 35:15). Apparently they established "guilds" for their sons and other musicians so they might carry on the worship traditions. Twelve psalms are attributed to Asaph (50, 73–83). This one deals with the age-old problem of why the righteous suffer while the ungodly seem to prosper (37; 49; Job 21; Jer. 12; Hab. 1:13ff). Asaph could not lead the people in divine worship if he had questions about the ways of the Lord, but he found in that worship the answer to his problems. Note five stages in his experience.

The Believer: Standing on What He Knows (v.1)

The French mystic Madame Guyon wrote, "In the commencement of the spiritual life, our hardest task is to bear with our neighbor; in its progress, with ourselves; and in the end, with God." Asaph's problems were with God. Asaph affirmed "God is," so he was not an atheist or an agnostic, and he was certain that the God he worshiped was good. Furthermore, he knew that the Lord had made a covenant with Israel that promised blessings if the people obeyed Him (Lev. 26; Deut. 28–30). The phrase "a clean [pure] heart" means, not sinlessness, but total commitment to the Lord, the opposite of verse 27. (See 24:4 and Matt. 5:8.) But it was these foundational beliefs he stated that created the problem for him, because unbelievers don't face problems of this sort. If the Lord was good and kept His covenant promises, why were His people suffering and the godless prospering? This first verse marked both the beginning and the end of his meditations. He came full circle. Note that he used "surely" or "truly" in verses 1, 13, and 18, and that "heart" is used six times in the psalm (vv. 1, 7, 13, 21, 26). When pondering the mysteries of life, hold on to what you know for sure, and never doubt in the darkness what God has taught you in the light.

The Doubter: Slipping from Where He Is Standing (vv. 2–3)

The Hebrew word translated "but" in verses 2 and 28, and "nevertheless" (yet) in verse 28, indicates a sharp contrast. In verse 2, the more he measured his situation against that of the ungodly, the more he began to slip from his firm foundation. There is a difference between doubt and unbelief. Doubt comes from a struggling mind, while unbelief comes from a stubborn will that refuses surrender to God (v. 7). The unbelieving person *will not believe*, while the doubting person struggles to believe but cannot. "Prosperity" in verse 3 is the familiar Hebrew word *shalom*. It's an act of disobedience to envy the wicked (37:1; Prov. 3:31; 23:17; 24:1, 19).

The Wrestler: Struggling with What He Sees and Feels (vv. 4–14)

From Asaph's viewpoint, the ungodly "had it made." They were healthy (vv. 4–5) and had no struggles in either life or death (Job 21:13,23). They were proud of their wealth and stations in life, and they wore that pride like jewelry. They used violence to get their wealth and wore that violence like rich garments. Like an overflowing river, their hard hearts and evil minds produced endless ideas for getting richer, and they frequently spoke words of opposition against the Lord in heaven. The words of the arrogant would "strut through the land" and take possession of whatever they wanted. But the greatest tragedy is that many of God's people don't seem to know any better but follow their bad example and enjoy their friendship! (v. 10). These ungodly men are sinning, but their foolish followers are "drinking it all up." (For drinking as a metaphor for sinning, see Job 15:16; 34:7; Prov. 4:17; 19:28; Rev. 14:8.) To encourage their hard hearts and quiet their evil consciences, the wicked affirmed that God didn't know what they were doing (Ps. 10).

Based on the evidence he could see around him, Asaph came to the wrong conclusion that he has wasted his time and energy maintaining clean hands and a pure heart (vv. 13 and 1, and see 24:4 and 26:6). If he had ever read the book of Job, then he had missed its message, for we don't serve God because of what we get out of it but because *He is worthy of our worship and service regardless of what He allows to come to our lives.* Satan has a commercial view of the life of faith and encourages us to serve God for what we get out of it (Job 1–2), and Asaph almost bought into that philosophy. (See also Dan. 3:16–18.)

The Worshiper: Seeing the Bigger Picture (vv. 15–22)

Before going public with his philosophy and resigning his office, Asaph paused to consider the consequences. How would the younger believers in the land respond if one of the three sanctuary worship leaders turned his back on Jehovah, the covenants, and the faith? To abandon the faith would mean undermining all that he had taught and sung at the sanctuary! The more he pondered the problem, the more his heart was pained (see vv. 21–22), So he decided to go to the sanctuary and spend time with the Lord in worship. There he would be with other people, hear the Word and the songs of praise, and be a part of the worshiping community. After all, Jehovah isn't a problem to wrestle with but a gracious Person to love and worship—especially when you are perplexed by what he is doing.

God is awesome in His sanctuary (68:35 NIV), and when we commune with Him, we see the things of this world in their right perspective.

Asaph did get a new perspective on the problem when he considered, not the circumstances around him but the destiny before him. He realized that what he saw in the lives of the prosperous, ungodly people was not a true picture but only pretense: "you will despise them as fantasies" (v. 20 NIV). In New Testament language, "the world is passing away, and the lust of it ..." (1 John 2:17 NKJV). Although God can and does give success and wealth to dedicated believers, worldly success and prosperity belong to the transient dream world of unbelievers, a dream that one day will become a nightmare. (See Luke 12:16–21.) Asaph was humbled before the Lord and regained his spiritual balance.

The Conqueror: Rejoicing over God's Goodness (vv. 23–28)

The psalm opened with "Truly God is good to Israel," but Asaph wasn't sure what the word "good" really meant. (See Matt. 19:16–17.) Is the "good life" one of wealth and authority, pomp and pleasure? Surely not! The contrast is striking between Asaph's picture of the godless life in verses 4–12 and the godly life in verses 23–28. The ungodly impress each other and attract admirers, but they don't have God's presence with them. The Lord upholds the righteous but casts down the wicked (v. 18). The righteous are guided by God's truth (v. 24) but the ungodly are deluded by their own fantasies. The destiny of the true believers is glory (v. 24), but the destiny of the unbelievers is destruction (vv. 19, 27). "Those who are far from You shall perish" (AMP). The ungodly have everything they want except God, and the godly have in God all that they want or need. He is their portion forever (see 16:2). The possessions of the ungodly are but idols that take the place of the Lord, and idolatry is harlotry (Ex. 34:15–16; 1 Chron. 5:25). Even death cannot separate God's people from His blessing, for the spirit goes to heaven to be with the Lord, and the body waits in the earth for resurrection (vv. 25–26; 2 Cor. 5:1–8; 1 Thess. 4:13–18).

When the worship service ended and Asaph had gotten his feet firmly grounded on the faith, he left the sanctuary and told everybody what he had learned. He had drawn near to God, he had trusted God, and now he was ready to declare God's works. "Yet in all these things we are more than conquerors through Him who loved us" (Rom. 8:37 NKJV).

Psalm 74

Psalm 73 deals with a personal crisis of faith, but Psalm 74 moves to the national scene and focuses on the destruction of the temple in Jerusalem by the Babylonians in 587–86 B.C. The author is obviously not the Asaph of David's day but a namesake among his descendants. Psalm 79 is a companion psalm, and you will find parallel passages in the book of Lamentations (4/2:6–7; 7/2:2; 9/2:6, 9) and Jeremiah (6–7/10:25; 1, 13/23:1). Even though the prophets had warned that judgment was coming (2 Chron. 36:15–21), the fall of Jerusalem and the destruction of the temple were catastrophic events that shook the people's faith. As he surveyed the situation, Asaph moved from despair to confidence and in the end affirmed that all was not lost.

The Sanctuary: "The Lord Has Rejected Us!" (vv. 1–11)

This was a logical conclusion anyone would draw from beholding what the Babylonians did to the city and the temple (Lam. 5:20–22). But the Lord had promised not to abandon His people (Deut. 4:29–31; 26:18–19), for they were His precious flock (77:20; 78:52; 79:13; 100:3; Num. 27:17), and He was the Shepherd of Israel (80:1). Israel was the tribe of His inheritance, and the future of the Messianic promise depended on their survival. (The Authorized Version reads "rod" in v. 2, and the word can also be translated "scepter." Num. 17 shows the connection between rods and tribes.) He had redeemed them from Egypt and made them His inheritance (Ex. 19:5; 34:9; Deut. 32:9), and He had come to dwell with them on Mt. Zion. The word "remember" (v. 2) doesn't mean "call to mind," because it's impossible for God to forget anything. It means "to go to work on behalf of someone."

Why did God permit a pagan nation to defeat the Jews and destroy their holy city and sacred temple, and why was He doing nothing about it?

The people of Judah thought that the presence of the temple was their guarantee of security no matter how they lived, but the prophet Jeremiah refuted that lie (Jer. 7). Jeremiah even used the phrase "everlasting (perpetual) ruins" (v. 3; Jer. 25:9) and warned that the temple would be destroyed and the nation taken into captivity. Many times in the past, God had intervened to save Israel, but now He seemed to be doing nothing. Asaph prayed, "Lift up your feet! Take your hand out of your garment! Get up and plead our cause!" (vv. 1, 11, 22). Do something!

Shouting their battle cries, the Babylonian soldiers brought their pagan ensigns into the holy precincts of the temple and began to chop at the gold-covered panels of the walls (see 1 Kings 6:18–22). The sanctuary was where God had met with His people (Ex. 29:42), yet He didn't come when they needed Him. The word "synagogues" in verse 8 (KJV) means "meeting places," for there were no synagogues until after the Jews returned to their land following the captivity. There was only one temple and one altar for sacrifices, but there must have been other places where the people met to be taught the Scriptures and to pray. Babylon was determined to show its power over the God of Israel. God's messengers had already warned the leaders and the people that judgment was coming, but they refused to listen. Therefore, the Lord didn't raise up any new prophets (Lam. 2:9). As far as the captivity was concerned, the question "How long?" (vv. 9–10) was answered by Jeremiah (25; 29:10). As far as the length of Babylon's destroying and disgracing Israel's capital city and temple, there was no answer. The people felt that they were cast off forever (v. 1), desolate forever (v. 3), humiliated forever (v. 10), and forgotten forever (v. 19). If we had been there, perhaps we might have felt the same way.

The Throne: "The Lord Reigns!" (vv. 12–17)

Verse 12 is the central verse of the psalm and the turning point in Asaph's experience. He lifted his eyes by faith from the burning ruins to the holy throne of God in the heavens and received a new perspective on the situation. (The Asaph who wrote 73 had a similar experience. See 73:17.) No matter how discouraging his situation was, Asaph knew that God was still on the throne and had not abdicated His authority to the Babylonians. Jeremiah came to the same conclusion (Lam. 5:19) "Thou/You" is the important pronoun in this paragraph. God brings "salvations" (plural) on the earth (v. 12; see 44:4), so Asaph reviewed the "salvation works" of God in the past. The Lord orchestrated Israel's exodus and the defeat of the "monster" Egypt (vv. 13–14; Ex. 12–15). He provided water in the wilderness (15a; Ex. 17; Num. 20) and opened the Jordan River so Israel could enter Canaan (15b; Josh. 3–4). Asaph even reached back to creation (v. 16; compare 136:7–9; Gen. 1–2) and the assignment of territory to the nations (v. 17a; Gen. 10–11; Acts 17:26). What a mighty God! What a mighty King! When the outlook is bleak, try the uplook.

The Covenant: "The Lord Remembers Us!" (vv. 18–23)

Since righteousness and justice are the foundation of His throne (89:14), it was logical for Asaph to move in his thoughts from God's throne to God's covenant with Israel (Lev. 26; Deut. 28–30). Asaph knew the terms of the covenant: if Israel obeyed the Lord, He would bless them; if they disobeyed, He would chasten them; if they confessed their sins, He would forgive them. If the Babylonians were mocking the Lord as they destroyed the city and temple, the Jews had mocked the prophets that God sent to them to turn them from their idolatry (2 Chron. 36:16). Israel had not honored God's name but had turned His temple into a den of thieves (Jer. 7:11). Asaph saw the nation as a defenseless dove that had no way of escape. Had the kings and leaders listened to their prophets and led the nation back to the Lord, all this carnage and destruction would have been averted. *But the Lord was paying attention to His covenant!* That was why He was chastening His people. Asaph was concerned about the glory of God's name and the survival of God's people. It was

243

God's cause that was uppermost in His mind. The prophet Jeremiah had preached about the dependability of God's covenant (Jer. 33:19–26), and Asaph was asking God to fulfill His purposes for the nation.

The nation had been ravaged, the city of Jerusalem had been wrecked, and the temple had been destroyed and burned—*but the essentials had not been touched by the enemy!* The nation still had Jehovah God as their God, His Word and His covenant had not been changed, and Jehovah was at work in the world! God is at work in our world today, and we need not despair.

Psalm 75

This psalm by Asaph may be read as the "digest" of a worship service called to thank the Lord for what He had done for His people. Because of the warning against boasting (vv. 4–7), some students associate the psalm with King Hezekiah and Jerusalem's deliverance from the Assyrian invaders (Isa. 36–3 7). They also associate 76, 77, and 78 with that great event. Sennacherib's officers certainly boasted about their achievements, but when the right time came, God destroyed the Assyrian army encamped around Mt. Zion. The tune "Destroy Not" is used with 57, 58, and 59. Now let's go to the worship service.

We Begin with an Invocation of Praise (v. 1)

True worship centers on the Lord and not on us, our personal problems, or our "felt needs." We praise God for who He is— His glorious attributes—and for His wonderful works (see 44:1–8; 77:12; 107:8, 15). God's name is a synonym for God's person and presence (Deut. 4:7; Isa. 30:27). He is indeed "a very present help in trouble" (46:1), and when God's people call on the Lord, they know He will hear them. We thank the Lord for all He has done and we tell others about His wonderful works. Though God wants us to bring our burdens to Him and seek His help, worship begins with getting our eyes of faith off the circumstances of life and focusing them on the Lord God Almighty.

We Hear the Lord's Message (vv. 2–5)

If we expect the Lord to receive our words of praise, we must pay attention to His Word of truth as it is read, sung, and preached. The message delivered here was twofold: a word of encouragement for believers (vv. 2–3) and a word of warning to the godless (vv. 4–5). As we see the wicked prosper in their evil deeds, we often ask God "How long?" (See 10:6; 74:9–10; 79:5; 89:46; 94:34; and Rev. 6:9–11.) God assured His people that He had already chosen the appointed time for judgment and that His people could wait in confidence and peace because He had everything under control. The Lord has His times and seasons (102:13; Acts 1:7), and He is never late to an appointment. It may seem to us that the foundations of society are being destroyed (11:3; 82:5), and the "pillars" of morality are falling down, but the Lord knows what He is doing (46:6; 1 Sam. 2:8). Jesus Christ is on the throne and holds everything together (Col. 1:17; Heb. 1:3).

But there is also a message for the godless (vv. 4–5), and it warns them not to be arrogant and deliberately disobey the will of God. Before it lowers its head and attacks, a horned beast proudly lifts its head high and challenges its opponent, and the ungodly were following this example. The Hebrew word translated "lift up" is used five times in this psalm (vv. 4, 5, 6, 7, 10), and in verses 4–5, it is associated with arrogance that leads to trouble. A "stiff neck" and proud speech are marks of an insolent and rebellious person, not one who is bowed down in submission to the Lord (Deut. 31:27; 2 Kings 17:14; 2 Chron. 36:13; Jer. 7:26).

We Apply God's Message Personally (vv. 6–8)

How easy it is to hear God's message, leave the meeting, and then forget to obey what we heard! The blessing doesn't come in the hearing but in the *doing* of God's Word (James 1:22–25). The word translated "lifted up" or "exalted" in verses 6, 7, and 19 has to do with God delivering His people from trouble and setting them free. ("Promotion" in v. 6 KJV has nothing to do with getting a better job or being highly publicized.) The arrogant were lifting themselves up only to be cast down by God, but the humble wait on the Lord and He lifts them up (1 Peter 5:6). A Jew could search in any direction—east, west, or the desert (south, Egypt)—and he would never find anybody who can do what only God can do. Why is north omitted? To look in that direction would mean seeking help from the enemies, Assyria and Babylon! (See Jer. 1:13–16; 4:6; 6:22–26.) The Lord delivered Joseph and made him second ruler of Egypt. He delivered David and made him king of Israel. He delivered Daniel and made him third ruler of the kingdom. (See 1 Sam. 2:7–8 and Luke 1:52–53.)

The cup (v. 8) is a familiar image of judgment (Job. 21:20; Isa. 51:17, 22; Jer. 25:15ff; Rev. 16:19; 18:6). The Jews usually drank wine diluted with water, but this cup contained wine mixed with strong spices, what they called a "mixed drink." (Prov. 23:30). If the believers went home from the worship service trusting the Lord to deliver them and judge their enemies, the ungodly should have gone home concerned about future judgment. The Lord Jesus Christ drank the cup for us (Matt. 26:36–46), but those who refuse to trust Him will drink the cup of judgment to the very dregs.

We Close with Praise and the Fear of the Lord (vv. 9–10)

"As for me" (v. 9 NASB) indicates decision on the part of the psalmist. Asaph had participated in the sanctuary worship and helped lead the music, but he, too, had to make a decision to obey the Lord and tell others about Him. Witness and praise go together. "The God of Jacob" is a frequent title for Jehovah in The Psalms (20:1; 24:6; 46:7; 81:1, 4; 84:8; 94:7; 114:7; 132:2, 5; 146:5). It's easy for us to identify with Jacob, who was not always a great man of faith, and yet God deigns to be called by Jacob's name! What an encouragement to us! The fact that God will one day judge the wicked ought to motivate us to share the gospel with them, and the fact that God's people ("the righteous") will be exalted ought to humble us and give us faith and courage in the difficult hours of life.

Psalm 76

The background of this psalm is probably God's judgment of the Assyrian army as recorded in Isaiah 37–38 and 2 Kings 18–19. Other "Zion" psalms include 46, 48, 87, 126, 132, and 137. But the emphasis in this psalm is on the God who accomplished the victory and not on the miracle itself. God's mighty works reveal the greatness of His character and His power (75:1). Sennacherib's officers boasted of their king and his conquests, but their dead idols were no match for the true and living God (115:1–18). Asaph shares four basic truths about Jehovah God.

God Wants Us to Know Him (vv. 1–3)

When the northern kingdom of Israel was taken by the Assyrians in 722 B.C., many godly people moved into Judah where a descendant of David was on the throne and true priests ministered in God's appointed temple (2 Chron. 11:13–17; 15:9). Asaph named both Israel and Judah, for though the kingdoms had been divided politically, there was still only one covenant people in the sight of the Lord. God's name was great in Judah and Jerusalem (47:1–2; 48:1, 10; 77:13), but it needed to be magnified among the neighboring nations, for that was Israel's calling (v. 11; Gen. 12:1–3; Isa. 49:6). "You who are far away, hear what I have done; and you who are near, acknowledge My might" (Isa. 33:13 NASB).

Jehovah had chosen Judah to be the ruling tribe (Isa. 49:10) and Jerusalem to be the site of His holy sanctuary (Ezra 7:19; Zech. 3:2). When the Assyrian army camped near Jerusalem and threatened to attack, the angel of the Lord visited the camp and killed 185,000 soldiers. All their abandoned implements of war were but silent monuments to the power of the God of Israel.

"Salvation is of the Jews" (John 4:22), and if we are to know the true and living God, we must read the Bible, a Jewish book, and trust the Lord Jesus Christ, the Son of God who came through the Jewish nation and died for the sins of the world. The true and living God is the God of Abraham, Isaac, and Jacob, and the God and Father of our Lord Jesus Christ (2 Cor. 1:3; Eph. 1:3; 1 Peter 1:3).

God Wants Us to Trust Him (vv. 4–6)

When you read in 2 Kings and Isaiah the account of Assyria's invasion of Judah, you see how difficult Hezekiah's situation was and how much faith he needed to trust God for victory. But the God of glory, more resplendent than the brightest light and more majestic than the mountains, wiped out the Assyrian soldiers as they slept. Instead of Assyria plundering Jerusalem, Jerusalem plundered Assyria, and the Assyrian lion was defeated by the Lion of Judah (Isa. 14:24–27; Nah. 2:11–13). The God of Jacob (v. 6; see 75:9) not only put an end to those soldiers and their chariot horses, but He took the weapons (v. 3) and put the fear of the Lord into their leaders (v. 12). Why? Because King Hezekiah, the prophet Isaiah, and the elders of Judah in Jerusalem all listened to God's Word and put their faith in the Lord. "For I will defend this city to save it for My own sake and for My servant David's sake" (Isa. 37:35 NASB). "So faith comes from hearing, and hearing by the word of Christ" (Rom. 10:17 NASB).

God Wants Us to Fear Him (vv. 7–9)

The fear of the Lord is a major theme in this psalm (vv. 7, 8, 11, 12). It means, of course, the reverential awe, the respect and veneration that belong to God alone. God's people love Him and rejoice in Him, but they also "[w]orship the Lord with reverence, and rejoice with trembling" (2:11 NASB). "No one can know the true grace of God," wrote A. W. Tozer, "who has not first known the fear of God" (*The Root of the Righteous*, p. 38). The Lord had been longsuffering toward Sennacherib's officers as they blasphemed His name and threatened His people, but then He revealed His wrath, and the siege was over that never really started. The question asked in verse 7 is also asked in 130:3 and Revelation 6:17, and it is answered in Ezra 9:15. We rejoice that "God is love" (1 John 4:8, 16), but we must remember that "our God is a consuming fire" (Heb. 12:29).

From His throne in heaven, the Lord announced the verdict and the trial was over (v. 8). There could be no appeal because God's court is the very highest and His judgment leaves the defendants speechless (Rom. 3:19). "The earth feared, and was still" (v. 8 NASB). According to verses 9 and 10, God's judgments accomplish at least three purposes: they bring glory to God as they reveal His justice and holiness; they punish the wicked for their evil deeds; and they bring salvation to those who trust the Lord. (See 72:4.)

God Wants Us to Obey Him (vv. 10–12)

Compared to the wrath of God, the wrath of man is nothing. The more men rage against Him, the more God is glorified! The longer Pharaoh refused to submit to God, the more Egypt was destroyed and the more God was glorified (Ex. 9:16; Rom. 9:14–18). Scholars have wrestled with the translation of the second line of verse 10, and some translations append a note stating that "the meaning is uncertain" or "the Hebrew is obscure." The idea expressed seems to be that the Lord isn't agitated about man's wrath but wears it like a sword (or a garment) and will use it against His enemies at the right time.

Instead of resisting the Lord—a losing battle—we should be grateful to Him for rescuing us (v. 9) and saving us from our sins. Asaph spoke to the Jewish believers and told them to keep the promises they made to the Lord when Jerusalem was in danger. How easy it is to make vows and not keep them! (Eccl. 5:1–6). The Lord's great victory should also have witnessed to the neighboring nations and motivated them to go to Jerusalem with gifts to worship Him. (See 2 Chron. 32:23.) The psalm begins at Jerusalem and its environs (vv. 1–6), then moves to the entire land of Israel (vv. 7–9), and now it reaches the whole earth (v. 12). There will be a day when the rulers of the earth will bow to Jesus Christ and worship Him as King of Kings (Isa. 2:1–4; 11:1ff; Rev. 19:11–16).

Psalm 77

This appears to be a companion psalm to 74, which also lamented the destruction of Jerusalem and the captivity of Israel. Both deal with the Lord's apparent rejection of His people (74:1; 77:7), and both look for renewed hope back to the Exodus (74:12–15; 77:16–19). When Jerusalem fell, many Jews were slain and many were taken captive to Babylon. Asaph may have been in Jeremiah's "circle" and left behind to minister to the suffering remnant (Jer. 30–40). But Asaph himself was suffering as he lay in bed at night (vv. 2, 6) and wrestled with the meaning of the terrible events he had witnessed. In this psalm, he described how he moved from disappointment and despair to confidence that the Lord would care for His people.

The Darkness of Despair (vv. 1–9)

Unable to sleep, Asaph began by *praying* (vv. 1–2), then moved into *remembering* (vv. 3–6), and finally found himself *questioning* (vv. 7–9). In times of crisis and pain, prayer is the believer's natural response, and Asaph reached out his hands in the darkness and cried out to the Lord. He was God's servant and had led the people in worship in the temple, yet he found no comfort for his own heart. When he remembered the Lord and pondered the matter (v. 3; see 6, 11–12), he only groaned, for it seemed that the Lord had failed His people. But had He? Wasn't the Lord being faithful to His covenant and chastening Israel for their sins? Their very chastening was proof of His love (Prov. 3:11–12). Asaph remembered the former years when Israel enjoyed God's blessing, and he also recalled the songs he had sung at the temple, even when on duty at night (134; see 42:8; 92:2; Job 35:10). He had lifted his hands in the sanctuary and received the Lord's blessing, but now he lifted his hands and received nothing.

It isn't a sin to question God, for both David and Jesus asked the Lord the same question (22:1; Matt. 27:46), but it is a sin to demand an immediate answer or to suggest that God needs our counsel (Rom. 11:33–36). Asaph asked six questions, all of which dealt with the very character and attributes of God.

Has He rejected us? No! He is faithful to His Word
(Lam. 3:31–33).
Will He ever again show favor to Israel? Yes! (Ps. 30:5.
Isa. 60:10)
Has His unfailing love vanished forever? No! (Jer. 31:3)
Have His promises failed? No! (1 Kings 8:56)
Has He forgotten to be gracious? No! (Isa. 49:14–18)
Is He so angry, He has shut up His compassions? No!
(Lam. 3:22–24)

It has well been said that we should never doubt in the darkness what God had told us in the light, but Asaph was about to do so. No matter what His hand is doing in our lives, His heart has not changed. He still loves us and always will.

The Dawn of Decision (vv. 10–12)

During the crisis experiences of life, there comes a time when we must get ourselves by the nape of the neck and shake ourselves out of pity into reality, and that's what Asaph did. The repeated "I will" indicates that he had come to the place of decision and determination. "It is my grief, that the right hand of the Most High has changed" (v. 10 NASB). That would be grief indeed if the character of God had altered! "God has deserted His people, and this is a burden I must bear!" He was wrong, of course, because the Lord doesn't change (102:26; Num. 23:19; 1 Sam. 15:29). But he was right in that, by an act of will, he abandoned his former posture of doubt and determined to see the matter through, come what may. He decided to meditate on what God had done for Israel in the past and to learn from His deeds what He was intending for His people.

The Day of Deliverance (vv. 13–20)

The pronouns suddenly change from "I" and "my" to "Thee" and "Thou," referring to the Lord. When we look at our circumstances, we focus on ourselves and see no hope, but when we look by faith to the Lord, our circumstances may not change *but we do*. Asaph didn't completely solve his problems, but he did move out of the shadows of doubt into the sunshine of communion with the Lord and confidence in Him.

First, he *looked up* by faith and rejoiced in the greatness of God (vv. 13–15). He realized that God's ways are always holy, that He is a great God, and that His purposes are always right. See Exodus 15:11, 13, 14, and 16. Then Asaph *looked back* to Israel's exodus from Egypt (Ex. 12–15) for proof of the grace and power of the Lord. Would God have bared His mighty arm to redeem Israel only for their destruction? No! These are the descendants of Jacob whose twelve sons founded the twelve tribes of Israel. These are the brethren of Joseph, whom God sent to Egypt to preserve the nation. Why preserve them if He planned to destroy them? The Exodus account says nothing about a storm, although it does mention a strong wind (Ex. 14:21). Some think that verses 17–18 refer to creation rather than to the Exodus, and creation does magnify God's power and glory (but see Gen. 2:5–6).

As believers, we look back to Calvary, where the Lamb of God gave His life for us. If God the Father did not spare His own Son for us, will He not give us everything else that we need (Rom. 8:32)? There is a wonderful future for the people of God!

Finally, Asaph realized afresh that the Lord was the Shepherd of Israel (v. 20; see 74:1; 78:52, 70–72; 79:13; 80:1). Just as He called Moses and Aaron (Num. 33:1) and David (78:70–72) to lead His flock, so He would appoint other shepherds in the years to come. One day, the Good Shepherd would come and give His life for the sheep (John 10). Asaph had some struggles during this difficult period in his life, but in the end, he knew he could trust the Lord to work out everything for good, and like an obedient sheep, he submitted to the Shepherd. That is what we must do.

Psalm 78

This is a history psalm; see 105, 106, 114, 135, and 136. The German philosopher Hegel said that the one thing we learn from history is that we don't learn from history. If you study the Bible and church history, you discover that God's people make that same mistake. As Asaph reviewed the history of his people, he saw a sad record of forgetfulness, faithlessness, foolishness, and failure, and he sought to understand what it all meant. These things were written for the profit of believers today (1 Cor. 10:11–12), so we had better heed what Asaph says. As A. T. Pierson said, "History is His story."

The psalm concludes with the coronation of David, but the mention of the temple in verse 69 indicates that David's reign had ended. "Ephraim" in verse 9 probably refers, not to the tribe, but to the Northern Kingdom (Israel) that had split from Judah and Benjamin when Rehoboam became king (1 Kings 12). The leaders of Israel abandoned the faith of their fathers and established a religion of their own making, while the people of Judah sought to be faithful to the Lord. In this psalm, Asaph warned the people of Judah not to imitate their faithless ancestors or their idolatrous neighbors and disobey the Lord. He admonished them to know the Scriptures and teach them to their children. Judah had the temple on Mt. Zion, the covenants, the priesthood, and the Davidic dynasty, and all this could be lost in one generation (see Judg. 2). Since Israel is a covenant nation, she has the responsibility of obeying and honoring the Lord, and this psalm presents three responsibilities God expected His people to fulfill.

Protecting the Future (vv. 1–8)

Where would we be today if over the centuries the remnant of Jewish spiritual leaders had not preserved the Scriptures for us! Until the New Testament was completed near the end of the first century, the only Bible the early church had was the Old Testament. It was God's law that each generation of Jewish people pass on God's Word to the next generation (71:18; 79:13; 102:18; 145:4; see Ex. 10:2; 12:26–27; 13:8, 14; Deut. 4:9; 6:6–9, 20–25), and this law applies to His church today (2 Tim. 2:2). In telling the "praises of the Lord"—His deeds worthy of praise—Asaph helped his readers understand an enigma in their history. (See Matt. 13:35.) He explained why God rejected the tribe of

Ephraim and chose the tribe of Judah and David to be king, and why He abandoned the tabernacle at Shiloh and had a temple built on Mt. Zion. Future generations needed to understand this so they would obey the Lord and do His will. Asaph did not want the people to imitate the "exodus generation" that died in the wilderness, or the third generation in Canaan that turned to idols, or the ten tribes that forsook the Lord and established a new kingdom and a false religion. The nation had been stubborn and rebellious (vv. 8, 37; Deut. 21:18) and had suffered because of their disobedience. On the positive side, Asaph wanted the future generations to trust God, to learn from the past, and to obey God's Word (v. 8). Only then could they be sure of the blessing of the Lord. That principle still applies today.

Understanding the Past (vv. 9–64)

Asaph reviewed the past, beginning with the apostasy of Ephraim (vv. 9–11) and continuing with Israel's sins in the wilderness (vv. 12–39) and in Canaan (vv. 54–64). One of the causes of their rebellion was that they forgot God's victory over the gods of Egypt and His deliverance of Israel from bondage (vv. 12–13, 40–53). They also did not take to heart His care for them during their wilderness journey. "Those who cannot remember the past are condemned to repeat it" (George Santayana).

The apostasy of Ephraim (vv. 9–11). This passage refers to the Northern Kingdom of Israel. When the ten tribes broke away from Judah and Benjamin, they informally adopted the name of their strongest and largest tribe, Ephraim. Joseph's sons, Manasseh and Ephraim, were adopted and blessed by Jacob, who made Ephraim the firstborn (Gen. 48:8–20; see Deut. 33:13–17). This added to the tribe's prestige. Moses' successor, Joshua came from Ephraim (Num. 13:8) and so did Jeroboam, the founding king of Israel/Ephraim (1 Kings 11:26; 12:16ff). Proud and militant, the tribe created problems for both Joshua (Josh. 17:14–18) and Gideon (Judg. 8:1–3). The tabernacle was in Shiloh, which was located in Ephraim, and this also added to the honor of the tribe. Like a warrior fleeing from the battlefield, Israel turned back from following the Lord, disobeyed Him, and forgot what He had done for them. For the image of the "bow," see also verse 57 and Hosea 7:16. By opening this long historical section with a description of the apostasy of the Northern Kingdom, Asaph was warning Judah not to follow their example.

The nation's sins in the wilderness (vv. 12–39). Asaph now returned to the account of the sins of the whole nation, before the political division after Solomon's death. The Jews forgot what the Lord did for them in Egypt when He sent the plagues to Egypt and delivered the Jewish people at the Exodus. The people saw one miracle after another as the Lord exposed the futility of the Egyptian gods and goddesses (Ex. 12:12; Num. 33:4), but the memory soon faded. (Asaph will again mention the Egyptian experience in vv. 40–53.) God led the nation both day and night and miraculously provided water for all the people. In verses 15–16, he combined the water miracles of Exodus 17:1–7 and Numbers 20:1–13. But the people would not trust the Lord but tempted Him by asking for food, "a table in the wilderness" (vv. 17–31). He sent manna, the "bread of heaven," as well as fowl to eat (Ex. 16; Num. 11), but He judged them for their insolence and fleshly appetite. Sometimes God's greatest judgment is to give us what we want. (See vv. 21, 31, 49–50, 58–59, 62.) "He brought their days to an end in futility" (v. 33 NASB; 90:7–12) at Kadesh Barnea when they refused to enter the land (Num. 13–14). They wandered for the next thirty-eight years until the people twenty years and older all died (Num. 14:28–38). From time to time, God's discipline did bring them to their knees in temporary repentance, but their confessions were insincere flattery (v. 36) and they soon rebelled again. In His mercy, God forgave them and held back His wrath, but they were a generation that grieved His heart.

The forgotten lessons of Egypt (vv. 40–53). The people did not remember the demonstrations of God's power in sending the plagues to Egypt (Ex. 7–12; Num. 14:32–35) and in opening the Red Sea to set the nation free (Ex. 12–15). Asaph listed six of the ten plagues but did not mention the gnats (Ex. 8:16–19), the killing of the livestock (Ex. 9:1–7), the boils (Ex. 9:8–12), and the three days of darkness before the death of the firstborn (Ex. 10:21–29). After this great display of divine power, the people should have been able to trust the Lord in any situation, knowing that He was in control, but they grieved Him, provoked Him, and tempted Him to display His anger against them! Human nature has not changed. Spurgeon said that we are too prone to engrave our trials in the marble and write our blessings in the sand. They opposed the Holy One of Israel (v. 41; 71:22; 89:18), and He disciplined them time after time.

The sins in Canaan (vv. 54–64). After caring for the nation in the wilderness for thirty-eight years, the Lord brought them again to Kadesh Barnea (Deut. 1:1–2). There he reviewed their history and taught them God's Law as he prepared the new generation to enter the land and conquer the enemy. Often in his farewell speech (which we call Deuteronomy—"second law"), Moses exhorted them to remember and not forget what the Lord had said to them and done for them. They were a new generation, making a new beginning with a new leader (Joshua) and a new opportunity to trust God. Under Joshua's able leadership, they conquered the land and claimed their inheritance, and for two generations obeyed the Lord. But the third generation repeated the sins of their ancestors and forgot what the Lord had said and done (vv. 56–57; Josh. 2:7–10). The "faulty bow" image shows up again in Hosea 7:16. Instead of destroying the altars and idols, the Jewish people mingled with the people of the land and learned their evil ways, and God had to discipline His people by turning them over to their enemies (v. 59). The book of Judges records how seven different nations invaded the nation of Israel and how God raised up judges to deliver Israel when the people repented and turned to Him for help. During the days of Eli the high priest, the Lord severely punished the people and even allowed His ark to be taken captive by the Philistines (1 Sam. 1–7). This meant the end of the tabernacle at Shiloh. It was at Nob in Benjamin for a time (1 Sam. 21:22; 2 Sam. 6:1–2) and also at Gibeon in Benjamin (1 Kings 3:4). When David brought the ark to Mt. Zion (v. 68; 2 Sam. 6), he erected a tent there for the ark and there the ark remained until it was moved into the temple during the reign of Solomon (1 Kings 8:3–9).

It has well been said that a change in circumstances does not overcome a flaw in character, and the history of the Jewish nation illustrates the truth of that statement. Whether living in Egypt, journeying in the wilderness, or dwelling in their own land, the people of Israel were prone to want their own way and rebel against the Lord. When chastened, they feigned repentance, experienced God's help, and were forgiven, but before long, they were back in trouble again. But is any people or individual free from this malady? At least the Jewish writers who gave us the Bible were honest to record their sins as well as their achievements! The church today can learn from both (1 Cor. 10).

Appreciating the Present (vv. 65–72)

The statement in verse 65 is metaphorical, for the Lord neither gets drunk nor goes to sleep. During the time of Samuel and Saul, with the help of young David, Israel beat back her enemies, but it was when David ascended the throne that the nation achieved its greatest victories and experienced the greatest expansion of its boundaries. This is one reason why God rejected the tribe of Ephraim and chose the tribe of Judah, and why He abandoned the tabernacle at Shiloh in Ephraim and chose Mt. Zion for the site of the temple. Jacob had prophesied that the king would come from Judah (Gen. 49:10), and King Saul was from Benjamin. When the Lord directed David to capture Mt. Zion and make Jerusalem his capital city, it was an act of His love (47:4; 87:2). If Asaph wrote this psalm after the division of the kingdom, then he was reminding the people of Judah that they were privileged indeed to have Jerusalem, Mt. Zion, and a king from the line of David, *from which line the Messiah would come!* (See Luke 1:30–33, 66–79; Matt. 2:6.) If they appreciated these privileges, they would not follow the bad example of the Northern Kingdom and sin against the Lord by turning to idols.

Kings were called "shepherds" (Jer. 23:1–6; Ezek. 34) because God's chosen people were the sheep of His pasture (v. 52; 77:20; 100:3), and no one was better qualified than David to hold that title (2 Sam. 5:1–3). He loved his "sheep" (2 Sam. 24:17) and often risked his life for them on the battlefield. His hands were skillful, whether holding a sword, a harp, a pen, or a scepter, and, unlike his predecessor Saul, his heart was wholly devoted to the Lord. (On "integrity," see 7:8; 25:21; 26:1, 11; 41:12.) Integrity and skill need each other, for no amount of ability can compensate for a sinful heart, and no amount of devotion to God can overcome lack of ability.

Psalm 79

God gave His people victory over Egypt (77) and helped them march through the wilderness and then conquer Canaan (78). He also gave them King David who defeated their enemies and expanded their kingdom. But now God's people are captive, the city and temple are ruined, and the heathen nations are triumphant. (See also 74 for parallels: 79:1/74:3, 7; 79:2/74:19; 79:5/74:10; 79:12/74:10, 18, 22.) We see Asaph playing four different roles as he contemplates the defeat of Judah by the Babylonians. Each division of the psalm opens with an address to Jehovah: "O God" (v. 1); O Lord" (v. 5); "O God our Savior" (v. 9); and "O Lord" (v. 12).

The Mourner: Beholding God's Judgment (vv. 1–4)

Babylon was the leading nation in the conquest of Judah, but the neighboring nations (Ammon, Moab, Edom) were delighted to see the Jews defeated (vv. 4, 12; see 44:13, 80:6; 137:7; Ezek. 25). The land was God's inheritance (Ex. 15:17), and He shared it with the people of Israel who were His inheritance (28:9; 33:12; Deut. 4:20). They could live in the land and enjoy its blessings as long as they obeyed the covenant (Lev. 26; Deut. 28–30), but repeated rebellion would only bring painful discipline to them, including expulsion from the land (Lev. 26:33–39; Deut. 28:64–68). They would be defeated before their enemies (v. 1; Deut. 28:25) and the dead bodies left unburied, a terrible disgrace for a Jew (v. 2; Deut. 28:26; Lev. 26:30; and see Jer. 7:33; 8:2; 9:22). Her cities would be destroyed (v. 1; Deut. 28:52) and Israel would be reproached by her neighbors (vv. 4, 12; Deut. 28:37). Note how Asaph identified the Lord with the situation: "your inheritance ... your holy temple ... your servants ... your name."

The Sufferer: Feeling God's Anger (vv. 5–8)

The question "How long?" is found often in Scripture (see 6:3). God is not jealous *of* anyone or anything, for He is wholly self-sufficient and needs nothing, but He is jealous *over* His land and His people. (See 78:58; Ex. 20:5; Deut. 4:24; 6:15–16; 29:20.) He is jealous for His name (Ezek. 39:25), His land (Joel 2:18), and His inheritance (Zech. 1:14). Asaph doesn't deny that he and the people deserve chastening (v. 9), but if the Jews are guilty, then how much guiltier the heathen nations are that have attacked the Jews! He asked God to pour out His anger on the invaders because of what they have done to the land, the city, and the temple (vv. 6–7).

As the kingdom of Judah declined, their kings and leaders became less and less devoted to the Lord. There were a few godly kings, such as Asa, Josiah, Joash, and Hezekiah, but foreign alliances, idolatry, and unbelief combined to weaken the kingdom and ripen it for judgment. The sins of the fathers accumulated until God could hold back His wrath no longer (Gen. 15:16; Matt. 23:32–33; 1 Thess. 2:13–16). We are guilty before God for only our own sins (Deut. 24:16; Jer. 31:29–30; Ezek. 18), but we may suffer because of the sins of our ancestors (Ex. 20:5; 34:7; 2 Kings 17:7ff; 23:26–27; 24:3–4; Lam. 5:7; Dan. 9:4–14).

The Intercessor: Pleading for God's Help (vv. 9–11)

His concern was for the glory of God's name (vv. 9, 12), and he felt that a miraculous deliverance for Judah would accomplish that, but no deliverance came. Asaph was quick to confess his own sins and the sins of his contemporaries, for it was not only their ancestors who had disobeyed the Lord (v. 8). (See 25:11, 31:3, 65:3, and 78:38.) In ancient days, a nation's victory was proof that its gods were stronger than the gods of the enemy, so the Babylonians taunted the Jews and asked, "Where is your God?" (See 42:3, 10; 115:2.) Moses used this same argument when he pled with God to forgive the nation (Ex. 32:12; Num. 14:13).

Asaph was also concerned about the justice of God. Twice he mentioned the pouring out of blood (vv. 3, 10), the slaughter of people, for the blood was very sacred to the Jews (Lev. 17). The shedding of animal blood at the altar at least covered the sins of the worshipers, but to what purpose was the shedding of so much human blood? In verse 11, he prayed on the basis of the Lord's great compassion, perhaps remembering Jehovah's words to Moses (Ex. 33:12–23, and see Deut. 32:36). God had felt the burdens of the Jews when He called Moses to lead them out of Egypt (Ex. 2:24–25, 6:1–9), so surely He would have pity on the prisoners and those ready to die. The cross of Jesus Christ is for us today the only evidence we need that God loves us (Rom. 5:8).

The Worshiper: Promising to Praise God (vv. 12–13)

How could any person witness what Babylon did to the Jews and not cry out to God for retribution? (See 55 for a discussion of the imprecatory prayers in the Psalms.) God had chosen Babylon to chasten Judah for her sins, but the Babylonians had rejoiced at the privilege and had gone too far in their cruelty (Jer. 50:11–16; 51:24). Asaph's burden was that Babylon had reproached the Lord and not just punished His people, and he asked God to pay them back in like measure (see Isa. 65:6; Jer. 32:18; Luke 6:38). God's covenant with Israel often uses the phrase "seven times" (Lev. 26:18, 21, 24, 28; Deut. 28:7, 25). The prophet Jeremiah promised that God would judge Babylon for her sins (Jer. 50–51), and if Asaph knew of these prophecies, then he was simply praying for God to accomplish His will on earth.

The people of Judah were but sheep (vv. 74:1; 77:20; 78:72; 95:7; 100:3), but they had been ruthlessly slaughtered by their enemies, and God's name had been slandered. God had called His people to praise Him and to bear witness to the heathen nations (Isa. 43:21), and this is what Asaph promised to do if God would only deliver the people. There were sons of Asaph who left Babylon for Judah when the captivity ended, so Asaph's promise to the Lord was fulfilled (Ezra 2:41; 3:10; Neh. 7:44; 11:17, 22; 12:35–36).

Psalm 80

This is Asaph's prayer to God on behalf of the Northern Kingdom ("Israel," "Samaria") after it was taken captive by Assyria in 722–21 B.C. While "Joseph" can refer to the whole nation (77:15; 80:4–5), the mention in verse 2 of Ephraim and Manasseh (Joseph's sons) and Benjamin (Joseph's brother) suggests that the Northern Kingdom is meant. These are the children and grandchildren of Rachel, Jacob's favorite wife. Samaria, the capital of the Northern Kingdom, was located in Ephraim. The temple was still standing in Jerusalem (v. 1), and the fall of Samaria should have been a warning to Judah not to disobey the Lord. That Asaph would pray for Samaria and ask God for restoration and reunion for the whole nation indicates that some of the old rivalries were ending and that some of the people of Judah were concerned over "the ruin of Joseph" (Amos 6:6). It's unfortunate that it sometimes takes dissension, division, and destruction to bring brothers closer together. Joseph and his brothers are a case in point. The refrain "Restore us" (vv. 3, 7, 19) marks out the three requests Asaph made to the Lord for both kingdoms.

"Save Your Flock" (vv. 1–3)

Both in the Old Testament and the New, the flock is a familiar image of the people of God (23:1; 28:9 NASB, NIV; 74:1; 77:20; 78:52; 79:13; John 10; 1 Peter 5:1–4; Heb. 13:20–21). The request here is that the Lord might lead His people through this crisis as He led them safely through the wilderness. He led the way by the ark (the throne of God; Num. 10:33; 99:1; 1 Sam. 4:4

and 6:2) and the cloud (the shining forth of the glory of God; Num. 14:14; see 50:2, 94:1, Deut. 33:2). After the ark came the people of Judah, Issachar, and Zebulun. Next were the Levites from Gershom and Marari carrying the tabernacle structure, followed by Reuben, Simeon, and Gad. Then came the Levites from Kohath carrying the tabernacle furnishings, followed by Ephraim, Manasseh, and Benjamin, with Dan, Asher, and Naphtali bringing up the rear (see Num. 10). Asaph asked the Lord to "stir up His might" (7:6; 78:65) and bring salvation to His people. This reminds us of the words of Moses whenever the camp set out, "Rise up, O Lord! May your enemies be scattered" (Num. 10:35 NIV). The "shining of His face" of the refrain reminds us of the priestly benediction (Num. 6:22–27), and see 4:6; 31:16; 67:1; and 119:135. When God hides His face, there is trouble (13:1; 27:9; 30:7; 44:24; 69:17; 88:14). "Turn us again" (KJV) means "restore us to our former state of blessing and fellowship with the Lord." (See 85:4; 126:1,4; Lam. 5:21.)

"Pity Your People" (vv. 4–7)

The shepherd image blends in with the image of Israel as God's people: "We are his people and the sheep of his pasture" (100:3). But the Lord was now angry with His people, and His anger smoldered like a fire about to erupt and consume them. (See 74:1 and 79:5; Deut. 29:20; Isa. 65:5.) He was even angry at their prayers, or "in spite of" their prayers. [For "How long?" see 6:3. See also Lam. 3:8 and 44, and recall that God told Jeremiah not to pray for His wayward people (Jer. 7:16; 11:14; 14:11; and see 1 John 5:16).] During Israel's wilderness wanderings, God provided bread from heaven and water from the rock (Ex. 16–17; Num. 20), but now His people had only tears as both their food and drink. (See 42:3; 102:9; Isa. 30:20.) To make matters worse, the neighboring peoples were laughing at God's people (44:13–16; 79:4). Again we read the plaintive refrain (v. 7), but note that the "O God" of verse 3 now becomes "O God of hosts" ("God Almighty" NIV). Jehovah is the Lord of the armies of heaven and earth, but His people no longer marched in victory.

"Revive Your Vine" (vv. 8–19)

The image now changes to that of Israel the vine (Isa. 5:1–7; Jer. 2:21; 6:9; Ezek. 15:1–2; 17:6–8; 19:10–14; Hos. 10:1; 14:7; Matt. 20:1–16; Mark 12:1–9; Luke 20:9–16). Jesus used this image to describe Himself and His followers (John 15), and in Revelation 14:17–20, John wrote of "the vine of the earth," the corrupt Gentile nations in the end times. The Lord transplanted Israel from Egypt to Canaan, uprooted the nations in Canaan, and planted His people in the land of their inheritance. As long as the people obeyed the Lord, the vine grew and covered more and more of the land. The boundaries of the nation reached from the hill country in the south to the mighty cedars of Lebanon in the north, from the Mediterranean Sea on the west to the Euphrates on the east—and beyond (72:8; Ex. 23:21; Deut. 11:24; 2 Sam. 8:6; 1 Kings 4:24).

But the luxurious vine disobeyed the Lord, produced "worthless fruit" (Isa. 5:2), and felt the chastening hand of the Lord. He withdrew His protection and permitted the enemy to enter the land and ruin the vineyard. Asaph prayed that the Lord might forgive and once again bless His people. The word "branch" in verse 15 (KJV) is translated "son" in the *New American Stamdard Bible* and the *New International Version*, perhaps a reference to Jacob's words about Joseph in Genesis 49:22. Israel was called God's "son" (Ex. 4:22–23; see Hos. 11:1, which is a Messianic reference in Matt. 2:15), and Benjamin means "son of my right hand." While there may be Messianic overtones in verses 15 and 17 (see 110:1, 5), the main idea is that Israel is God's own people, His vine, and His chosen son. He planted the nation in Canaan, and He alone can protect and deliver them. He had treated the people like a favored son, just as Jacob had laid his right hand of blessing on Ephraim rather than the firstborn Manasseh (Gen. 48:12–20). They did not deserve His blessing, but in His grace He bestowed it. It is also possible that verse 17 refers to Israel's king and expresses hope in the Davidic dynasty.

The final refrain introduces a third name for God, borrowed

from verse 4: "O Lord God of hosts [Almighty NIV]." LORD is the name "Jehovah," which is the covenant name of God. The psalmist appealed to the covenant and asked God to be faithful to forgive His people as they called upon Him and confessed their sins (Lev. 26:40–45; Deut. 30:1–10). This is the Old Testament version of 1 John 1:9. Spiritually speaking, the roots of Israel are still strong (Rom. 11:1ff, especially vv. 16–24), and one day the vine and olive tree will be restored, and Asaph's prayer will be answered.

Psalm 81

The psalmist called the people together to worship the Lord, but then the Lord's messenger received a special message from God and delivered it to the people. The occasion was a stated feast on the Jewish calendar, but we are not told which feast it was. Passover is suggested by verses 5–7 and 10, but the mention of the new moon and the full moon (v. 3 NASB) suggests Trumpets and Tabernacles. The Jewish religious year begins in the month of Nisan (our March–April), during which the Feast of Passover is celebrated (Ex. 12). The civil year begins with Tishri (our September–October), the seventh month in the religious year, during which the Jews celebrate the Feast of Trumpets (first day, "Rosh Hashanna"), the Day of Atonement (tenth day, "Yom Kippur"), and the Feast of Tabernacles (days fifteen to twenty-two). (See Lev. 23:23–44 and Num. 29.) The first day would be new moon and the fifteenth day the full moon. The trumpets mentioned here are not the silver trumpets (Num. 10) but the "shofar," the ram's horn, as was used at Jericho (Josh. 6). This argues for the occasion being the Feast of Tabernacles, although perhaps Asaph conflated Passover and Tabernacles, for they go together. Passover celebrated the deliverance from Egypt and Tabernacles the Lord's care of His people during their wilderness years. Tabernacles was also a joyful harvest festival. The psalm reminds us of three different aspects of true worship.

Praising God's Name (vv. 1–5)

The leader called together the people (v. 1), the musicians (v. 2), and the priests to blow the trumpets (v. 3). In the Old Testament Law, you find stated times of worship (the weekly Sabbath, the annual feasts, etc.) as well as spontaneous times of worship (at the defeat of the enemy, for example). Both are essential to balanced worship, and both should focus on the goodness of the Lord. If all worship were personal and spontaneous, there would be diversity but no unity; but if all worship only followed a schedule, there would be unity and no diversity. Both voices and instruments were used in worship. The nation is called "Jacob, Israel, and Joseph" (vv. 4–5). Jacob and his wives built the family, and Joseph preserved them alive in Egypt. God gave Jacob the name "Israel," which means "he strives with God and prevails" (Gen. 32:22–32).

Hearing God's Word (vv. 6–10).

The last clause of verse 5 could be translated, "We heard a voice we had not known" (NIV margin), referring to the message God sent in verses 6–10. At some point in the festal celebration, a priest received God's message and declared it to the people. The emphasis in this psalm is on hearing the Word of God (vv. 6, 11, 13; see 95:7–11 and Heb. 3). Every seventh year at the Feast of Tabernacles, the priests read the book of Deuteronomy to the people, and perhaps this was one of those special sabbatical years. (See Deut. 31:9–13, and note the emphasis in Deuteronomy on "hearing God" [Deut. 4:1, 6, 10; 5:1; 6:3–4; 9:1].) It is delightful to sing praises to God and to pray, but if we want Him to listen to us, we must listen to Him.

Frequently the Lord reminded His people of their miraculous deliverance from Egypt (v. 6), the power of God that accomplished it, and the love of God that motivated it. He also reminded them of the covenant they accepted at Sinai (v. 7a; see Deut. 5:2–3). The people hearing this message were not at Sinai, but the decision of their ancestors was binding on them and their descendants. God's message also mentioned their failure to trust Him at Meribah (Ex.

17; Num. 20). At the Feast of Tabernacles, the priests poured out water in the temple to commemorate these events (John 7:37–39). The Lord emphasized that He would not tolerate His people worshiping idols (vv. 8–9; Ex. 20:1–4; Deut. 4:15–20). What could the false gods of the neighboring nations give to them? "Open your mouth wide and I will fill it" (v. 10 NASB).

Obeying God's Will (vv. 11–16)

Worship and service go together (Matt. 4:10; Deut. 6:13), and this means we must obey what the Lord commands. But the nation did not obey God's Word, and He had to destroy all the people twenty years and older (Num. 14:26ff). But this attitude of spiritual "deafness" and willful disobedience persisted even after Israel entered the Promised Land, as recorded in the book of Judges. (See 78:10, 17, 32, 40, 56.) The greatest judgment God can send is to let people have their own way (see Rom. 1:24, 26, 28).

Had His people obeyed Him, the Lord would have kept the promises in His covenant and blessed them with protection and provision (Deut. 28:15ff; Lev. 26:17–20; 27–31). When we disobey the Lord, not only do we feel the pain of His chastening, but we also miss out on the blessings He so desires to give us. The Lord gave Israel water out of the rock, but He was prepared to give them honey out of the rock (Deut. 32:13). He sent manna from heaven, but He would have given them the finest of wheat. The word "if" (v. 13) is small, but it carries big consequences (Deut. 5:29; 32:29; Isa. 48:18; Matt. 23:37).

Of all sad words of tongue or pen,
The saddest are these: "It might have been."
John Greenleaf Whittier

Psalm 82

In the previous psalm, Asaph described the Lord judging His people during one of their feast days, but in this psalm it is the judges of the people that He indicts. (See also 50 and 75.) The psalmist speaks in verse 1 and announces that the Judge will speak, and in verse 8, Asaph prays that God will bring justice to the whole earth. Between these statements, the Lord Himself speaks to the judges.

The Judge (v. 1)

Since God is the Lawgiver, He is also the Judge (Isa. 33:22), and the Judge of all the earth does what is right (Gen. 18:25). He presides over the congregation of Israel and over the judges of the nation. The Lord is not sitting at a bench, patiently listening to the presentation of the case, because God is Judge and jury and needs nobody to tell Him the facts. He knows what people are doing on the earth and will execute judgment righteously (11:4–7). In His court, there is no "defense" or "appeal." He is omniscient and His verdict is final. It is an awesome occasion: He is standing and about to announce His decision (Isa. 3:13–15).

The "gods" (vv. 1, 6) are not the false gods of the heathen, for such nonexistent gods are not Jehovah's judicial representatives on earth. Nor are these "gods" the holy angels, for angels cannot die (v. 7). These "gods" (*elohim*) are people who have been given the awesome responsibility of representing the Lord on earth and interpreting and applying His Law (Ex. 18:13–17; 21:6; Deut. 16:18–20; 17:2–13; 19:15–20; 21:2). Jesus made this clear in His quotation of verse 6 in John 10:34–36. It is a great responsibility to represent the Lord on earth (Lev. 19:15; Deut. 1:17; 16:19) and seek to execute justice by applying the law correctly. Civil servants are "ministers of the Lord" and will answer to Him for what they have done (Rom. 13).

The Judges (vv. 2–7)

"And what does the Lord require of you but to do justice, to love kindness, and to walk humbly with your God?" (Mic. 6:8 NASB). These judges did not do justly (v. 2) or love mercy (vv. 3–4), and they walked in defiance of God's will (v. 5). The pronoun "you" in verse 2 is plural, for the Lord is addressing all the guilty judges. They championed the causes of the guilty because they were bribed, and they failed to care for the orphans and widows. (See Ex. 22:21–24; Deut. 10:17–18; Isa. 1:17; 10:1–2; Jer. 5:28; 22:3, 16; Amos 2:7; 4:1; 5:11–12; 8:6; Ezek. 16:49; 18:12; 22:29.) Judges are to uphold the Law and not show partiality (Lev. 19:15; Deut. 16:19; Isa. 3:13–15; Mic. 3:1–4), a principle that also applies in the local church (1 Tim. 5:21). Even during the glorious days of Solomon's kingdom, the state officers were abusing people and disobeying the Law (Eccl. 5:8)—yet Solomon had asked for an understanding heart (1 Kings 3:9).

Does verse 5 describe the evil judges or the abused people? If the judges, then it is a terrible indictment against people who are supposed to know the Law and walk in its light (Isa. 8:20; 59:1–15; Rom. 1:21–22). But it's possible that the pronoun "they" in verse 5 refers back to the weak and needy people described in verse 4. The priests and Levites did not always do their jobs well, and the common people did not know the Law well enough to defend themselves. "My people are destroyed for lack of knowledge" (Hos. 4:6). When the Law of God is ignored or disobeyed, this shakes and threatens the very foundations of society (11:3; 89:14; 97:2), for God's moral Law is the standard by which man's laws must be judged.

The Judgment (vv. 6–8)

Though these people held high offices and were called "elohim—gods" (Ex. 21:6), they were only humans and would be judged for their sins. Privilege brings responsibility, and responsibility brings accountability. Jesus quoted verse 6 (John 10:34–36) to defend His own claim to be the Son of God. For, if the Lord called "gods" the imperfect human judges chosen by men, how much more should Jesus Christ be called "the Son of God," He who was set apart by the Father and sent to earth! In spite of their titles and offices, these judges would die like any other human and pay the price for their sins. When God the Judge ceased to speak, then Asaph added his prayer that God would bring justice to all the earth and not just to Israel (v. 8; 9:7–8). When the Lord comes to judge the earth, no one will escape and

His sentence will be just. Asaph's prayer echoes the church's prayer, "Thy kingdom come, Thy will be done on earth as it is in heaven" (Matt. 6:10).

Psalm 83

This is the last of the psalms identified with Asaph (50, 73–83). It describes a coalition of ten Gentile nations that attempted to wipe Israel off the face of the earth. Some students connect this psalm with Jehoshaphat's great victory over a smaller coalition (2 Chron. 20), although it's possible that the historian did not list all the nations involved. Second Chronicles 20:11 parallels 83:12, and 20:29 parallels 83:16 and 18, but these similarities are not proof that the psalmist wrote about the same event. Israel has been the object of hatred and opposition since their years in Egypt, but God has kept His promises and preserved them (Gen. 12:1–3). Pharaoh, Haman (the book of Esther), Hitler, and every other would-be destroyer of the Jews has ultimately been humiliated and defeated. This reminds us that the church of Jesus Christ is likewise hated and attacked by the world (John 15:18–19; 17:14), and like the Jews in Asaph's day, our defense is in prayer and faith in God's promises (Acts 4:23–31). Commenting on this psalm, Alexander Maclaren wrote, "The world is up in arms against God's people, and what weapon has Israel? Nothing but prayer." But is there any better weapon? As he saw the enemy armies surrounding Israel, Asaph lifted three heartfelt requests to the Lord

"Lord, See What Is Happening!" (vv. 1–8)

Two names of God open the psalm—Elohim and El, and two names close it—Jehovah and El Elyon (God Most High). The last name reminds us of Abraham's victory over the kings and his meeting with Melchizedek (Gen. 14:18–20). Asaph was troubled because the Lord had said nothing through His prophets and done nothing through His providential workings to stop the huge confederacy from advancing. Literally he prayed, "Let there be no rest to you" (see 28:1–2; 35:21–22;

39:12; 109:11; Isa. 62:6). These were God's enemies, attacking God's people, and threatening God's "protected ones" (see 27:5 and 31:21), so it was time for God to take notice and act!

The invaders were many, they were united, and they proudly lifted their heads as they defied the Lord God of Israel (see 2:1–3). They had secretly plotted together but were now "roaring like the sea" (v. 2 "tumult"; see 46:3). Their purpose was to destroy God's people and take possession of the land (v. 12). It appears that Moab and Ammon, the incestuous sons of Lot (Gen. 19), were the leaders of the coalition, encouraged by Assyria, which was not yet a world power (v. 8). Moab and Ammon would come from the east, along with the Ishmaelites, and Edom would come from the southeast along with their neighbor Gebal. Ishmael was the enemy and rival of Isaac (Gen. 21:1–21). The Hagerites lived northeast of Israel and the Amalekites lived southwest. The people of Philistia and Phoenicia (Tyre) were west of Israel. The enemy came against Israel from every direction and had the people surrounded!

"Lord, Do What Is Necessary!" (vv. 9–15)

Even if Jehoshaphat's situation was not the same as that described by Asaph, his prayer would have fit the occasion: "O our God, will You not judge them? For we have no power against this great multitude that is coming against us; nor do we know what to do, but our eyes are upon you" (2 Chron. 20:12 NKJV). Asaph remembered some of Jehovah's great victories in Israel's past history, especially Gideon's victory over the Midianites (vv. 9a, 11; Judg. 6–8) and the victory of Deborah and Barak against Sisera and Jabin (vv. 9b–10; Judg. 4–5). Endor is not mentioned in Judges 4–5, but it was a city near Taanach (Judg. 5:19), which was near Endor (Josh. 17:11). The phrase "as dung for the ground" (v. 10 NASB) describes the unburied bodies of enemy soldiers rotting on the ground. The enemy was defeated and disgraced. Oreb and Zeeb were commanders (princes) of the Midianite army, and Zeba and Zalmunna were Midianite kings (Judg. 7:25–8:21). The victory of Gideon ("the day of Midian") stood out in Jewish history as an example of God's power (Isa. 9:4; 10:26; Hab. 3:7). Asaph closed his prayer by asking God to send such a victory to Israel that the enemy soldiers would flee in panic and look like tumbleweeds and chaff blowing before the wind. Like a forest burning on the mountainside, their armies would be consumed. The image of God's judgment as a storm is found in 18:7–15, 50:3 and 68:4. If Asaph's prayer seems vindictive, remember that he was asking God to protect His special people who had a special work to see on earth. (See 55 for more on the "imprecatory psalms.")

"Glorify Your Name!" (vv. 16–18)

Before asking for their destruction, Asaph prayed that the enemy would be "ashamed and dismayed" and would turn to the true and living God. This is what happened in Jehoshaphat's day: "And the fear of God was on all the kingdoms of those countries when they heard that the Lord had fought against the enemies of Israel" (2 Chron. 20:29). King Hezekiah prayed a similar prayer for the invading Assyrians (Isa. 37:14–20). The armies of the ten nations depended on many gods to give them success, but the God of Abraham, Isaac, and Jacob defeated the armies and their gods! "Hallowed be Thy name" is the first request in the Lord's Prayer (Matt. 6:9) and must be the motive that governs all of our praying. The Most High God is sovereign over all the earth!

Psalm 84

The phrase "appears before God in Zion" (v. 7 NASB) suggests that this psalm was penned by a Jewish man who could not go to Jerusalem to celebrate one of the three annual feasts (Ex. 23:17; 34:23). For forty years after their exodus from Egypt, the Jews were a wandering people, but even after they had moved into the Promised Land, the three feasts reminded them that they were still pilgrims on this earth (1 Chron. 29:15), as are God's people today (1 Peter 1:1; 2:11). A vagabond has no home; a fugitive is running from home; a stranger is away from home; a pilgrim is heading home. The psalmist's inability to attend the feast did not rob him of the blessings of fellowship with the Lord. All who are true pilgrims can make the same three affirmations that he made.

My Delight Is in the Lord (vv. 1–4)

In his opening statement, the psalmist said two things: "The temple is beautiful" and "The temple is beloved by all who love the Lord." It was the dwelling place of the Lord, His house (vv. 4, 10), the place where His glory dwelt (26:8). Although God doesn't live today in man-made buildings (Acts 7:47–50), we still show special reverence toward edifices dedicated to Him. We can worship God anytime and anywhere, but special places and stated rituals are important in structuring our worship experience. The important thing is that we have a heart devoted to the Lord, a spiritual "appetite" that cries out for nourishing fellowship with the Lord (42:1–4; Matt. 5:6). The psalmist cried out for God with his entire being. He envied the birds that were permitted to nest in the temple courts, near the altar, as well as the priests and Levites who lived and worked in the sacred precincts (v. 4). How easy it is for us to take for granted the privilege of worshiping "the living God" (see 115:1–8), a privilege purchased for us on the cross.

My Strength Is in the Lord (vv. 5–8)

Though he had to remain at home, the psalmist's heart was set on pilgrimage, and the very map to Jerusalem was written on that heart. His love for God and His house helped him make right decisions in life so that he did not go astray. A geographic site named "the Valley of Baca" is nowhere identified in Scripture. "Baca" is a Hebrew word meaning "balsam tree," and the sap of this tree oozes like tears. The "Valley of Baca" is a name for any difficult and painful place in life, where everything seems hopeless and you feel helpless, like "the pit of despair." The people who love God expect to pass *through* this valley and not remain there. They get a blessing from the experience, and they leave a blessing behind. Like Abraham and Isaac, they "dig a well" (Gen. 21:22–34; 26:17–33), and like Samuel and Elijah, they pray down the rain (1 Sam. 12:16–25; 1 Kings 18). It's wonderful to *receive* a blessing, but it's even greater to *be* a blessing and transform a desert into a garden. True pilgrims "go from strength to strength" (Deut. 33:25; Isa. 40:28–31; Phil. 4:13) and trust God to enable them to walk a step at a time and work a day at a time. They are people of prayer who keep in communion with the Lord, no matter what their circumstances may be. "Blessed are those whose strength is in you" (v. 5 NIV).

My Trust Is in the Lord (vv. 9–12)

From pleading "Hear my prayer" (v. 8), the psalmist then lifted his petitions to the Lord, beginning with a prayer for the king (v. 9). A "shield" is a symbol of both the Lord (3:3; 7:10; 18:2, 30; Gen. 15:1) and Israel's anointed king (89:18; see 2 Sam. 1:21). But why pray for the king? Because the future of the Messianic promise rested with the line of King David (2 Sam. 7), and the psalmist wanted the Messiah to come. Believers today should pray faithfully for those in authority (1 Tim. 2:1–4).

When you walk by faith, you put the Lord and His will first, and you keep your priorities straight (v. 10). This is the Old Testament version of Matthew 6:33 and Philippians 1:21. According to the inscription, this psalm is associated with "the Sons of Korah," who were Levites assigned to guard the threshold of the sanctuary (1 Chron. 9:19), an important and honorable office. Their ancestor rebelled against God and Moses and was slain by the Lord (Num. 16; note "tents of wickedness" in 84:10 and Num. 16:26). Korah's children were not killed because of their father's sins (Num. 26:11) but continued to serve at the sanctuary. The psalmist didn't aspire to a high office ("gatekeeper" in 1 Chron. 9:19 is not the same word as "doorkeeper" in 84:10) but was willing to "sit at the threshold" of the temple, just to be close to the Lord.

To men and women of faith, the Lord is all they need. He is to them what the sun is to our universe—the source of life and light (27:1; Isa. 10:17; 60:19–20; Mal. 4:2). Without the sun, life would vanish from the earth, and without God, we would have neither physical life (Acts 17:24–28) nor spiritual life (John 1:1–14). God is our provision and our protection ("shield"; see references at vv. 8–9). He is the giving God, and He gives grace and glory—grace for the journey and glory at the end of the journey (see Rom. 5:1–2; 1 Peter 5:10). If we walk by faith, then whatever begins with grace will ultimately end with glory. God does not give us everything we want, but He bestows upon us all that is good for us, all that we need. (See 1:1–3.)

Although times of solitude and spiritual retreat can be very beneficial to us spiritually, believers today have constant open access into the presence of God because of the shed blood of Jesus Christ and His constant intercession for us in heaven (Heb. 7:25; 10:19–25). Do we delight in the Lord and seek Him? Do we depend on His strength? Do we walk and work by faith? Are we among those who walk uprightly (v. 11)?

Psalm 85

This psalm was probably written after the Jewish people returned to their land following their seventy years of captivity in Babylon (Jer. 29). Note the emphasis on *the land* (vv. 1, 9 and 12) and on God's anger against His people (vv. 3–5). God gave them favor with their captors, raised up leaders like Zerubbabel the governor, Joshua the high priest, and Ezra the scribe, and protected the Jewish remnant as they traveled to their war-ravaged land. When you read Ezra 6 and the prophets Haggai, Zechariah, and Malachi, you learn that life was very difficult for them in the land. They did not always obey the Lord or show kindness to each other, but they did make a new start. The Scottish preacher George H. Morrison said, "The victorious Christian life is a series of new beginnings," and he is right. It is a sin to disobey God and fall, but it is also a sin to stay fallen. We must always make a new beginning, and this psalm gives us some instructions that we can follow after times of failure and chastening.

Give Thanks to the Lord (vv. 1–3)

It should have been no surprise to the people of Judah that the Babylonians would invade their land, destroy their city and temple, and take them captive. After all, they knew the terms of the covenant (Lev. 26; Deut. 28–30), and time after time, the Lord had sent His prophets to warn them, but they would not listen (2 Chron. 36:15–21). Jeremiah had told the people that their captivity would last seventy years and then the Lord would restore a remnant to the land (Jer. 29). God protected the people as they made the long journey home. He forgave their sins and gave them a new beginning, and for this they thanked the Lord (Isa. 40:1–2). The Hebrew word *shuv* basically means "to turn or return," and it is used in verse 1 ("brought back"), verses 3, 4, and 8 ("turn"), and verse 6 ("again"). When we turn back to God, repent, and confess our sins, He turns back to us and restores us.

Ask Him for Renewed Life (vv. 4–7)

It is one thing for the nation collectively to have a new birth of freedom, but there must also be changes in individuals. The praise begun in verses 1–3 (possibly by a choir) now becomes prayer from the hearts of the people. Note that the word *us* is used six times, for it is the people who are praying, not the choir or worship leader. "Turn (restore) us" is the burden of their prayer. It has well been said that a change in geography will never overcome a flaw in character. The return of the people to the land was no guarantee that all of them had returned to the Lord. Not only were they concerned that God's chastening would end in their own lives, but they did not want it to be passed on to their children and grandchildren. The word "revive" simply means "to live again, to be renewed in life." (We must not confuse this with the modern meaning—"special meetings for winning the lost.") Establishing the nation, rebuilding the temple, and restoring the liturgy would not guarantee God's blessing on His people. They desperately needed His life at work within them. While in Babylon, had they heard or read Ezekiel's message about the dry bones (Ezek. 37), and did they long for the wind of the Spirit to blow upon their own lives and homes? New life is not something that we manufacture ourselves; new life can come only from the Holy Spirit of God. God gave a special message about this to Haggai (Hag. 2:1–9) and also to Zechariah (Zech. 4:6).

Listen for God's Message to You (vv. 8–13)

"I will hear" suggests that the worship leader or a prophet stepped forward and said, in effect, "Now it is time to be silent before God and listen for His message to us for this hour." God and His people were now reconciled and He was speaking peace to them (Jer. 29:11). "Saints" means "people who are set apart for God." Alas, Israel had a long record of "turning to folly"! According to the book of Judges, seven different nations were sent by God to chastise Israel; they repented, but they always lapsed back into idolatry again. After Solomon died, his son Rehoboam was a fool not to listen to the wise men of the land, and this led to a division of the kingdom. Jeroboam, ruler of the northern kingdom, manufactured his own religion and led the nation astray. How foolish! The task of God's people is to fear God and glorify Him (v. 9). The word "dwell" is the Hebrew word *shechinah*, and we speak of God's glory dwelling in the tabernacle (Ex. 40:34) and the temple (2 Chron. 7:1–3). Before the temple was destroyed, Ezekiel saw God's glory leave the structure (Ezek. 9:3; 10:1–4, 18–19; 11:22–23). When the Jewish remnant rebuilt the temple, the prophet Haggai promised that God's glory would return in an even greater way (Hag. 2:6–9).

In verses 10–13, the Lord announced future blessings that He would send if His people continued to walk with Him. Righteousness and peace—attributes of God—are personified and would "kiss" each other, for the warfare would be over. (See Isa. 32:17; Rom. 3:21–31 and 5:1–3.) Surely there is a glimpse here of the person and work of Jesus Christ, for only in Him can mercy and truth become friends, for if you tell the truth, you may not receive mercy! But the blessing changes the people, for truth springs up from the earth! God's people are faithful and walk in the truth. The psalmist described a world of holiness and harmony, a picture of the coming kingdom over which Christ shall reign. And what a harvest there will be, not only of food necessary for survival (Hag. 1:3–11) but of heaven-sent blessings that will bring joy to the land. As people walk through the land, God's righteousness will go before them and their way will be prepared. God's will shall be done on earth just as it is now done in heaven.

"Even so, come, Lord Jesus!" (Rev. 22:20).

Psalm 86

In the midst of a group of four psalms attributed to the Sons of Korah you find one psalm by David, the only Davidic psalm in the entire third book of Psalms. When David wrote it, he was facing some formidable enemies whom we cannot identify (v. 14), at a time when he was "poor and needy" (v. 1) and calling for God's help. The remarkable thing about the psalm is that it is a mosaic of quotations from other parts of the Old Testament, especially 25–28, 40 and 54–57, and Exodus 34. Since David wrote these psalms, he had every right to quote from them and adapt them to his present needs. At a time of danger, when he felt inadequate to face the battle, David found three encouragements in the Lord, and so may we today.

God's Covenant Is Secure (vv. 1–7)

His statement "I am holy [godly, devoted]" was not an egotistical statement but rather the declaration that David was a son of the covenant and belonged wholly to the Lord. It is the translation of the Hebrew word *hesed* (4:3; 12:1) and is the equivalent of "saints" in the New Testament, "those set apart by and for the Lord." The word is related to *hasid,* which means "mercy, kindness, steadfast love" (vv. 5, 13, 15). As he began his prayer, David pleaded for help on the basis of his covenant relationship with the Lord, just as believers today pray in the name of Jesus and on the basis of His covenant of grace (Luke 22:20; 1 Cor. 11:25; Heb. 10:14–25).

The psalm has many connections with the Davidic covenant (2 Sam. 7). We get the impression that David had the covenant text before him and selected verses from his psalm to parallel what the Lord had said to him and he had said to the Lord. David is called "servant" (7:5, 8, 19, 20, 25, 26, 29; 86:2, 4, 16), and both texts refer to the great things God had done (7:21; 86:10). The uniqueness of the Lord is another shared theme (7:22; 86:8) as well as Jehovah's supremacy over all the supposed "gods" (7:23; 86:8). In both, God's great name is magnified (7:26; 86:9, 11, 12). In his psalm, David used three basic names for God: Jehovah (vv. 1, 6, 11, 17), Adonai (vv. 3, 4, 5, 8, 9, 12, 15), and Elohim (vv. 2, 10, 12, 14). On the basis of God's covenant promises, David could "argue" with the Lord and plead his case. In verses 1–7, the word "for" usually signals one of David's persuasive reasons why the Lord should help him. In verse 5, he changes from "for I" to "for you" (vv. 5, 7, 10), climaxing in verse 10 with "For you are great." There are at least fourteen personal requests in the psalm, which suggests to us that effective praying is specific. David "cried [called]" and the Lord answered (vv. 3, 5, 7).

(For some of the citations and parallels in the Old Testament, see: **v. 1**—17:6; 31:2; 35:10; 37:14; 40:17; 70:5; **v. 2**—25:20; **v. 3**—57:1–2; **v. 5**—Ex. 34:6ff; **v. 6**—28:2; 55:1–2; **v. 7**—17:6; 77:2; **v. 8**—35:10; 71:19; 89:6; Ex. 8:10; 9:14; 15:11; **v. 10**—72:18; 77:13–14; **v. 11**—27:11; **vv. 12–13**—50:15, 23; 56:13; 57:9–10; **v. 16**—25:16.)

God's Character Is Unchanging (vv. 8–13)
"There is none like you!" (v. 8) is the confession of a man who truly knows God and remembered Israel's confession at the Exodus (Ex. 15:11). During ten years of exile in the wilderness of Judea, David had learned much about God's character and the way He worked in the lives of His people. God is great in who He is and what He does, and the false gods of all the nations are nothing. In spite of his present troubles, David the prophet (Acts 2:30) saw the day coming when all the nations would enter the Messianic kingdom (v. 9; see Rev. 15:3–4). God makes the

nations and assigns their boundaries and determines their destinies (Acts 17:22–28; Isa. 2:1–4; 9:6–7; 11:1–16). In verses 11–13, David focused on his own walk with the Lord. After he was delivered from danger, he wanted to walk so as to please and honor the Lord. "Unite my heart" means "I want to have an undivided heart, wholly fixed on the Lord." A perfect heart is a sincere heart that loves God alone and is true to Him (James 1:8; 4:8; Deut. 6:4–5; 10:12). He promised to praise God forever for delivering him from the grave (sheol), a hint here of future resurrection. (See 49:15 and 73:23–24.)

God's Glory Shall Prevail (vv. 14–17)

David's enemies were proud of themselves and their abilities, violent, and totally ignorant of and indifferent to the God of Israel. But David looked away from them to the Lord who had saved and guided him all his life. (His confession in v. 15 is based on Ex. 34:6ff; and see v. 5; 103:8–13; 116:5; 145:8; Neh. 9:17; and Jonah 4:2.) The apostle Paul tells us that knowing these attributes of God ought to lead people to repentance (Rom. 2:4). "The son of your handmaid" (v. 16) means "your devoted servant" (116:16; Ruth 2:13, 3:9; 1 Sam. 1:11, 12, 18). Children born to servants were considered especially faithful since they were brought up in the master's household (Gen. 14:14). Since David was the Lord's faithful servant, it was his Master's duty to protect and deliver him (143:11–12). But David wanted that deliverance to bring glory to the Lord and to demonstrate to the nations that Jehovah alone was God. It wasn't just warfare, it was witness, a "sign" of the goodness of the Lord to David. It was his way of praying, "Hallowed be Thy name" (Matt. 6:9). When our requests are in God's will and glorify His name, we can be sure He will answer.

Psalm 87

This is another psalm that extols the glory of Mount Zion (see 46–48, 76, 125, 129, 137). The writer was not indulging in arrogant nationalism but only seeking to glorify the God of Israel and the blessings He bestows. The psalm must be read on two levels. It is a prophecy of the future kingdom, when all nations will come to Jerusalem to worship (86:9; Isa. 2:1–5), and it is also a picture of the heavenly Zion where the children of God have their spiritual citizenship (Luke 10:20; Gal. 4:21–31; Phil. 3:20–21; Heb. 12:18–24). God promised that Abraham would have an earthly family, like the sands of the sea, which is Israel, and a heavenly family, like the stars of the heaven, which is the church (Gen. 13:16; 15:4–5). The psalm was probably written in the time of King Hezekiah, after the Assyrian army had been defeated and Babylon was on the rise (Isa. 36–39). Following this great victory, the neighboring nations, usually hostile to the Jews, honored Hezekiah and brought gifts to him as well as sacrifices to the Lord (2 Chron. 32:23). The psalmist shares three wonderful truths about the city of Jerusalem.

The City Is Built by God (vv. 1–3)

After the battle of the kings (Gen. 14:18), Abraham met Melchizedek, the king-priest of Salem (Jerusalem, "city of peace"; see 76:2), and Hebrews 7 informs us that Melchizedek is a type of Jesus Christ, our Priest-King in heaven. David chose Jerusalem for his capital city (2 Sam. 5:6–10), and the Lord validated that choice by putting His temple there. The nation of Israel was to be separate from the other nations both politically (Num. 23:9) and geographically. That is why God called Jerusalem "my city" (Isa. 45:13) and "the holy city" (Isa. 48:2; 52:1) and Zion "my holy mountain" (Isa. 11:9; 56:7; 57:13). It is "the city of the great King, the joy of all the earth" (48:2). It is "His foundation" from which He has built His great work of redemption (Isa. 14:32.). "Salvation is of the Jews," said Jesus (John 4:22), and were it not for Israel, the world would not have the knowledge of the true and living God, the inspired Scriptures, or the Savior. Jesus died and rose again outside the walls of Jerusalem, the Holy Spirit descended on the church meeting in Jerusalem on Pentecost, and it was from Jerusalem that the early Jewish believers scattered to carry the Gospel to the nations.

The phrase "the gates of Zion" refers to the city itself, a city God loves above all cities in the Holy Land. (See Deut. 7:6–9; 2 Chron. 6:5–6; Isa. 60:11–12; Zech. 1:14.) In Jerusalem was not only the temple of the true God, but also the throne of David, and it would be the Davidic line that would give us the Savior, Jesus Christ. In the end times, Jerusalem will be a center of controversy and conflict, but the Lord will rescue His beloved city (Zech. 12:1–13:1). But the prophets have written some "glorious things" about the future Jerusalem, and the apostles have written even more glorious things about the heavenly Jerusalem!

The City Is Inhabited by His Children (vv. 4–6)

The Lord is described as a king taking a royal census and registering individual names ("this one … that one …"), but the remarkable thing is that these people are Gentiles and that God is making them His own children and citizens of His holy city! Even more, the nations named are the avowed enemies of the Jews! The emphasis in all three verses is on *birth*, indicating that the people who enter the future glorious kingdom will experience a "new birth" and belong to the family of God. Like Paul, they will be citizens by birth (Acts 22:25–29) and not by purchase. The phrase "those that know me" indicates more than an intellectual appreciation of the Lord. It describes a personal relationship with Him, like that of husband and wife (Gen. 4:1; 19:8; 1 Sam. 2:12; 3:7).

"Rahab" refers to Egypt (89:10; Isa. 51:9), Israel's enemy in the south, and the word means "arrogant, boisterous." Egypt enslaved the Jews and yet will share with them citizenship in the city of God and membership in the family of God! (Isa. 19:18–25). Israel's northern enemy, Babylon, would one day destroy Jerusalem and ravage the kingdom of Judah, and the Jews would vow to pay her back (137:1, 8–9), but she, too, will be part of the glorious kingdom! Philistia and Tyre on the west were always a threat to Israel, but they will be included. Ethiopia is "Cush," a nation in Africa. Of course, of all these nations, only Egypt is still on the map, but the message is clear: when the Lord establishes

His glorious kingdom, and Messiah reigns from Jerusalem, Israel's enemies will be transformed into fellow citizens. Through the preaching of the Gospel today, this miracle is happening in His church (Eph. 2:11–22; Gal. 3:26–29). The Old Testament prophets promised that believers from all the nations of the earth would be included in Messiah's reign (Isa. 2:1–5; Mic. 4:1–5; Zech. 8:23; 14:16–20), and so did the psalmists (22:27; 46:10; 47:9; 57:5, 11; 98:2–3; 99:2–3). "For the earth will be filled with the knowledge of the glory of the Lord, as the waters cover the sea" (Hab. 2:14 NKJV).

The City Enjoys His Abundant Blessings (v. 7)

As citizens of Zion and the children of God, the Jews and Gentiles not only live together but they sing together and play musical instruments as they rejoice in God's blessings. Jerusalem is one of the few ancient cities that was not built near a great river, and it was always a problem to supply enough water, especially during a siege. To help solve this problem, King Hezekiah had ordered an underground water system constructed (2 Kings 20:20; 2 Chron. 32:30). The word translated "fountains" or "springs" refers to "living water" and not water brought up from a well. A fountain or spring symbolizes the source of something, as Jacob is the "fountain" from which the nation came (Deut. 33:28). All blessings, especially spiritual blessings, will flow from the Lord who reigns in the City of David, just as today we draw upon the wealth found only in our exalted Lord (Rom. 2:4; 9:23; 11:33; Eph. 1:3; 2:4–10; 3:8; Phil. 4:19; Col. 1:27). The image of a river of living water is found also in 36:8–9; 46:4; 89:6; Ezekiel 47; John 7:37–39; and Revelation 22:1–2.

Psalm 88

Heman, the son of Joel, was a temple musician during the reign of David (1 Chron. 6:33, 37; 15:17; 16:41–42; 2 Chron. 35:15) and is the most likely candidate for the authorship of this psalm. Second choice is Heman, the son of Mahol, one of the wise men during the reign of King Solomon (1 Kings 4:31). The Hebrew words *mahalath* and *leannoth* mean "sickness" and "for singing" or "for humbling." The first word probably refers to a sad melody to accompany this somber song, and the second might identify the purpose of the psalm, to bring us low before the Lord. This is the last "sons of Korah" psalm in the psalms and is perhaps the most plaintive song in the entire book. In the Hebrew text, the psalm ends with the word *hoshek*, "darkness," and there is no closing note of triumph as in other psalms that begin with pain and perplexity. The psalm speaks of darkness (vv. 1, 6, 12, 18), life in the depths (vv. 3–4, 6), the immanence of death (vv. 5, 10–11), feelings of drowning (vv. 7, 16–17), loneliness (vv. 5, 8, 14, 18), and imprisonment (v. 8). Heman was a servant of God who was suffering intensely and did not understand why, yet he persisted in praying to God and did not abandon his faith. Not all of life's scripts have happy endings, but that does not mean that the Lord has forsaken us. From Heman's experience, as recorded in this psalm, we can discover four instructions to follow when life falls apart and our prayers seemingly are not answered.

Come to the Lord by Faith (vv. 1–2)

Heman's life had not been an easy one (v. 15) and now it had grown even more difficult, and he felt that death was very near (vv. 3, 10–11). But he did not give up! He still trusted in God, whom he addressed as "LORD—JEHOVAH" four times in this prayer (vv. 1, 9, 13, 14). "Jehovah" is the name of the Lord that emphasizes His covenant relationship with His people, and Heman was a son of that covenant. Heman also addressed Him as "God—Elohim," the name that expresses His power. The phrase "God of my salvation" indicates that Heman had trusted the Lord to save him, and the fact that he prayed as he did indicates that his faith was still active. Three times we are told that he cried to the Lord, and three different words are used: verse 1—"a cry for help in great distress"; verse 2—"a loud shout"; verse 13—"a cry of anguish." He was fervent in his praying. He believed in a God who could hear his prayers and do wonders (vv. 10, 12), a God who loved him and was faithful to His people (v. 11). All of this is evidence of faith in Heman's heart, even though he spoke as though he was ready to give up. He prayed day and night (vv. 1, 9) and trusted that no obstacle would come between his prayers and the Lord (v. 2; 18:6; 22:24; 35:13; 66:20; 79:11). No matter how we feel and no matter how impossible our circumstances, we can always come to the Lord with our burdens.

Tell the Lord How You Feel (vv. 3–9)

There is no place for hypocrisy in personal prayer. One of the first steps toward revival is to be completely transparent when we pray and not tell the Lord anything that is not true or that we do not really mean. Heman confessed that he was "full of troubles" and felt like a "living dead man." He was without strength and felt forsaken by the Lord. Old Testament believers did not have the full light of revelation concerning death and the afterlife, so we must not be shocked at his description of sheol, the world of the dead. The Lord does not forget His people when they die, nor does He cease to care, for "to be absent from the body" means to be "present with the Lord" (2 Cor. 5:6–8). (See 25:7; 74:2; and 106:4.)

But Heman also told the Lord that *He* was responsible for his servant's troubles! God's hand put him into the pit (sheol, the grave), and God's anger was flowing over him like breakers from the sea (see 42:8). Whatever sickness he had was caused by the Lord and made him so repulsive that his friends avoided him (see 31:1). He was without health, without light, and without friends—and he felt like he was without God! He was a prisoner and there was no way to escape. Like Job, Heman wanted to know why all this suffering had come to him.

Defend Your Cause Before the Lord (vv. 10–14).

The saintly Scottish minister Samuel Rutherford (A.D. 1600–1661), who suffered much for his faith, wrote, "It is faith's work to claim and challenge lovingkindnesses out of all the roughest strokes of God." He also said, "Why should I tremble at the plough of my Lord, that maketh deep furrows in my soul? I know He is no idle husbandman; He purposeth a crop." Hamen's argument is simply that his death will rob God of a great opportunity to demonstrate His power and glory. Of what service could Hamen be to the Lord in sheol?

The spirits of the dead will not arise in the world of the dead and do the Lord's bidding (see Isa. 14:9–11), but Heman could serve the Lord in the land of the living. (See 30:8–10; 115:17.) Before he went to the sanctuary to assist in the worship, Heman prayed to the Lord for healing and strength, and at the close of a busy day, he prayed again. During his daily ministry, he heard the priestly benediction: "The Lord bless you, and keep you; the Lord make His face to shine upon you and be gracious to you; the Lord lift up His countenance on you, and give you peace" (Num. 6:24–26 NASB)—but the blessing did not come to him! He felt rejected and knew that God's face was turned away from Him. But he kept on praying!

Wait for the Lord's Answer (vv. 15–18)

We do not know what this affliction was that came to him early in life, but it is painful to think that he suffered all his life long and all day long (vv. 15, 17). He could not even look back to a time in his life when he enjoyed good health. The billows that almost drown him (v. 7) now became fiery waves of torment (v. 16) as God's "burning anger" went over him (see 42:7). The flood was rising and he felt he was about to drown (see 130:1), and there was nobody near enough to rescue him. He was alone! The darkness was his friend because it hid him from the eyes of those who observed his sufferings and may have said (as did Job's friends), "He must have sinned greatly for the Lord to afflict him so much!"

But he continued to pray and to look to God for help! "Though he slay me, yet will I trust him" (Job 13:5). "I would have despaired unless I had believed that I would see the goodness of the Lord in the land of the living. Wait for the Lord; be strong, and let your heart take courage; yes, wait for the Lord" (Ps. 27:13–14 NASB). The Lord always has the last word, and it will not be "darkness." We should never doubt in the darkness what God has taught us in the light.

Psalm 89

If the author is the wise man Ethan of Solomon's reign (1 Kings 4:31), then verses 39–45 describe the invasion of Shishak and the Egyptian army recorded in 1 Chronicles 12, which occurred during the reign of Solomon's son Rehoboam. But this invasion did not mean the end of the Davidic dynasty, which is the major theme of this psalm. However, the invasion and captivity of Judah by the Babylonians did mean the end of the Davidic dynasty, so this psalm could have been written after that crisis by an unknown "Ethan." Young King Jehoiachin had already been taken captive to Babylon and Zedekiah, his uncle, named king in his place (2 Kings 24), and Jeremiah had announced that none of Jehoiachin's sons would ever sit on David's throne (Jer. 22:24–29). What, then, becomes of God's covenant that promised David a throne forever (vv. 3, 28, 34, 39, and see 2 Sam. 7)? Does Jehovah no longer keep His promises? The faithfulness of the Lord is the major theme of this psalm (vv. 1, 2, 5, 8, 14, 33, 49). Of course, God's great promises to David have their ultimate fulfillment in Jesus Christ, the Son of David (Luke 1:26–38, 68–79). The psalm gives us four assurances about the faithfulness of the Lord.

God Is Faithful in His Character—Praise Him (vv. 1–18)

The psalm opens on a joyful note of worship with praise to God from the psalmist (vv. 1–4), in heaven (vv. 5–8), and on earth (vv. 9–13), and especially from the people of Israel (vv. 14–18), who rejoice in the Lord all day long (v. 16). The psalmist sings (v. 1), the angels praise (v. 5), and even the mountains sing for joy (v. 12). Ethan praised the faithfulness of God's character (vv. 1–2) and His covenant (vv. 3–4), about which he has much to say (vv. 3, 28, 34, 39). Because he wanted to instruct and encourage the coming generations (see 78:1–8), Ethan wrote down his praise and his prayer. God had sworn to David that his dynasty and throne would continue forever (vv. 28–29, 35–36, 49; 2 Sam. 7:13), but future generations of Jews would live without any king, let alone a king from David's line. Ethan wanted them to know that God's mercy (lovingkindness NASB; love NIV) was being built up (v. 2) even though the city and temple had been torn down and the crown and throne of David had been cast down (vv. 39, 44). God was still on His throne (v. 14), and David's line ("seed") was secured forever in Jesus Christ, the Son of God (vv. 4, 29, 36–37; see Heb. 1:8; 5:6; 7:28; 10:12; 13:8, 21; Rev. 11:15). The "sure mercies (lovingkindnesses, v. 1) of David" will never fail (Isa. 55:3; Acts 13:34). God had not forsaken His servant David (vv. 3, 20, 39; 2 Sam. 7:5, 8, 20, 21, 25–29).

Heaven is a place of worship, and the angels praise the Lord for His glorious attributes (vv. 5–8; see Rev. 4 and 5), for there is no god like Him (Ex. 15:11). But the earth joins the hymn and even the mighty waves of the sea obey Him and praise Him. The tumultuous sea is an image of the nations (93:3; Isa. 17:12–13; Rev. 13:1; 17:15), so Ethan mentioned God's victory over Egypt (Rahab, 87:4; Isa. 51:9). The "scattering" of God's enemies (v. 10) reminds us of Numbers 10:35. Hermon is an imposing mountain to the far north, near Damascus, and Tabor is a much smaller mount about fifty miles southwest of Hermon. Ethan heard the mountains singing praises to God, just as Isaiah did centuries before (Isa. 55:12).

If any people on earth have a right to praise God, it is the nation of Israel, God's chosen people. They had a holy land, given to them by God, a royal dynasty chosen by God, and the light of the holy law that guided their steps in the ways of the Lord. They had a holy priesthood to serve them and bless them (v. 15; see Num. 6:24–26), men who would blow the trumpets to signal the special holy days and feasts ("the joyful sound"; see 81:1). In verse 18, "our shield" (NASB, NIV) refers to their king (84:9), now in captivity. In many Jewish synagogues today, verses 15–18 are recited on their New Year's Day after the blowing of the shofar.

God Is Faithful to His Covenant—Trust Him (vv. 19–29)

From verse 19 to verse 37, it is the Lord who speaks and reminds us of what He did for David. The question in the mind of the writer was probably, "If you did so much for David, why then did you break your covenant and reject us?" What was the vision and to whom was it given? God gave Samuel the message that David would succeed Saul (1 Sam. 13:13–15 and 16:1–13), and He gave Nathan the message that David would not build the temple but would have a "throne forever" and a "house" (family) built by the Lord (2 Sam. 7:1–17). The Lord may have led Ethan to rehearse this important information because the generations living after the exile needed to know it. Israel had a tremendously important ministry to fulfill in bringing the Messiah into the world, and He would come through the family of David. (Be sure to refer to 2 Sam. 7:1–17, for vv. 19–29 are a summary of the promises the Lord made to David.)

In a sovereign act of grace, the Lord *elected* David to be king of Israel (vv. 19–20). Their first king, Saul of Benjamin, was never supposed to establish a dynasty because he was not from the royal tribe of Judah (Gen. 49:10). David had proved himself before the Lord even before he stepped out on the stage of history and killed Goliath (1 Sam. 17:32–37). He had been faithful over a few things, and now the Lord would promote him to greater things (see Matt. 25:21). The Lord who elected David also *equipped* him to fight battles, lead the army, and build the kingdom (vv. 21–23). Even as a youth, he was known for his military prowess. The Lord *exalted* David, because David was a humble man who would not promote himself (vv. 24–27). Indeed, God helped David to expand the borders of the kingdom so that it reached from the Mediterranean Sea on the west to the Tigris and Euphrates Rivers on the east (see Ex. 23:31). It was David's close relationship to the Lord and his desire to exalt the Lord alone that made him a success (v. 26). David was the eighth son in Jesse's family (1 Sam. 16:13), but God made him His firstborn, the honored son that received the greatest inheritance. David's greater Son, Jesus Christ, was also called "the firstborn" (Rom.

8:29; Col. 1:15, 18; Heb. 1:6; Rev. 1:5). If David was "the highest of the kings of the earth" (v. 27 NASB), then he was "King of kings" like our Savior (see Rev. 17:14 and 19:16). Finally, the Lord *established* David and promised him a throne and a dynasty forever (v. 4; 2 Sam. 7:13, 16, 24–26, 29, 31), a promise fulfilled in Jesus Christ.

God Is Faithful in His Chastening (vv. 39–45)

Again, Ethan faced the question: "If God did so much for David, why did his throne and crown fall in defeat and disgrace?" The answer: because the terms of His covenant declare that the same Lord who blesses the obedient will also chasten the disobedient. The principle applied not only to David's successors on the throne (vv. 30–37; 2 Sam. 7:12–15) but also to the nation of Israel collectively (Deut. 28). "For whom the Lord loves He corrects, just as a father the son in whom he delights" (Prov. 3:12 NKJV; Heb. 12:3–11). Because of their disobedience and self-will, many of the kings of Judah were chastened by the Lord, but the Lord never broke His promise to David. The "witness" in verse 37 is probably the Lord Himself in heaven (see NASB), but the constancy of the heavenly bodies is also a witness to the faithfulness of the Lord's promises (Gen. 8:20–22; Jer. 31:35–36; 33:19–26).

Ethan told the Lord what He had done to Judah's anointed king, the descendant of David. The Lord was angry with the kings because of their sins, especially idolatry (v. 38), so He permitted the Babylonians to come and ravage the land, destroy Jerusalem, and burn the temple (vv. 40–41). To Ethan, the Lord was actually aiding the enemy! (vv. 42–43). But the glory had once more departed from the temple (v. 44; see 1 Sam. 4:21–22; Ezek. 8:1–4; 9:3; 10:4, 18; 11:22–23) because the leaders had turned their backs on the Lord and turned to idols. It appears that verse 45 applied especially to King Jehoiachin, who was but eighteen years old when he became king and reigned for three months and ten days (2 Kings 24:8). He became a captive in Babylon for thirty-seven years.

God's Faithfulness Will Never Cease—Wait for Him (vv. 46–52)

Ethan looks ahead (vv. 46–48) and asks the painful question, "How long, O Lord?" (See 6:3 for other references.) Surely he knew the prophecy of Jeremiah that the people would be in exile for seventy years and then permitted to return to their land (Jer. 25:1–14; 29:4–14), but when you are in the midst of the storm, you long for God to deliver you as soon as possible. To Ethan, it all seemed so futile. Life is short, all people will die, and God's people had to spend their days in exile. Then Ethan looked back (v. 49) and asked what had happened to the great lovingkindnesses the Lord had shown to David. But God's love had not changed; it was Judah's love for the Lord that had waned. Like any good parent, God shows His love to His children either by blessing their obedience or chastening them for their disobedience, but in either situation, He is manifesting His love.

Finally, Ethan looked around and felt keenly the reproaches of the enemy (vv. 50–51). The king of Judah was now a common prisoner in a foreign city! No doubt Jehoiachin was paraded shamelessly in Babylon as living proof that the gods of Babylon were greater than Judah's God. How the Babylonians must have enjoyed following the parade and taunting the captive Jews, especially the anointed king!

Verse 52 is not a part of the original psalm but forms the conclusion of Book III of The Psalms (see 41:13 and 72:18–19). But it expresses a great truth: no matter how much we suffer because of the sins of others, and no matter how perplexed we may be at the providential workings of the Lord, we should still be able to say by faith, "Praise the Lord! Hallelujah!" And our fellow sufferers ought to respond with, "Amen and amen! So be it!"

That's the way of trust—faith in the faithfulness of the Lord.

Book I

1. The word "man" is generic and includes both men and women.

2. The Hebrew word letz means "to mock, to scorn." In modern Hebrew, letzen means "a clown."

3. V. 1 can be translated "has not walked … has not stood … has not sat." The only person who ever lived that way on earth was Jesus Christ, and in Him, we have the righteousness of God (2 Cor. 5:21).

4. See Gen. 18:19, Ex. 33:12, 2 Sam. 7:20 and 2 Tim. 2:19 for other examples of this meaning of the word "know."

5. The word for "Son" is bar, which is Aramaic, and not the familiar ben, which is Hebrew. But the Spirit is speaking to Gentile nations outside the nation of Israel.

6. The "communal laments" are 36, 44, 60, 74, 79, 80, 83, 90, 112, 137.

7. In The Psalms, the Lord is also called "God of my salvation" (27:9), "God of my strength" (27:9), "God of my mercy" (59:17), "God of my praise" (109:1) and "God of my life" (42:8).

8. For other "intrigue" psalms, see 17, 25, 27–28, 31, 35, 41, 52, 54–57, 59, 63, 64, 71, 86, 109, 140, 141. These involved the plots of either King Saul or Absalom.

9. Since they deal with similar themes, Pss. 9 and 10 have parallel statements. See 9:10/10:1, 18; 9:20–21/10:12,18; 9:13/10:4, 12–13; 9:19/10:11; 9:6/10:16.

10. See *Double-Speak* by William Lutz (1989) and *The New Double-Speak* (1996), both published by HarperCollins.

11. *Earth and Altar* (IVP, 1985), p. 111.

12. For a comparison of Matt. 5–7 and Ps. 15, see Appendix 70 of *The Companion Bible*, by E. W. Bullinmger (London: Lamp Press.)

13. *Dialogues of Alfred North Whitehead*, compiled by Lucien Price (New American Library, 1964), pp. 223–224.

14. *Critique of Practical Reason*, p. 2.

15. *Reflections on The Psalms* (NY: Harcourt Brace Jovanovich,

1958), p. 63.

16. *The Future of Life* (NY: Alfred A. Knopf, 2002), chapter 1.

17. Some interpret the picture as the bridegroom leaving the marriage pavilion after consummating the marriage, rejoicing that now "two had become one." Either way, David saw the sunrise as a time of joy as he faced the day, and also as a time of determination to reach the goals set for the day.

18. This may explain why Ps. 19 is appointed in the church lectionary to be read on Christmas Day.

19. *The Road Less Traveled* (NY: Simon and Schuster, 1978), p. 15.

20. For other important "one thing" statements in Scripture, see Josh. 23:14; Ecc. 3:19; Mark 10:21; Luke 10:42; 18:22; John 9:25; Phil. 3:13.

21. David said "I have sinned" more than once (2 Sam. 12:13; 24:10, 17; 1 Chron. 21:8, 17; Ps. 41:4 and 51:4). For others who also said "I have sinned," some of them insincerely, see: Ex. 9:27; 10:16; Num. 22:34; Josh. 7:20; 1 Sam. 15:24, 30; 26:21; Matt. 27:4; Luke 15:18, 21.

22. London: Geoffrey Bles, 1950; page 81.

23. *The Journals of Jim Elliot*, edited by Elizabeth Elliot (Revell, 1978), p. 174.

BE WORSHIPFUL

*A study guide for personal reflection
or group discussion.*

Chapter Two
Book I: Psalms 1 — 41

Psalm 1

1. What does Psalm 1 identify as the key to success? How do you measure true success?

2. According to Psalm 1, what conditions must you meet in order to be "blessed"? Are you willing to meet these conditions?

3. What will you do this week to be a blessing to others?

Psalm 2

4. What evidence of rebellion against God do you see in international events? In national events? In local events? In the lives of your coworkers? How can you help reconcile at least one person to Christ?

5. What do you learn from this psalm about God's sovereignty? How does knowing God is sovereign help you face life's challenges?

Psalms 3, 4

6. What do Psalms 3 and 4 have in common? Can you praise God even in difficult circumstances? If so, why? If not, why not?

7. According to Psalm 4:1, David was desperate for God to answer his prayer. Why does God sometimes delay His answer to an urgent prayer? What helpful lessons have God's delays taught you?

Psalms 5, 6

8. What is an imprecatory psalm? Should believers today offer imprecatory prayers? Why or why not?

9. How should a believer's life contrast with the life of an unbeliever?

10. Have you ever felt that God deserted you? What did you later discover? How can suffering patiently strengthen your faith and enlarge your sphere of Christian influence?

11. How can you be confident that God is steering even your harshest circumstances toward His ultimate goal for your life?

Psalm 7, 8

12. Have you ever been falsely accused? How did you respond? What advice can you give other falsely accused believers?

13. What keeps God from snuffing out the rebellious today, once and for all?

14. What does creation teach you about God? How does knowing that God created such a vast universe make you feel about His love for you, such a small "speck" on Planet Earth?

Psalm 9

15. How has God proved to be your stronghold? What might you say to a person who fears for his or her safety in a climate of terror and uncertainty?

Psalm 10

16. What personal reasons might a person have for refusing to believe in the existence of God. What do you believe is the strongest evidence that God exists?

17. Is it harder to persuade "down and outers" or "up and outers" to believe in God? Explain.

Psalm 11

18. Having to choose between fear and faith, David chose faith. What fears must your faith overcome? What Bible promise gives you great comfort when you feel threatened?

Psalm 12

19. Dishonesty and deception characterized David's culture. What big lies are circulating today in education? In politics? In religion? In the secular media?

20. Why is it so important to accept God's Word as absolute truth?

Psalm 13

21. A fugitive on the run from King Saul, David felt abandoned by God. But faith eventually displaced doubt, and he exchanged a

dirge for a doxology. When have you felt abandoned by God? What chased the gloom away and restored your hope?

22. How can you live above the circumstances?

Psalm 14

23. Would you agree that a believing twelve year old is wiser than an atheistic philosopher? Defend your answer.

24. Why might those who deny God's existence purposely refuse to believe?

Psalm 15

25. Good works cannot procure our salvation, but they ought to prove our salvation (Ephesians 2:8–10). What good works do you believe prove most convincingly that a person has received salvation?

26. David longed for heaven. What aspects of heaven are you longing for? If someone asked, "What's so great about heaven?" how would you respond?

27. David stressed the value of integrity, honesty, and sincerity. How might Christians practice these virtues at home, in church, and in the business community?

Psalm 16

28. This Messianic psalm radiates with joy. David derived unbridled joy from a personal relationship with the Lord. Read John 16:9–11. How can believers experience the joy of the Lord?

29. How does verse 11 explode the false notion that heaven is a boring place?

Psalm 17

30. David's enemies were hurling false accusations against David, therefore David longed for the Lord to vindicate him. What is the best defense against false accusations? Why is the Lord our best defense attorney?

Psalm 18

31. David referred to the Lord in this psalm as his "rock," "shield," and "horn, meaning the Lord was his refuge, protector, and strength. What metaphors can you use to tell what the Lord means to you?

32. This psalm affirms the victory the Lord had given David over his enemies. Identify a recent victory the Lord gave you, and write a four-line poem of praise for that victory.

Psalm 19

33. David worshiped the God who had created nature. Why is it wrong to worship nature instead of God? Can we learn all we need to know about God by simply observing nature? Why or why not?

34. What have you learned from Scripture recently about God and His ways? How does the Bible impact your daily life in positive ways?

Psalm 20

35. This was a prayer offered before battle. What impending battles can you pray about?

Psalm 21

35. How do we respond to answered prayer? David and his people responded with thanksgiving. What answered prayer will you thank God for? How will you face the future, knowing He has been faithful in the past?

Psalm 22

36. What depictions of Christ's crucifixion do you find in this psalm?

37. How should the fact that Jesus will return to earth in glory affect the way a believer lives today?

Psalm 23

38. Why do sheep represent believers so well? What kinds of duties did shepherds provide in Bible times? How do those duties correspond with those performed by pastors?

39. How can a person enjoy the Good Shepherd's peace, care, and guidance?

Psalm 24

40. What event in David's life seems to correspond with the writing of this psalm? How is this psalm connected with Palm Sunday?

41. In view of terrorism, crime, and a declining commitment to morality, do you see any hope for our planet? If so, what is your hope based on? Do you agree or disagree that Christians are optimistic pessimists? Why?

Psalm 25

42. This psalm teaches us to submit ourselves to the Lord in meekness. How does meekness differ from weakness?

43. What enemies did God help David conquer? What "enemies" will you conquer with His help?

Psalm 26

44. David had to contend with hypocrites. What help do you find in Psalm 26 for contending with hypocrites?

Psalm 27

45. Where was David living when he wrote this psalm? How would you worship the Lord if you lived in an area that had no churches?

Psalm 28

46. What changed David's sobbing into singing? How has being the victim of unjust treatment worked for your spiritual good?

Psalm 29

47. When did you last observe God's glory in nature? How does it make you feel to know that God is Lord of heaven and earth?

Psalm 30

48. David's pride had brought chastening. What are some damaging effects of sinful pride? What do you see as the purpose for God's chastening in the lives of His errant children?

49. How can a disobedient believer enjoy renewed intimacy with the Lord?

Psalm 31

50. Who quoted verse 5? Who quoted verse 6? What attitude or attitudes did David show in Psalm 31 that you want to develop in your life?

Psalm 32

51. Why is this psalm appropriately called a "penitential psalm"? What do these words mean: transgression, iniquity, guile, forgive, and impute?

52. How does sinning negatively impact a believer?

53. How can a sinning believer recover the joy of salvation?

Psalm 33

54. This psalm is devoted entirely to praise. What role should praise play in congregational worship? How can a congregation keep praise from becoming merely a lifeless routine?

Psalm 34

55. What threefold witness of what the Lord does for His own do you find in this psalm? What has the Lord done for you today that merits your praise?

Psalm 35

56. What did David ask the Lord to do for his enemies? To his enemies? What is the best course of action to follow when you are falsely accused, criticized, or slandered?

Psalm 36

57. What evidence do you see that the human heart is corrupt? What are some consequences of a corrupt heart?

58. Describe the love that issues from God's heart.

Psalm 37

59. What issue did David address in this psalm? How do you resolve this issue in your own situation?

Psalm 38

60. What was David's physical condition when he wrote this psalm? What situation(s) do you need to place in the Lord's hands?

Psalm 39

61. What precaution did David refer to in the opening verse of this psalm? What offensive speech may slip from your mouth occasionally? How will you deal with this weakness?

62. Knowing that life is brief, how will you make the most of it?

Psalm 40

63. What has impressed you most about the way the Lord has worked in your life? Why are sacrifices no substitute for obedience? What motivates you to obey the Lord?

Psalm 41

64. What four questions does this psalm prompt us to ask?

65. Has a trusted friend disappointed you, perhaps even betrayed you? How do we know the Lord will never disappoint or betray us?

Chapter Three
Book II: Psalms 42 − 72

Psalms 42, 43

66. These two psalms were likely written as one. If you prepared a brief biographical sketch of their author, what would you include?

67. If an unbeliever asked, "Where is your God?" how would you respond? What reasons do believers have to sings songs in the night to the Lord?

68. The writer longed to return to the holy city and God's sanctuary. How strongly do you look forward to worshiping God with fellow believers at your place of worship? How can increase your anticipation of worship? How can increase others' anticipation of worship?

Psalm 44

69. On what occasion did Israel sing this psalm? Do you sometimes doubt God's presence? Do you think God is withdrawing His blessing from America? Explain.

70. How might personal tragedy be one of the best things a believer experiences?

Psalm 45

71. This wedding psalm prompts us to contemplate the attractiveness and glory of Jesus, our King and Bridegroom. What aspects of Jesus' majesty and love do you find most appealing?

Psalm 46

72. The word "trouble" (v. 1) describes the unhappy situation of being trapped in a corner. What encouragement does this psalm bring to those who feel trapped by some difficult circumstances?

73. Which command in this psalm means, "Take your hands off! Relax!"? Can you identify a situation when you released your grip and turned the matter over to the Lord? If so, what resulted from placing the matter in the Lord's hands?

Psalm 47, 48

74. When will God reign over the nations? How does this prospect help you cope with unsettling world events?

75. What changes do you expect to see worldwide when God makes His city "secure forever" (48:8)?

Psalm 49

76. What are some valuable things money can't buy? What is "a root of all kinds of evil"? (See 1 Tim. 6:10.)

Psalm 50

77. This psalm depicts God as "the mighty One, God, the LORD." How might such a lofty concept of God elevate our worship to a

higher level of spiritual significance? Do you agree or disagree that believers and unbelievers alike are humanizing God? Explain.

Psalm 51

78. How is all sin first and foremost an assault on God?

79. What is your response to the excuse that we're just human and therefore can't help but sin? Do you think the Church is becoming more tolerant of sexual sins? Explain.

80. What link, if any, do you see between a blameless life and the effectiveness of the gospel? Do you agree or disagree that Christians must sow a few wild oats so they can better understand non-Christians?

Psalms 52, 53

81. "Mighty man" in Psalm 52 may be identified as our "big shot." But what will become of self-acclaimed big shots at the hands of God? Big shots may harass the righteous, but who will have the last laugh?

82. How does God sustain His people when they are clearly a persecuted minority?

Psalm 54

83. Recall a time in your life when you progressed from danger to confidence in the Lord to praise of the Lord. What advice would you give a believer who is experiencing relentless persecution?

Psalm 55

89. In what period of David's life was this psalm most likely composed? Where did David look for help when everything seemed to be crumbling around Him? Why is it so much better to look above us when looking around us detects calamity?

Psalm 56

90. David vowed to sacrifice to the Lord and to serve Him. Do you think it is wise to make vows to the Lord? If not, why not? If so, what are a few appropriate vows?

Psalms 57, 58

91. David prayed and praised from a cave when he was a fugitive. How do prayer and praise transform our gloomiest days into glorious days?

92. David indicted lawless leaders in Psalm 58. Do you agree or disagree that a leader's private life has no bearing on his ability to lead the nation? Why or why not?

Psalms 59, 60

93. Can believers trust God to protect them from evildoers? If so, how do you explain the fact that every year thousands of believers die at the hands of wicked men? What purpose might those deaths serve?

94. Why is it impossible for a believer to live endlessly in defeat? How can we apply Psalm 60:12 to our lives?

Psalm 61

95. David prayed, "Hear my cry." What requests do you urgently want the Lord to hear?

96. David longed for the Lord's presence. How should your life reflect the truth that the Lord is with you always?

Psalm 62

97. How could David be so calm when his enemies were so aggressive? What can you learn from David about meeting adversity with calm confidence in the Lord?

Psalm 63

98. How thirsty are you for God? How might you develop a greater desire for God? How would you get along spiritually if you were suddenly separated from your local church and Christians friends? How would you worship and sustain your interest in spiritual matters?

Psalm 64

99. What strategies do you learn from Psalm 64 for winning life's battles?

100. Why do we need to know Satan's modus operandi? What weapons are available to us as we wrestle against Satan and his forces? (See Eph. 6:10–19.)

Psalms 65—68

101. What does "crown the year" (65:11) suggest? What qualities of the Lord will you praise Him for today? Which of His gracious works will you praise Him for today?

102. How do we know from Psalm 66 that the Lord loves the whole world?

103. What part can you have in inviting all nations to "shout with joy to God" (66:1)?

104. According to Psalm 67:1, 2, why did the psalmist ask God to bless Israel? Are blessings supposed to be hoarded or shared? How can you share with others the blessings you have received from the Lord?

105. How does the Song of Deborah (Judg. 5) parallel Psalm 68?

106. How does it encourage you to know the King is coming? How will the world be different when the nations submit to Him?

Psalm 69

107. In this psalm David prayed for judgment on his enemies. How do the following verses picture Jesus' suffering for us: 1–4a, 7–9, 12, 19, 21?

Psalm 70, 71

108. What reasons can you cite to "rejoice and be glad" in the Lord (70:a)?

109. How does recounting the Lord's faithfulness in the past (71:22) help entrust your future to Him?

Psalm 72

110. Who do you believe authored this psalm, David or Solomon? Why?

111. Verse 6 predicts Israel's king will be "like rain falling on a mown field, like showers watering the earth." How does trusting Jesus bring refreshing showers into your life?

112. What aspects of Jesus messianic kingdom are you most looking forward to? Why?

Chapter Four
Book III: Psalms 73 – 89

Psalm 73

113. What can you relate about Asaph, the author of this psalm? Would you describe him as a godly man? Why or why not?

114. Are you troubled by the fact that many wicked people prosper? Why does their prosperity trouble you?

115. How does this psalm help you take your focus off the current prosperity of the wicked and place it on "the big picture"?

Psalm 74

116. The psalmist believed God had rejected His people. When are you most apt to feel that God has rejected you?

117. What promises has God given His people to remind us in hard times that He will not fail us?

Psalm 75

118. What elements of true worship does this psalm reveal? Have you worshiped the Lord today, incorporating these elements?

Psalm 76

119. What event in Israel's history most likely frames the message of this psalm? What role do you see God occupying in modern history? How would you contrast His strength and the strength of today's super powers?

120. Knowing God is sovereign over earth's rulers, what can you trust Him to do in your life?

Psalm 77

121. Unable to sleep because he lamented the destruction of Jerusalem and Israel's captivity, Asaph committed the matter to the Lord. What problems or unanswered questions have kept you awake? What might encourage you to commit those matters to the Lord?

122. What do you find significant about the shift from "I" and "my" to "You" in this psalm?

Psalm 78

123. This is a history psalm. Why do you agree or disagree that all history is His story?

124. How can believers best ensure that the next generation will remember God's wonderful works and appreciate His unchanging character?

Psalm 79

125. What cruel nation is described in verses 1–4? Why did God allow His people to suffer at this enemy's hands?

126. Under what circumstances might God allow an enemy to inflict harm to our nation? If such a tragedy occurred, what purpose might it accomplish?

127. Why is the fulfillment of God's will always the best thing that could happen to us?

Psalm 80

128. Based on his prayer for the Northern Kingdom, what do you conclude about Asaph's character? Should believers pray for their rivals? If so, what might they ask for? What does the "vine" represent in this psalm? How did Jesus use the imagery of a vine and its branches in John 15?

Psalm 81

129. What feasts in the Jewish calendar can you name?

130. The psalmist invited God's people to "sing for joy." What reasons do believers have to sing for joy?

131. What were the costs of Israel's disobedience? What are some costs of disobedience today?

Psalm 82

132. Asaph prayed that God would bring justice to the earth. Do you believe Asaph's prayer will be answered. If so, when and how?

133. If a nation's leaders reject God, what are some likely consequences? What do you believe Christians can do to encourage their national leaders to honor God?

Psalm 83

134. What is the best weapon against aggression? How consistently do you use this weapon?

Psalm 84

135. The psalmist longed for "the courts of the LORD" (v. 2). If you had to be absent from church for an extended period, what would you miss the most? Why?

136. God's people pass through painful places occasionally. How might that experience bless them? How might it make them a blessing to others?

137. The psalmist valued a day in the house of God more highly than "a thousand elsewhere." Why should believers place a higher value on worship and fellowship than on a life of comfort in partnership with the wicked?

Psalm 85

138. How long were the Jewish people exiles in Babylon? Verse 6 links revival and joy. Do you believe revival or spiritual renewal always produces joy? Explain.

139. What picture of Jesus' person and work do you see in verse 10: "Love and faithfulness meet together; righteousness and peace kiss each other"?

140. How does it help you to embrace the future knowing "the LORD will indeed give what is good" (v. 12)?

Psalm 86

141. This psalm depicts David as inadequate to face a battle. Is a sense of inadequacy helpful or harmful when we face life's battles? Explain.

142. What characteristics of God, cited in this psalm, strengthen your faith?

143. Why is it good to know "there is none like you, O LORD"?

144. David asked God to grant him His strength (v. 16). For what specific task or trial do you need God's strength?

Psalm 87

145. Why is Zion, Jerusalem, so cherished by the Jews? What future will Jerusalem and its inhabitants ultimately enjoy?

146. Jesus provides living water for His followers. Describe the satisfaction you have in Jesus and contrast it with the thirst unbelievers experience.

Psalm 88

147. The psalmist, Heman, endured pain and suffering, yet he kept on praying. How do you explain the fact that some believers experience ongoing pain and suffering in spite of their prayers? Did the Lord promise us an easy road? What did He promise (see Matt. 28:20b)?

148. Heman questioned the Lord's fairness (v. 14). Why do you agree or disagree that it is all right to question the Lord's fairness?

Psalm 89

149. How does nature praise the Lord?

150. How can your words glorify the Lord? How can your life praise Him?

The Word at Work Around the World

A vital part of Cook Communications Ministries is our international outreach, Cook Communications Ministries International (CCMI). Your purchase of this book, and of other books and Christian-growth products from Cook, enables CCMI to provide Bibles and Christian literature to people in more than 150 languages in 65 countries.

Cook Communications Ministries is a not-for-profit, self-supporting organization. Revenues from sales of our books, Bible curricula, and other church and home products not only fund our U.S. ministry, but also fund our CCMI ministry around the world. One hundred percent of donations to CCMI go to our international literature programs.

CCMI reaches out internationally in three ways:

· Our premier International Christian Publishing Institute (ICPI) trains leaders from nationally led publishing houses around the world.

· We provide literature for pastors, evangelists, and Christian workers in their national language.

· We reach people at risk—refugees, AIDS victims, street children, and famine victims—with God's Word.

Word Power, God's Power

Faith Kidz, RiverOak, Honor, Life Journey, Victor, NexGen — every time you purchase a book produced by Cook Communications Ministries, you not only meet a vital personal need in your life or in the life of someone you love, but you're also a part of ministering to José in Colombia, Humberto in Chile, Gousa in India, or Lidiane in Brazil. You help make it possible for a pastor in China, a child in Peru, or a mother in West Africa to enjoy a life-changing book. And because you helped, children and adults around the world are learning God's Word and walking in his ways.

Thank you for your partnership in helping to disciple the world. May God bless you with the power of his Word in your life.

For more information about our international ministries, visit www.ccmi.org.

Additional copies of this and other
Victor products are available
from your local bookstore.

❖ ❖ ❖

If you have enjoyed this book,
or if it has had an impact on your life,
we would like to hear from you.

Please contact us at:

VICTOR
Cook Communications Ministries, Dept. 201
4050 Lee Vance View
Colorado Springs, CO 80918
Or visit our Web site:
www.cookministries.com

Victor®

The Bible Teacher's Teacher